Protection of the Right to Seek and Obtain Asylum under the African Human Rights System

Refugees and Human Rights

VOLUME 12

The *Refugees and Human Rights* Series aims to meet the increasing need for literature which probes the nature and causes of forced migration, the modalities and procedures employed when refugees present themselves, and the manner in which the human rights of refugees are, or should be, promoted and protected.

The titles published in this series are listed at brill.com/rehr

Protection of the Right to Seek and Obtain Asylum under the African Human Rights System

By

Chaloka Beyani

MARTINUS NIJHOFF PUBLISHERS

LEIDEN · BOSTON
2013

Library of Congress Cataloging-in-Publication Data

Beyani, Chaloka.
Protection of the right to seek and obtain asylum under the African human rights system / By Chaloka Beyani.
p. cm. -- (Refugees and human rights ; v. 12)
Includes index.
ISBN 978-90-04-16341-6 (hardback : alk. paper) -- ISBN 978-90-04-22861-0 (e-book) 1. Human rights--Africa. 2. Civil rights--Africa. I. Title.
KQC572.B49 2012
342.608'3--dc23

This publication has been typeset in the multilingual "Brill" typeface. With over 5,100 characters covering Latin, IPA, Greek, and Cyrillic, this typeface is especially suitable for use in the humanities. For more information, please see www.brill.com/brill-typeface.

ISSN 1387-6031
ISBN 978-90-04-16341-6 (hardback)
ISBN 978-90-04-22861-0 (e-book)

This book is printed on acid-free paper.

Printed by Printforce, the Netherlands

Contents

Preface

The year 2011 commemorated the thirtieth anniversary of the African Charter on Human and Peoples' Rights 1981. *Protection of the Right to Seek and Obtain Asylum under the African Charter on Human and Peoples' Rights* is a timely publication which reflects on this anniversary and deals with a recurrent humanitarian subject whose effect on humanity is tragic. The study builds on important international initiatives that were aimed at bolstering the condition and framework of refugee protection in Africa from 1990 to 2002. These initiatives included the joint United Nations (UN) and African Union (AU) Conference held in Addis Ababa in 1994, the Lawyers Committee for Human Rights field research study that was published as *African Exodus* (1995), the Comprehensive Implementation Plan (CIP) that was adopted by the AU and United Nations High Commissioner for Refugees (UNHCR) Meeting of Governments and Non-Government Technical Experts held in Conakry, Guinea, in March 2000, in commemoration of the 30th Anniversary of the 1969 *AU Convention Governing the Specific Aspects of Refugee Problems in Africa*. The CIP is regarded as the effective regional complement to the International Agenda for Refugee Protection 2002.

The author participated in all these studies, events and activities, and the present study builds on these efforts by providing an additional dimension to the protection of refugees in Africa. In doing so, the study takes a different perspective based on human rights, drawing upon the framework of the ACHPR and other applicable law drawn from the *International Covenant on Civil and Political Rights* (ICCPR) 1966, the *Convention Against Torture and Other Cruel, or Inhuman or degrading Treatment or Punishment* (CAT) 1984, the *European Convention for the Protection of Human Rights and Fundamental Freedoms* (ECHR) 1950 and the *American Convention on Human Rights* (ACHR) 1969, and other human rights instruments. The growing importance of the role and application of human rights in the protection of refugees was underscored when the United Nations

High Commissioner for Refugees and the African Commission on Human and Peoples' Rights reached conclusions and recommendations on the complementary role of the African Commission in the protection of refugees. The conclusions and recommendations in question were agreed between UNHCR and the African Commission at their consultative meeting held between in Addis Ababa, 20 and 21 March 2003.

The study has been prepared over a period of years. An original draft was 'field tested' in seminars and training sessions with scholars, lawyers, non-governmental organisations, protection officers from UNHCR, and refugees in East Africa, Southern Africa and West Africa. Specific factual and legal conditions of refugees and asylum seekers were taken into account in these regions, although the issues of protection are not peculiar to the regions concerned. They are synonymous with the general problems encountered in the protection of refugees all over Africa.

Conservative estimates are that Africa is host to upwards of six million refugees. The findings of the UN/AU Addis Ababa Conference in 1994 echo the alarming truth that, civil wars, internal armed conflicts, repressive regimes, bad governance and lack of respect for human rights, are key causes of instability, massive displacement of populations and the movement of persons across borders, seeking refuge in other states. Rape, murder, abduction, sexual slavery, forced marriages, amputations and mutilations, police harassment and extortion, unlawful and arbitrary arrests, insecurity, and denial of human rights, including economic, social and cultural rights-food, clean water, adequate standards of health and shelter, and education characterise the protection needs of refugees in Africa and elsewhere.

Acknowledgements

This Study is the product of combined field-based research and practice on the protection of the right to seek and obtain asylum under the African Charter on Human and Peoples' Rights 1981. The thirtieth anniversary of the Charter in 2011 is an occasion on which to reflect on significant developments relating to one of Africa's most perennial and recurrent problem, namely the quest for asylum by millions who seek it under a legal framework of human rights, in addition to international refugee law. The book covers these developments by examining the content and scope of the right to seek and obtain asylum under the Charter as well as the practice of the African Commission on Human and Peoples' Rights in so far as this right is concerned.

Special support in the preparation of the book was received from a number of distinguished individuals and institutions without whom the initial study would have been impossible to undertake. Therefore, my profound thanks are due considerably to all persons and institutions whose tremendous work and dedication contributed to the completion of this work.

Sincere appreciation goes to the Ford Foundation whose grant supported the preparation of the original commentary, the research, and training workshops convened to discuss and test the application of its content and practicability in East Africa, Southern Africa and West Africa. The benevolence and sustained commitment of the Ford Foundation to the cause of persons and populations in distress in Africa is outstanding and must be placed on record for generations to come. Special and heartfelt thanks to Taryn Higashi, Akwasi Aidoo, then of the Ford Foundation, and Joseph Gitari of the Ford Foundation. They all gave great personal and professional support while tolerating my involvement in the Great Lakes peace process in 2005-2006.

Warm thanks to the Windle International Trust for facilitating the preparation of the study and for coordinating and administering the organisation of the workshops in particular. Immeasurable thanks to Robin Shawyer and Anne Lloyd-Williams at Windle International Trust for their unfailing confidence and personal commitment throughout the various phases of the preparation and completion of the project.

I must express a debt of gratitude to the formidable support from Chidi Odinkalu of the Open Society Justice Initiative, and Monette Zard, then at the International Council of Human Rights, and now at the Ford Foundation. Both offered impeccable professional and practical advice and starred in the research-led training of the participants at the workshops on the use the study. Chidi led and contributed to the use and procedures of the African Commission, while Monette led and contributed to the need for advocacy and protection techniques. I must also thank Bonaventure Rutinwa especially for his insight and undertaking a stirring training session at the Southern African Workshop at very short notice. Special appreciation to Ibrahima Kane of the Open Society Foundation for East Africa, for leading the discussion on the institutional aspects of the African Human Rights System at the final research and training workshop in Nairobi in 2006.

My special appreciation is for Abi Gitari and Muthoni Kamau, then of the Refugee Consortium of Kenya, Zonke Majodina then of the South African Human Rights Commission, and Sadikh Niass of WARIPNET in West Africa, for their research assistance and skill as regional coordinators who ably organised and coordinated the regional research and training workshops in Nairobi, Pretoria, and Dakar respectively, and who utilised their own expertise and experience to ensure that the study reflected the regional realities of human rights and refugees in East Africa, Southern Africa, and West Africa. Deep felt thanks to Deirdre Clancy, Dismas Nkunda, and Olivia Bueno, all of the Refugee Rights International, for accepting to organise the final research and training workshop on the applicability of the study in Nairobi in 2006. George Okoth-Obbo deserves special mention for taking time from his former duties as Director of the Division of International Protection at UNHCR to attend the final Workshop and offered concise reflections.

Finally, I have to thank Anne Bayefsky as Editor of the series in which the book is published, Lindy Melman editing the manuscript, and the publishers Martinus Nijhoff. Thanks to Zahra Ashfar who, as Research Assistant, was able to chase footnotes, and prepare the initial table of cases and index.

However, I personally remain responsible for any omissions or failings in this work.

Chaloka Beyani
London School of Economics

Table of Cases

Table of Instruments

Chapter 1

Introduction

1. *Scope of the Study*

Because of its inclusive refugee group eligibility to asylum, the regional system of protecting refugees in Africa is well considered to be the most generous of its kind in the world.[1] However, since its establishment over forty years ago, the character of refugee flows and the climate for refugee protection has changed remarkably in the 21st century. This necessitates an appraisal of the manner of application of the existing regime of principles, institutions and methods of protection which are operative in Africa. The objective is to strengthen the viability of refugee protection well into this millennium by inquiring into the applicability of the present framework of protection in the light of the underlying protection concerns. Significant protection issues are indicated and evaluated by reference to the legal principles which have so far rendered the protection of refugees endurable between African states. Specific recommendations are made to add strength and durability to the present system of protection.

There is a growing band of authoritative literature on the general protection of human rights under the *African Charter on Human and Peoples' Rights* 1981[2] (the

---

1 See below, p. 36.

2 AU Doc. CAB/LEG/67/3 rev. 5, or 21 *I.L.M.* 58 (1982). The major works are by U.O. Umozurike, *The African Charter on Human and Peoples' Rights* (Martinus Nijhoff, 1997); V.O. Orlu Nmehielle, The African Human Rights System: Its Laws, Practice, and Institutions (Martinus Nijhoff, 2001); R. Murray, The African Commission on Human and Peoples' Rights (Oxford, Hart, 2000); R. Murray and M. Evans (eds.), Documents of the African Commission on Human and Peoples' Rights

African Charter). However, the specific application of the African Charter and the role of the African Commission and Court on Human and People's Rights in the protection of asylum seekers and refugees have not received adequate attention within the existing literature. This underlies the general problem that refugees are a neglected category of persons and inadequate consideration of their protection in the literature on the African Human Rights system exacerbates their vulnerability. Indeed, many scholars and advocates of refugee protection in Africa have expressed a great deal of intellectual frustration at the lack of legal accountability for the failure of some States to accord refugees the protection which they are entitled to in international human rights law.

One specific means of bringing about such accountability is the exercise of the right of individual or collective petition by, or on behalf of, refugees under the African human rights system. Inevitably, the exercise of such a right begs an inquisition into the law of the forum concerned. It is on this premise that this Study seeks to lay out the legal basis and processes by which academics, lawyers, refugees, and civil society can have better recourse to the complementary protection of refugees under the framework of the African Charter on Human and Peoples' Rights. The Study is designed to provide a 'reader friendly' analytical guide to the applicable standards of African Charter under which the right of individual petition can be invoked by refugees as human beings with equal entitlement to protection and respect for the worthiness and value of their human dignity.

The underlying basis of the Study is that the prospect offered by the African Charter should be explored to provide protection to refugees when national legal systems fail to do so and the resulting failure cannot be remedied by other agents of protection, including the United Nations High Commissioner for Refugees (UNHCR), the African Union, and Non –Governmental Organisations. This Study is also an educational and training aid on such use, and on how refugee protection feeds legally into the process of protecting human rights under the African Charter, with suitable examples drawn from other human rights systems, such as the human rights treaty bodies of the United Nations, the European and Inter-American human rights systems.

The Study has been prepared over a period of three years in which an original draft was the subject of field research, participatory analysis, and testing by academics, lawyers, members of civil society, and refugees in East Africa, Southern Africa and West Africa. The objective was to ensure that the Study would address and reflect the realities and modality of protecting refugees under the African Charter.

Bearing that in mind, the process of preparing this Study has been a very functional, dynamic and collaborative one, involving constant input from scholars,

(Oxford, Hart, 2001) V.O. Orlu Nmehielle, The African Human Rights System: Its Laws, Practice, and Institutions (Martinus Nijhoff, 2001) M.D. Evans and R. Murray (eds.), *The African Charter on Human and Peoples' Rights: The System in Practice, 1986–200* (Cambridge University Press, 2002); F. Ouguergouz, *The African Charter on Human and Peoples' Rights: A Comprehensive Agenda for Human Dignity and Sustainable Democracy in Africa* (Martinus Nijhoff: 2003).

State officials, and civil society groups from around Africa who work with, and advocate on behalf of refugee rights, as well as from refugees and asylum-seekers themselves. Three regional consultations took place in the course of research for the Study – in East Africa in June 2002, West Africa in September 2002 and Southern Africa in November 2002 – where groups from each of these sub-regions came together to discuss the Study in light of the protection challenges within their national and sub-regional contexts. In all some 60 groups and participated in the research workshops. These were coordinated by a network of academics that included the author from the Law Department of the London School of Economics, the Refugee Law Project at the University of Makerere, the Centre for the Study of Forced Migration and the Faculty of Law of the University of Dar-res-Salaam, and the Human Rights Centre and Faculty of Law of the University of Pretoria.

These workshops were a valuable opportunity for individuals and groups to underpin the substance of the Study, the challenges of protection concerning refugees in Africa, and to discuss the potential for working collaboratively to meet these challenges. They were also a useful opportunity to initiate a dialogue with respect to the development of protection techniques and strategies in the area of human rights and refugees based on the competence of the African Commission and Court on Human and Peoples' Rights. A team of researchers drawn from East, West and Southern Africa, provided material on the problems faced by refugees in these regions and channelled different perspectives from around Africa into the Study on a continuous basis, in between formal workshops and consultations. The Study reflects the themes that emerged from the workshops. With the preparation of this Study, the expectation is that it illuminates the beginning of a process and that many of the ideas and strategies it contains will continue to be applied and become translated into concrete action over time.

The principal focus on refugees in this Study derives from the fact that, unlike internally displaced persons who remain under the precarious legal responsibility of their own States, refugees are uniquely and legally vulnerable persons who are forced to flee their own States in search of safety and protection in States to which they do not belong. Providing such protection has long been the objective of the law relating to the status of refugees in international law.[3] However, a major point of weakness in the legal arrangements for protecting refugees under existing international refugee law is the absence of an international court or treaty body to which they can present their claims for protection when such protection is denied or neglected. As a result even the few rights which are intended to apply to

[3] See, A. Bayefsky (ed.,) *Human Rights and Refugees, Internally Displaced Persons and Migrant Workers* (Martinus Nijhoff, 2006); A. Bayefsky and J. Fitzpatrick, *Human Rights and Forced Displacement* (Martinus Nijhoff, 2000); B.S.Chimni (ed.,) *International Refugee Law: A Reader* (Sage Publications, 2000); E. Feller, V. Turk and F. Nicholson, *Refugee Protection in International Law: UNHCR's Global Consultations on International Protection* (Cambridge University Press 2003); G. Goodwin-Gill and J. MacAdam, *The Refugee in International Law* 3rd ed., (Oxford, 2007); J. Hathaway, The Law of Refugee Status (Butterworths, 1991); J. Hathaway, *The Rights of Refugees under International Law* (Cambridge, 2005); A. Grahl-Madsen, The Status of Refugees in International Law (Leyden, 1966–1972).

refugees under the *United Nations Convention Relating to the Status of Refugees* 1951, as complemented by the *African Union Convention Governing the Specific Aspects of Refugee Problems in Africa* 1969, are difficult to invoke against States that deny protection to refugees.

In the period of human rights, this problem may be tackled in Africa by using the regional human rights system in which the right to seek and obtain asylum is recognised as a human right capable of legal application alongside other human rights contained in the African Charter. Not only does this offer the possibility for asylum seekers and refugees to exercise the right of individual petition by taking their cases to the African Commission or Court to seek protection for their rights in the event of denial, neglect, or violation by host States, but there is also now greater willingness on the part of the African Commission to apply human rights to refugees and nationals of third States.

A prime example of this can be seen in the case of *Rencontre Africaine pour la Defense des Droits de l'Homme* (*RADDHO*) *v. Zambia*,[4] which concerned the mass expulsion of West African nationals from Zambia in early 1990s. In holding against Zambia for breach of its human rights obligations under the African Charter, the Commission required African States 'to secure the rights protected in the Charter to all persons within their jurisdiction, nationals or non-nationals'. In this way, States in Africa can be held accountable before their own regional system of human rights in the way in which they treat refugees, their nationals- including internally displaced persons- and nationals of third States. However, unlike 'refugee specific treaties' that typically contain obligations for the receiving States, human rights obligations under the African Charter are two dimensional in that they reach out to the receiving States as well as States of origin, and thus provide refugees with the possibility to advance legal claims against the host States and their own States of origin.[5]

A further advantage in the use of the African human rights system lies in the fact that it includes within it the prospect for applying the 1951 UN and 1969 AU Conventions on Refugees respectively, as well as other regional arrangements in which refugees are entitled to freedom of movement and residence in regions, such as the Community of West African States.[6]

2. *Structure and Organisation*

The Study is structured and organised as follows. Chapter Two outlines the background to the evolution of refugee protection in Africa. After that, each of the key

[4] Communication 71/92, *Compilation of Decisions on Communications of the African Commission on Human and Peoples' Rights*, p. 367.

[5] C. Beyani, 'State Responsibility for Refugee Flows and Displaced Persons with respect to the Country of Origin' *International Journal of Refugee Law* 7 (1995).

[6] C. Beyani, *Human Rights Standards and the Movement of People within States* (Oxford, 2000) pp See below, pp. 20–21.

sections of the Study's relevant Chapters has a guiding comment on the important issues of law to consider, followed by an analysis of the way in which the essential standards of human rights and refugee law should be applied to protect refugees, and a Concluding Reflection on important activities and procedures that ought to be followed to achieve that end.

In this format, Chapter Three begins with an outline of the application of the relevant aspects of international law relating to the African Charter. The aim of this is to convey the basics of the system of law in which the Study is situated, and of the obligations of States to incorporate or implement the Charter in national law. This Chapter also establishes the relationship between human rights and refugees in order to establish the basis for the application of human rights in the context of refugee protection, and to underline the practical use of the Charter to protect the rights of refugees.

Chapter Four examines the procedures by which refugees may exercise the right of individual protection before the African Commission or Court. It identifies procedural and practical difficulties that should be tackled and borne in mind when doing so. The main issues covered in this part of the Study are: the identification of cases that are appropriate for consideration by the African Commission on Human and Peoples' Rights; the preparation of a case to protect refugee rights effectively and to identify which rights are involved, as well as the factors that should be taken into account. The latter are based upon the procedures established by the African Commission concerning the lodging of complaints and how these procedures apply to refugee cases. The challenge of presenting a case concerning refugee rights in the light of the relevant and appropriate jurisprudence of the African Commission is also considered.

Chapter Five highlights the necessity for concerted efforts to devise useful techniques and strategies for enhancing the protection of refugees through regional cooperation or solidarity. The Chapter proposes cooperation and partnerships between civil society, the United Nations High Commissioner for Refugees (UNHCR), academic institutions and legal practitioners within and between the sub-regions of East Africa, Northern Africa, Southern Africa, and West Africa. In addition, the Chapter examines the use of reporting procedures by the African Commission in the context of asylum. The role of national institutions is considered in this regard. There is emphasis on the importance of following up on the decisions made by the Commission to ensure that the States concerned comply with these decisions, in relation to the individual refugee in whose favour a decision is made, and in respect of other refugees similarly affected by any such decision.

Chapter Six presents a general case study prepared for the purpose of teaching and training. The main issues in the case study are teased out and a summarised approach on how to deal with them is provided. Other case studies drawn from East, Southern, and West Africa, which participants from those regions prepared for workshops and seminars that were held in the course of drafting the

Study are also laid out. Appendices of important documents that are crucial to the protection of refugees in Africa complete the structure of the Study. These include the relevant agreements or treaties adopted by African States and an illustrative chart regarding African States that have ratified, or agreed to be bound by, the African Charter is provided.

Chapter 2

Background

1. *Introduction*

The writing of this Study follows important international initiatives that were aimed at bolstering the system of refugee protection in Africa from 1990 to 2002. The initiatives include the joint United Nations (UN) and African Union (AU) Conference in Addis Ababa in 1994, research by the Lawyers Committee for Human Rights which was published as *African Exodus* (1995), the Comprehensive Implementation Plan (CIP) that was adopted by the AU and UNHCR meeting of States and Non-Government Technical Experts held in Conakry, Guinea, in March 2000, in commemoration of the 30th Anniversary of the *AU Convention Governing the Specific Aspects of Refugee Problems in Africa* 1969. The CIP is regarded as the effective regional complement to the *International Agenda for Refugee Protection* 2002.

The present Study complements these important steps. However, it differs in that its framework of reference is based on human rights, drawing upon the African Charter and other applicable law drawn from the *International Covenant on Civil and Political Rights* 1966, the *Convention against Torture and other Cruel, Inhuman or Degrading Treatment or Punishment* 1984, the *European Convention for the Protection of Human Rights and Fundamental Freedoms* 1950 and the *American Convention on Human Rights* 1969, and other relevant human rights instruments. The growing importance of the role and use of human rights in the protection of refugees was underscored when, after the first preparatory seminar for this Study was held in Nairobi in 2003, the Office of the United Nations High Commissioner for Refugees and the African Commission on Human and Peoples' Rights reached conclusions and recommendations on the complementary role of the African Commission in the protection of refugees. The conclusions and recommendations in question were agreed between the Office of the High Commissioner for Refugees and the African Commission at their consultative meeting held in Addis Ababa, between 20 and 21 March 2003.[1]

Research for this Study was carried out over a period of three years. In this period, specific factual and legal problems experienced by refugees and asylum seekers were taken into account in East Africa, Southern Africa and West Africa. It became clear in the seminars that the issues of protection that surfaced were not peculiar to the regions concerned. They are synonymous with the debilitating conditions encountered in the protection of refugees all over Africa.[2]

Conservative estimates are that Africa is host to upwards of six million refugees.[3] The findings of the UN/AU Addis Ababa Conference in 1994 exhort the continuing alarming scenario that civil wars, internal armed conflicts, repressive regimes, bad governance and lack of respect for human rights are key causes of instability, massive displacement of populations and movement of persons across borders, seeking refuge in other States. Rape, murder, abduction, trafficking, sexual slavery, forced marriages, amputations and mutilations, police harassment and extortion, unlawful and arbitrary arrests, insecurity, and denial of human rights, including economic, social and cultural rights, i.e., food, clean water, adequate standards of health, and education, characterise the protection needs of refugees in Africa and elsewhere.[4]

2. *Evolution and Trends*

The quest for establishing an African regional system for the protection of refugees evolved from the agenda for African solidarity in the struggle against colonialism which lay at the heart of the creation of the then Organisation of African Unity (OAU, which was succeeded by the African Union or AU in 2000) in 1963. From the very beginning, the AU was eager to establish a system of protection which would reflect and resolve specific refugee concerns in Africa. A characteristic of this concern was that of large numbers of persons who were compelled to

1 This document is reproduced in the Appendices to the Study at p. 232.

2 See Chapter Six in which these issues are laid out in the form of problems identified by the participants.

3 For details, please consult UNHCR, *2005 Global Refugee Trends: Statistical overview of Populations of Refugees, Asylum-Seekers, Internally Displaced Persons, Stateless Persons, and other Persons of Concern to UNHCR*, 9th June 2006. Available at: http://www.unhcr.org/statistics/STATISTICS/4486ceb12.pdf.

4 African Union and the United Nations, *The Addis Ababa Document on Forced Population Displacements in Africa*, 8–10th September 1994, Addis Ababa. See recommendation 1 on 'Root Causes of Refugee Flows and other Forced Population Displacements'. See further, Lawyers' Committee for Human Rights, *African Exodus*, New York, 1995).

leave their countries of origin by factors other than individualised persecution or the risk thereof.

The genesis of this idea was first formulated in the *Kampala Draft Declaration* 1964[5] which represented a concrete initiative at defining the applicable standards of protecting refugees in Africa. That *Declaration* affirmed the classical persecution based standard contained in the *Convention Relating to the Status of Refugees* 1951,[6] read together with the *Protocol Relating to the Status of Refugees* 1967. It also listed three additional elements that were thought to characterise the situation of refugees in Africa, namely, persons who:

a. Had been uprooted by political, racial, social, religious or other similar turmoil or upheaval;
b. Risked injury to their life, physical integrity or liberty in the event of returning to their country of origin;
c. Did not in law or in fact enjoy the protection of their country of origin or had compelling reasons for not doing so.

Underlying these conceptions was the phenomenon of mass refugee out-flows in circumstances that were said to be unique to Africa. In the prevailing struggle for decolonisation in the 1960's, the causes of flight and the corresponding lack of protection were connected to the liberation struggle against colonial rule, with the result that commitment to the protection of refugees became a solid expression of solidarity between African States.

This commitment led to the convening of the first *African Conference on the Legal, Economic, and Social Aspects of the African Refugee Problem* in Addis Ababa, Ethiopia, in 1967. By way of definition, the Conference noted that in Africa, refugees were persons who had been obliged to leave their State of nationality under the pressure of an illegal act, such as aggression by another State, or as a result of an invasion, wholly or partially, of their State.

Two specific recommendations were adopted for concrete action at that Conference. One was to create an AU institutional structure for the protection of refugees in the form of a Bureau for the Placement, Education, and Training of African Refugees (the Bureau for Refugees). Another was to adopt an African instrument which, in addition to containing the definition of a refugee under the 1951 Convention, would define specific standards which characterised the African refugee situation. These recommendations led to the creation of the Bureau for Refugees in Africa, which was established on 1 March 1968,[7] and the adoption of the *Convention Governing the Specific Aspects of Refugee Problems in Africa* (the AU

5 UN. Doc. MHCR/175/66. Opposing drafts were made in 1965 and 1966, but they contained no specific provisions relating to the specific character of the African refugee problem.

6 *Text*:2545 *United Nations Treaty Series 137*; UNHCR, *Collection of International Instruments* (Geneva, 1995) p. 10; *entry into force 1954*.

7 Lawyers' Committee for Human Rights, *African Exodus*, pp. 139–166; J. Oloka-Onyango, 'Plugging the Gaps: Refugees, OAU Policy and the Practices of Member States in Africa' in United Sates Committee for Refugees, *Issue Brief* (1996).

Convention) by the Assembly of Heads of State and Government of the AU on 10 September 1969.[8]

A main objective of the Bureau was to provide opportunities for the education and training of refugees. The Bureau was to act as a clearing base for the resettlement of refugees between host countries; in the spirit of African solidarity, it was expected that host States would be called upon to resettle and place refugees on the basis of fixed quotas.

In addition, the Bureau would mediate in disputes arising from alleged breaches by refugees of national laws of the host State where such breaches gave rise to arbitrary arrest or expulsion.[9] In seeking to effectively implement the AU Convention, the Bureau worked functionally with the High Commissioner for Refugees, member States of the AU, and non-governmental organisations. Although African States displayed positive political will towards the Bureau, the projection of its mandate was severely curtailed by an acute shortage of resources. Professor Joe Oloka-Onyango's on site assessment of the function of the Bureau in Addis Ababa during the preparation of the study on *African Exodus* in 1995 showed that the Bureau was largely under resourced, dysfunctional and ill-equipped for this purpose.

Yet from the 1980's, the mandate of the Bureau started to expand considerably to include coordinating humanitarian assistance and monitoring the conditions and welfare of refugees. After the formal creation of the African Union in 2000, the Bureau was merged into the newly created Division of Humanitarian Affairs, Refugees and Displaced Persons, which took an additional dimension as the operational unit of the AU Commission and acts as a Secretariat to all the organs of the African Union on matters concerning forced displacement.[10]

Thus, in addition to refugees, the Division's mandate now includes the welfare of internally displaced persons. In July 2004, the Executive Council of the African Union requested its Commission 'to collaborate with relevant cooperating partners and other stakeholders to ensure that Internally Displaced Persons are provided with an appropriate legal framework to ensure their adequate protection and assistance'.[11] Upon this decision, the Division for Humanitarian Affairs completed a draft *Convention for the Protection and Assistance of Internally Displaced Persons in Africa 2006*.[12] An outline of the draft was first approved by the Ambassadors and Ministers of the African Union in Ouagadougou, Bukina Faso, 29th May-2nd June 2006, and the draft Convention was adopted by the Ministers

8 *Text*:14 691 *United Nations Treaty Series*; UNHCR, *Collection of International Instruments, Vol.II* (Geneva, 1995) p. 3; *entry into force 1974*.
9 C. Amate, *Inside the AU: Pan-Africanism in Practice* (London, 1986) p.473.
10 Patrick Tigere and Rita Amukhobu, 'The African Union's Institutional Framework for responding to Forced Displacement in Afrca' *African Union Policy Review*, (Addis Ababa, 2006) p.53. Sadly, Patrick Tigere, then Chief of the Division, passed on in November 2006. May his soul rest in peace.
11 African Union, *Decision on the Situation of Refugees, Returnees and Displaced Persons*, Executive Council Decision EX/CL/Dec.127.
12 C. Beyani, 'The Elaboration of a Legal Framework for the Protection of Internally Displaced Persons in Africa', *Journal of African Law*, 50, 2(Cambridge, 2006) 1–11.

on 11th November 2008, while the Convention itself was finally adopted by the Heads of State of the African Union on 22nd October 2009[13] in Kampala. The aim behind the Convention is to provide legal protection for internally displaced persons in parallel to the AU *Refugee Convention*.

The regional dimension of the AU *Refugee Convention* is apparent in the official status it enjoys as the effective regional complement to the 1951 Convention in Africa. This means that there exists a legal basis for the dual application of the principles contained in both of these treaties, and a collaborative partnership in the protection methods and institutions of the United Nations and the AU exists. The AU *Refugee Convention* was designed as a purposefully distinct treaty whose scope and definition of refugees sought to reflect the reality of refugee out-flows in Africa. Its history, as outlined above, shows that it was framed to provide the broadest possible inclusive protection to the masses of people whose lives, safety, and well-being were endangered by the disruption brought about by decolonisation. Thus, under Article 1(2) of the Convention, the term refugee also applies,

> to every person who, owing to external aggression, occupation, foreign domination or events seriously disturbing internal order in either part or the whole of his country of origin or nationality, is compelled to leave the habitual place of residence in order to seek refuge in another place outside of the country of origin or nationality.

The framework of the Convention contains a solid commitment to providing asylum and cementing solidarity between African States within the institutional framework the AU, UNHCR and non-governmental organisations. The protection features of the Convention are based on mass admission, non-refoulement, prohibition on subversive activities, burden or responsibility sharing, and voluntary repatriation.

Evidence of apparent legal commitment by African States to the protection of refugees lies in the fact that nearly all of them have ratified or acceded to the UN and AU Refugee Conventions.[14] While conceding that ratification or accession by itself is not sufficient, none the less the deed of commitment lies initially in the willingness of States to accept formal obligations. Notwithstanding this, the truth is that the African system of refugee protection has faced mounting challenges throughout the period in which it has existed. At times, its resilience has been bolstered crucially by a combination of regional and international strategies.

The first of these was the *Arusha Conference on the Situation of Refugees in Africa* in 1979.[15] This Conference served as a catalyst for revitalising refugee protection in Africa by assessing the difficulties of protection and taking full stock of the

---

[13] The Convention for the Protection and Assistance of Internally Displaced Persons in Africa 2009 was prepared, drafted, and negotiated by the present author. See, C. Beyani, 'The Elaboration of a Legal Framework for the Protection of Internally Displaced Persons in Africa' *Journal of African Law* 50(2006) 187–197.

[14] *Supra*, note.....above.

[15] See *Recommendations From the Pan-African Conference on the Situation of Refugees in Africa* 7–17 May 1979, UN Doc. A/AC.96/INF.158.

principles and institutions of protection at that time. The Conference renewed African vigour towards refugee protection by endorsing the viability of the principles of protection and burden (responsibility) sharing in post-colonial Africa, and recognised the need for the publicity and teaching of refugee law. That Conference also added momentum to the regional commitment to the principles and institutions of protection under the UN and AU Conventions and endorsed the establishment of corresponding national institutions for protecting refugees. Moreover, the delegates at the Conference made an important connection between the right to asylum and the protection of human rights in Africa, thus reinforcing the principle of asylum in terms of human rights, while condemning those practices which threatened the protection of asylum, e.g. the expulsion of refugees.[16]

Quite obviously, recognition of the importance of the right to seek asylum in Africa at the Arusha Conference in 1979 pre-dated the African Charter on Human and Peoples' Rights in 1981. Inclusion of the right to seek and obtain asylum in the African Charter in 1981 was therefore central to the strategy of enhancing the protection of refugees within the framework of human rights. Although the subsequent initiatives mentioned at the beginning of this Study continued to endorse the vitality and centrality of the right to seek and obtain asylum, none of them outlined how this right could be used in theory and practice. This Study responds to this void specifically.

If the recommendations of the *Arusha Conference* served as a telling blue print for invigorating the premises of refugee protection in Africa, then subsequent international conferences envisioned an equation, within this regional approach, between protection and assistance, development aid to refugees, returning refugees, and displaced persons. In other words, the frontiers of protection began to expand in the 1980's to include assistance and development aid; terms such as 'returnees' and 'displaced persons' entered the vocabulary of protection and assistance, in addition to the central focus on refugees as such.

The gestation for these developments were the first and second *International Conferences on Assistance to Refugees in Africa,*[17] *ICARA* 1 in 1980 *and ICARA* II in 1982,[18] which laid emphasis on burden (responsibility) sharing and recommended the provision of humanitarian assistance as a matter of necessary relief and care to refugees, having regard to their needs during the emergency phase of their flight; continuity and expansion in long-term solutions related either to voluntary repatriation or settlement in host States; and technical and capital support to host States, and States of origin that received returning refugees, appeared on the

16 Ibid. These recommendations were endorsed in G.A. Res. 34/61, 29th November 1979.

17 G.A. Res. 34.42, 25th November, 1980 requested the Secretary General of the United Nations to convene ICARA I.

18 G.A. Res. 37/197, 18th December 1982, requested the Secretary General of the United Nations to convene ICARA II and set out the aim of the Conference in terms of development assistance to refugees in Africa.

protection agenda as new elements of international assistance additional to previously ongoing development programmes. Special structures for assistance were called for which would bring about complementarity between refugee-related aid and development assistance, with the High Commissioner remaining the fulcrum of protection and the delivery of assistance to refugees mainly.

Subsequently, SARRED[19] – the Oslo *Declaration and Plan of Action on the Plight of Refugees, Returnees, and Displaced Persons in Southern Africa* carried this approach to sub-regional level by articulating basic principles on humanitarian assistance as a component of protection extending to burden sharing, relief, recovery and development assistance for refugees, returning refugees, and displaced persons in Southern Africa. This approach extended to the Great Lakes Region in 1994 when a *Regional Conference on Assistance to Refugees, Returnees, and Displaced Persons in the Great Lakes Region* was convened in Kigali, Rwanda.[20]

If any lesson is to be learnt from the strategies of protection, assistance and development aid, it is that they injected vitality into the system of protecting refugees in Africa in ways which sustained it into the early to mid 1990s. Clearly the capacity of the system to cope with mass refugee flows was enhanced by means of international solidarity in sharing the burden of responsibility as well as in promoting the viability of voluntary repatriation by linking it directly to assistance for returnees. But it is also fair to say that as important as they are, the *ICARA* and *SARRED* initiatives were short lived steps which did not become part of the regular system of refugee protection, and their substantive recommendations should have been placed on a stronger and sure legal footing than before in order to have ensured outcomes based on international obligations of result, in so far as these would have been possible.

With the benefit of hindsight, it is safe to observe that *Arusha, ICARA and SARRED* were standard-setting Conferences expressing international consensus on the stock of measures that should have been accomplished as obligations for the effective protection of refugees in Africa.

The circumstances in which refugee flows occurred in the late 1990s to the 2000s bear witness to serious indications that continuity in the viability of the African system of protection could not be guaranteed in the wake of new challenges that have affected the climate of refugee protection. It is important to acknowledge these changes, to note the challenges which they pose, and to assess the strategic premises that are fundamental to effective methods of refugee protection in Africa.

---

19 *International Conference on the Plight of Refugees, Returnees, and Displaced Persons in Southern Africa, Oslo 22–24 August 1988, SARRED* Doc. 88/5, 24 August 1988. See also G.A Res. 42/106, 7th December 1987.

20 G.A. Res. 49/7, 25th October 1994.

3. *The Changing Climate of Refugee Protection in Africa*

No one denies that there are complex concerns knocking repeatedly and with tremendous impact at the foundations of the legal and institutional structures for protecting refugees in Africa today. These concerns are self-evident and they do give rise to a growing set of complicated challenges which have affected the effectiveness of the system. Unless these are tackled effectively, the adverse consequences arising from the failure to do so will depreciate further the quality of the entire system of international protection for refugees.

The challenges appear on several inter-related fronts. First of all, there is the challenge of granting protection to extra-ordinary large numbers of refugees and internally displaced persons in the context of on-going internal and external conflicts in States of origin as well as in some of the host States. The reality is that dimensions of large population movements that are not managed have a deprecating effect on the capacity of host States, cause severe depreciation in infrastructure (roads, bridges, airports) and serious degradation of the environment, .e.g., soil erosion, and deforestation, as refugees or internally displaced persons search for energy, firewood, and food. These catastrophes produce long-term detrimental consequences, which host States are left to grapple with on their own, in the course of discharging international obligations.

Armed protection for the safety and security of refugees, internally displaced persons, and humanitarian personnel has become an essential pre-requisite of protection. In the normal scheme of things, such protection would derive from the responsibility of the States concerned. However, there is the problem that the nature of the conflicts which give rise to refugee flows and the phenomenon of internal displacement fundamentally disables States, and with the collapse of governmental authority in given cases, e.g., Somalia, non-state actors fill this 'vacuum' with impunity, disregarding the safety or protection of the civilian population, refugees, displaced persons and humanitarian workers.

The wide scale use of land mines in armed conflicts and the ease with which small arms can be acquired and put to indiscriminate use compromises the safety and physical protection of refugees, internally displaced persons, and humanitarian workers. Landmines also hinder the effective implementation of 'return based' solutions because safety and physical integrity upon return cannot be guaranteed, nor can reintegration and development assistance be pursued to restore socio-economic and political normality or stability. On the one hand, awareness about desisting from methods of warfare which employ landmines must be orchestrated; on the other hand, international resources must be mobilised to help clear the scourge of landmines if return oriented solutions are to be effective.[21]

An imperious challenge is the change in the character of refugee flows in the form of mixed or composite out-flows of refugees, combatants or armed elements,

---

21 The *Ottawa Antipersonnel Landmines Convention* 1997 entered into force in 1998 after receiving the fortieth ratification from Bukina Faso. The majority of the ratifying States are African.

and migratory movements. In the past, these stood out as unusual and isolated incidents. From the mid-1990s to date, and seemingly for the foreseeable future, mixed out-flows have become a general feature of the character of refugee flows in Africa. Defeated or fleeing armies and insurgents are all taking advantage of the system of refugees, for their own protection as well so as to pursue military operations against States of origin in the guise of refugees. In turn, States of origin and allied States whose security is threatened by the incidence of armed attacks emanating from the consequence of mixed case loads consider refugees and refugee camps as targets for attack directly or by proxy forces. No humanitarian system of protection can be expected to function effectively in these circumstances.[22]

The source of the problem, namely, the necessity to isolate combatants and militia from ordinary refugee populations is acknowledged in principle.[23] Not only are there massive logistical problems involved in screening very large refugee populations, but attending to the problem of mixed out-flows also requires military or security presence to protect refugees or internally displaced persons and humanitarian personnel in particular. Even if there is goodwill on their part, many host States face competing internal claims of their own, which affect their logistical, resource and military capacity for dealing with such challenges adequately. Compounding this is a distinct lack of willingness on the part of the international community to support or build the capacity of host States as part of the general international legal obligations to protect refugees. Unless these concerns are addressed effectively, a number of host States will come to formulate unilateral positions on matters of refugee protection. Inevitably, the unpredictable composition of massive refugee movements will be considered to constitute threats to national, as well as, regional peace and stability.

This calls for a broader socio-political and legal approach in which threats to national, or regional peace and stability, are juxtaposed alongside the obligations to protect refugees and internally displaced persons. The Great Lakes Region took such an approach in 2006 in the context of preventing recurrent armed conflicts and creating conditions for peace, stability, and development in conditions of post-conflict reconstruction.[24]

African experience has shown that where the cause of flight arises from impunity and massive violations of human rights, the consequences of such violations tend to affect the stability of host States and entire sub-regions. This was the case with regard to the political consequences that flowed when genocide was perpetrated in Rwanda in 1994. A regional armed conflict between States, the first of its kind since the end of the second world war, ensued in 1998 in the Democratic

---

22 Lawyers' Committee for Human Rights, *Refugees, Rebels and the Quest for Justice* (New York, 2002) pp. 1–118.

23 C. Beyani, 'The Legal Criteria for the Separation of members of Armed Forces, Armed Bands, and Militia from Refugees in the Territories of Host States' in *Special Issue of the International Journal of Refugee Law,* 12 (2000) 251–271.

24 C. Beyani, 'Second Summit of the International Conference on the Great Lakes Region: Pact on Security, Stability and Development in the Great Lakes Region', 46 *ILM* (2007) 173–184.

Republic of the Congo between six States, namely, Rwanda and Uganda on the one hand, and Angola, Democratic Republic of the Congo, Namibia, and Zimbabwe, with assistance from Chad, Libya, and Sudan on the other hand. In this climate, the pack of available solutions appeared to diminish until 2004 when the Great Lakes peace process set in under the International Conference on Peace and Security and elaborated a comprehensive framework of peace, security, and stability in which the protection of refugees and internally displaced persons features prominently.[25]

4. *'Solution' Oriented Trends*

The African system is notable for being directly inclined to the repatriation of refugees to their countries of origin. It was thought that repatriation would set in after the wars of national liberation. Aside form that, a repatriation oriented system appeared to be an eventual remedy for a system based on the *en masse* admission of refugees by host States. However, massive refugee out-flows in Africa continued beyond the spectre of armed liberation struggles. The perceived remedy also diminished in the face of the perpetual being of refugees.

In any case, the propriety of repatriation may, in certain cases, clash with the necessity to evacuate refugee populations from host States to other States when there is a threat to their physical security or safety that may overwhelm a host State. Inherent weaknesses in repatriation based solutions are that renewed outflows after evacuation or repatriation are often prone to recur because of renewed conflict, as in the case of Liberia in the 1990's, or population growth amidst shrinking resources, including land, as in Rwanda since 1998, and because of the lack of overall sustainable development and meaningful reintegration programmes in the countries of origin.

It is poignant that the magnitude of the challenges has grown at a moment in time when the syndrome of 'refugee fatigue' has set in. As a result, international and regional solidarity for the cause of refugee protection appears to be faltering. Several factors account for this state of affairs. First, there are no longer 'power based' strategic interests to be pursued in Africa in the aftermath of the cold war and international interest in the political dimensions that created refugees problems, such as thwarting communism or capitalism, has correspondingly waned. Secondly, there is not in place a serviceable system of international solidarity which regularly nourishes the principle of burden or responsibility sharing in order to enhance the capacity of the entire system of refugee protection. Thirdly, as Professor Bonaventure Rutinwa has observed, many African States are increasingly becoming inward looking.[26] This may be in response to internal political

---

25 www.icglr.org.

26 B.Rutinwa, 'End of Asylum? The Changing Nature of Refugee Policies in Africa' (UNHCR Working Paper No. 5, Geneva, 1999). Available at: http://www.unhcr.org/cgi-bin/texis/vtx/research/opendoc.pdf?tbl=RESEARCH&id=3ae6a0c34.

accountability for the plight of their own populations as part of the emerging process of democratic accountability and, or, due to the economic and social dislocation brought about by the international policy of economic structural adjustment and the privatisation of public utilities.[27]

Despite all these factors, the responses to the prevailing challenges have been formidable, though somewhat fragmented. Most strikingly, the AU has signalled its determination to address the root causes of refugee out-flows and displacement as 'basically and foremost an African responsibility'.[28] Amongst the root causes identified are armed conflicts, gross violations of human rights, natural calamities, drought and famine. The vision is for Africa to tackle these, and for the international community to assist in that effort.[29] In essence, this suggests a partnership between Africa and the international system in dealing with the situation of refugees and internally displaced persons. Before examining what this partnership entails, there should be regard to the issue of the political resolution of African States to address the root causes of refugee out-flow.

The political will of African States to tackle the situation of root causes is demonstrated amply in the inauguration in 1993 of the *Central Organ of the AU Mechanism for Conflict Prevention, Management and Resolution.*[30] Preventive diplomacy, early warning, peace keeping, and conflict resolution are the hall marks of this system on the political front. On the economic front, the agenda encourages regional and sub-regional economic and political integration anchored in the *Abuja Treaty establishing the African Development Community* 1991.

Within this agenda, sub-regional bodies have displayed increased interest and concern for refugees in the context of establishing conditions of regional stability that are favourable to economic integration and development. Thus ECOWAS (The Economic Community for West African States), and SADC (the Southern African Development Community) have established defence and conflict prevention mechanisms which have been actively engaged in conflicts in West Africa, including Sierra-Leone and Liberia, and in the Democratic Republic of the Congo respectively; IGAD (the Inter-Governmental Authority on Development) has also established a conflict prevention mechanism and has pledged to find lasting and durable solutions to the problem of conflict and refugees in the horn of Africa, particularly in Somalia where Ethiopian armed forces intervened in 2007 and the African Union has sent ill-equipped peace keeping forces.

---

27 See AU Council of Ministers, *Relaunching Africa's Economic and Social Development : The Cairo Agenda for Action, Report of the Seventeenth Extra-ordinary Session of the Council of Minsters*, CM/1892(LXII), 1995.

28 *Secretary-General's Report on the Root Causes of the Refugee Problem in Africa*, CM/1605 (LIII) Rev.I).

29 Ibid.

30 *Report of the Secretary-General on the Establishment, within the AU, of Mechanism for Conflict Prevention, Management and Resolution* 1993; *AU's Position Towards the Various Initiatives on Conflict Management: Enhancing AU's Capacity in Preventive Diplomacy, Conflict Resolution and PeaceKeeping*, Central Organ/MEC/MIN/3 (IV).

The treaty frameworks establishing some of these bodies carry specific objectives for the harmonisation of national laws and policies on the free movement of persons, goods and services, rights of residence and establishment, immigration and refugee laws. Specific standards and structures for the protection of refugees are proposed in this context.[31] The sub-regional bodies are making progress towards the consolidation of free movement generally, which will eventually ease the situation of refugees with regard to their movement and residence in the sub-regions to which they belong.

So far as the matter of partnership is concerned, the underlying dynamics are predominantly institutional. For a start, the AU's Committee of Ministers has reiterated the Union's commitment to take bold measures to solve the problem of refugees. The Committee has reiterated the importance of a partnership predicated on solidarity between African peoples and Governments on the one hand, and the international community on the other. This is viewed as a necessary condition for a successful system of refugee protection in Africa. In operating a limited system of burden or responsibility sharing, the Committee has called for international support in the provision of material, financial, and moral assistance in tackling the problems of protection while recognising that African responsibility is paramount. In reality, this should be regarded as part of a broad international responsibility for the protection of refugees in which African States have disproportionately bone the brunt of expenditure in human, economic, material and unquantifiable resources.

The obligations to protect refugees are international in character and scope and thus touch upon the interests of the international community as whole.

Institutional responses to alleviating the plight of refugees have grown out of cooperation between the UNHCR and the AU. As a result, cognate strategies aimed at tackling the abiding challenges have been formulated in an array of recommendations contained in the *Addis Ababa Document on Refugees and forced population displacements in Africa 1994; the Bujumbura Plan of Action and the Kampala conference 1998* which addressed the protection of refugees in the light of security concerns by States, and established the basis for redressing the relationship between protection, humanitarian assistance, and reconstruction, based on longer-term post-conflict peace-building measures. These were followed by the CIP adopted by the AU and UNHCR in 2000 in Conakry. The CIP contained recommendations on concretely strengthening the protection of refugees in Africa; a task force was established to assist the AU/UNHCR Implementing Committee to identify priorities of protection.[32]

No less significant was the response of the Secretary General of the United Nations who lent support to the efforts taken by UNHCR and the AU and highlighted the necessity for coordinating the system of humanitarian assistance with

31 See for example, ECOWAS, *A.L.M.* (1991) 3; SADC 32 *I.L.M.*(1993) 116.
32 See http://www.unhcr.org/publ/PUBL/3e23eb6e0.pdf.

specific reference to the protection of refugees and displaced persons.[33] The Secretary General has also examined the specific issue of security for refugees, humanitarian personnel, and host States in the Great lakes Region.[34] His recommendations however carried wider significance going beyond that region.[35] They endorsed an overall strategy involving protection, assistance, repatriation, and the reintegration of refugees and internally displaced persons as well as longer-term regional efforts, towards national reconciliation, rehabilitation and reconstruction. Specific recommendations included giving assistance to the military forces of host States to enable them to protect refugees, isolate military elements, protect humanitarian operations, and the option of deploying international peacekeeping forces to carry out these purposes.

Although the political context in which the character of the refugee problem is changing, the substantive premises, principles and institutions upon which the African refugee regime are based, namely, mass out-flows, protection and assistance, including burden or responsibility sharing, and return oriented solutions, have remained the same. If anything, these should be developed further to cement a pro-active (as opposed to a reactive or responsive) system of protection whose dimensions should be the subject of specific protocols or agreements reflecting the changing political climate.

5. *Issues of Protection*

There are a considerable number of issues affecting the protection of refugees in Africa. For the purpose of this study, the most germane few can be identified as follows.

5.1. *Group Eligibility*

Group eligibility, i.e., the admission as refugees of significantly large numbers of asylum seekers on the *prima facie* basis is quintessentially a progressive founding basis of the system of refugee protection in Africa. This does pose a major dilemma, which is that the inclusive nature of such protection raises, in practice, a tension between *en masse* admission and the necessity to exclude combatants, militia, and other persons who must be excluded from protection under Article 1(F) of the 1951 Convention because there are serious reasons to believe that they have committed international crimes, serious non-political crimes, or engaged in activities contrary to the United Nations or the African Union.

By its very character, group eligibility circumvents the determination of refugee status on an individual basis and yet it is the individualised determination

33 United Nations, *Report of the Secretary -General on the work of the Organisation* (New York, 1998).
34 *Report of the Secretary- General on Security in the Rwandese Camps*, S/1994/1308, 18 November 1994.
35 Ibid.

procedures that are crucial to undertaking exclusion. In practice, massive influxes of refugees certainly overwhelm individual status determination procedures. That represents a conundrum of all sorts that is difficult to deal with in theory and in practice. Yet refugee status obtained by virtue of group eligibility co-exists legally with refugee status obtained by virtue of individual determination procedures. In theory, both forms of status should be legally equal. But this is not the case in practice. African State practice subjects urban asylum seekers to individual determination procedures while applying group eligibility procedures to groups of asylum seekers residing in the rural areas.

This difference of treatment is not justified where the cause of flight is the same for urban and rural asylum seekers. To eliminate such differentiated treatment, there must be harmonised procedures and institutions for determining refugee status based on the principle under the AU Convention that asylum is a peaceful humanitarian act not to be regarded as an unfriendly act.[36] The obligations of African States in this respect derive directly from their membership of the AU to use their best endeavour to receive and to secure the settlement of refugees within their territories. For these reasons, the AU Refugee Convention has to be regarded as the *lex specialis.*

5.2. *Protection*

A major protection issue concerns the protection of the rights of refugees after lawful admission to the territories of the receiving States. The main basis for determining the rights of refugees is clearly the 1951 Convention. On the whole, that Convention is not the exclusive source of reference for such rights. Although its preamble pays homage to the United Nations Charter 1945 and the Universal Declaration of Human Rights 1948, it does not holistically employ the language of 'rights'; its obligations accord treatment to refugees on the basis of either the national or minimum international standard of treatment. Inevitably, refugees are entitled potentially to the full scope of human rights stipulated in human rights treaties, subject to the consent of the host States to such treaties, to the extent that the protection of those rights is consistent with their status as refugees. Economic, social and cultural rights as regards food, health, adequate housing or shelter, work, education, and are basic to refugees, although they are not often given specific protection as such.

The common assumption that humanitarian assistance to refugees in general meets the requirements of these rights is inadequate. The rights in question provide standards of protection for refugees and they are a legal guide for the conduct of those responsible for such protection when it comes to determining the form, quality and manner of assistance. In addition to protection offered by the 1951 Convention, refugee women and children require specific forms of protection that are specified in the standards contained in the *Convention on the Elimination of All*

[36] See Article II, *AU Convention Governing the Specific Aspects of Refugee Problems in Africa.*

Forms of Discrimination Against Women (CEDAW) 1979, the *Convention on the Rights of the Child* (CRC) 1989, the *African Charter on Human and Peoples' Rights,* the *African Charter on the Rights and Welfare of the Child* 1990, and the *Protocol to the African Charter on Human and Peoples' Rights on the Rights of Women in Africa* 2003.

Non-discrimination by reference to gender, protection against sexual abuse, exploitation and extortion, trafficking, and ensuring reproductive health and care, are crucial to refugee women. The best interests of the child, non-discrimination, protection against trafficking and recruitment in armed forces or armed groups, and mounting recovery or rehabilitation programmes for children are specific areas of protection for refugee children.

There is an endemic problem of statelessness in Africa, despite the existence of international obligations against statelessness and towards stateless persons,[37] as well as decisions of the African Commission against rendering persons stateless and expelling refugees illegally.[38] The phenomenon of statelessness in Africa has not been given the full attention it deserves; it essentially requires the elaboration of a Protocol to the African Charter on Human and Peoples' Rights centred on the right to nationality and the prohibition of statelessness by arbitrary deprivation of nationality.[39]

5.3. *Security*

The prohibition of subversive activities[40] on the part of refugees goes to the root of the civilian nature of refugee protection as well as the civilian character of refugee camps. Clear choices must be made by those wishing to receive protection as refugees and those who wish to engage in armed military action. Refugee camps are not the place for the latter; the civilian and humanitarian character of refugee camps is based on the concept of demilitarisation or absence of military activity which is crucial to humanitarian operations. But the state of affairs is such that armed protection for refugees and humanitarian workers, as indicated in the United Nations' Secretary General's report, is a necessary component of protection.

To strengthen protection, the establishment of camps for refugees must be consistent with the principle of safe location which requires, for reasons of security, that refugees be settled as far as possible from the frontier of their countries of origin.[41] This principle has not always been observed with the result that refugee

---

[37] *Convention Relating to the Status of State less Persons* 1954; Convention on the *Reduction of State lessness* 1961; and *Convention for the Reduction of Cases of State less Persons* 1973.

[38] *Modise v Botswana* (Nationality and State lessness) Decision of the African Commission, 21st Ordinary Session, April 1997; *Organisation Mondale Contre La Torture, and others v Rwanda* (Asylum and expulsion) Decision of the African Commission, 20th Ordinary Session, October 1996.

[39] For a comprehensive analysis of th problems involved, see B. Manby, *Struggles for Citizenship in Africa* (London, Zed Books, 2009).

[40] Article III, *AU Convention Governing the Specific Aspects of Refugee Problems in Africa.*

[41] Article II(6), *AU Convention Governing the Specific Aspects of Refugee Problems in Africa..*

camps continue, in some cases, to be located perilously close to the border of the State of origin. Safe location connotes the combined criteria of distance and safety, not the arbitrary location of thirty kilometres from the frontier of the country of origin. It relates to the distance which, having regard to all circumstances pertaining to the risk of insecurity, guarantees the location of refugees in safety. The principle of safe location should also be applied in situations of conflict so that refugees are located safely away from areas of conflict. In the event that refugees must be evacuated from areas of armed conflict in the receiving States, safe location to other areas should be considered to be an overbidding principle.

5.4. *Voluntary Repatriation*

Refugee protection in Africa is return oriented. Voluntary repatriation is the legal anchor in terms of Article V of the Convention.[42]

> The essentially voluntary character of repatriation shall be respected in all cases and no refugee shall be repatriated against his will.

Voluntary repatriation is a species of the right to return, but it is based upon the consent and willingness of refugees to return to their States of origin when the circumstances which caused them to flee revert to normality. How 'normal' such normality should be is, is a huge question. Sometimes the mere conclusion of peace agreements, cease fire, elections, and the adoption of new constitutions, are taken or mistaken for normal circumstances that permit repatriation. Repatriation that is ill-judged or which results from diminishing resources is more likely to exacerbate original causes of flight than provide a durable solution.

In practice, voluntary repatriation takes many forms, e.g., organised, spontaneous, induced or coerced. The basic legal issue to ensure is the voluntariness of repatriation, which provides a safeguard against refoulement, coercion or inducement to return. Specific problems which stand in the way of the right to return include land mines, land constraints, breakdown in infrastructure etc. To be durable, voluntary repatriation must be informed and linked to addressing the root causes as well as integration, resettlement, and reconstruction programmes which should offer targeted forms of redress and building the capacity to absorb returning refugees, and confidence building measures. To provide effective legal protection, tripartite agreements under which repatriation exercises are conducted must be justiciable before the courts of the host States and the States of origin. As a corollary, such agreements may be challenged before the African Commission or Court in situations where a breach of a right of a refugee descends directly from their implementation.

[42] Article V(1), *AU Convention Governing the Specific Aspects of Refugee Problems in Africa.*

6. *Concluding Reflections*

This Chapter has provided a contextual background to the situation of refugees in Africa and the attendant problems of their protection. The framework of human rights is significant to addressing protection that is founded on the UN and AU Conventions on refugees. It is clear that diplomatic, political, and development based techniques are essential components of protection. A study on the application of the African system of human rights to the protection of refugees does not by itself provide a comprehensive formula of protection or solutions. But it does illuminate the way in which the right to seek and obtain asylum under the African Charter is protected for asylum seekers and refugees.

Chapter 3

The Applicable Legal Framework

1. *Introduction*

Human rights law is widely regarded as one of the most important branches of international law. The role of human rights is to govern the behaviour and conduct of States towards all human beings in their jurisdiction or control and to establish national and international accountability for such behaviour or conduct. Human rights are mainly defined by standards on how human beings ought to be treated and protected by States as stipulated in international agreements that such States accept to be bound by voluntarily.[1] These agreements are themselves governed by international law, as the law applicable to the relations and activities of States, International Organizations, individuals and other participants whose international participation is regulated by international law.

The African Charter on Human and Peoples' Rights is an example of a regional agreement relating specifically, as it does, to the protection of human rights in Africa. African Heads of States adopted this Charter in Nairobi, Kenya, in 1981; the Charter itself became effective as a regional legal instrument when it entered into force in 1986. Apart from Morocco, all African States have ratified or accepted the provisions of the Charter as formally binding and applicable upon and between them.

1 In the context of the sources of international law and the settlement of disputes, Article 38(1)(a) of the Statute of the International Court of Justice refers to such agreements as 'international conventions, whether general or particular, establishing rules expressly recognised by the contesting States'.

In 1987 the African Commission on Human and Peoples' Rights (referred to as 'the African Commission' in short) was established under Article 30 of the Charter, with the mandate of overseeing and ensuring the promotion and protection of human and peoples' rights in Africa. More recently, the Commission was supplemented by an African Court of Human and Peoples' Rights as created under the *Protocol on the Establishment of an African Court on Human and People's Rights* adopted in Ouagadougou, Burkina Faso, in 1998. This *Protocol* entered into force in December 2003,[2] and the African Court itself was created in January 2006. Never the less, barely two years later, the African Court of Human and Peoples' Rights was merged legally, with the yet to be established Court of Justice of the African Union, under the *Protocol on the Statute of the African Court of Justice and Human Rights* 2008,[3] which was adopted in that year in Sharm El-Sheikh, Egypt. As if the merger were not enough, almost a year later, the AU Assembly[4] requested 'the African Union Commission, in consultation with the African Commission on Human and Peoples' Rights, and African Court on Human and Peoples' Rights, to examine the implications of the Court being empowered to try international crimes such as genocide, crimes against humanity and war crimes.'

This process is still developing, but the pace at which these developments have taken place has not given the African Court on Human and Peoples' Rights time to settle and function as a court expected to pass legally binding decisions. Conferring the Court with criminal jurisdiction in particular has far reaching implications on its viability in the long term as a justice, human rights, and criminal justice Court. However, it holds out a prospect to prosecute those who would commit persecution as a crime against humanity in relation to refugees and internally displaced persons in Africa.

This discussion on institutional developments should lose sight of the fact that both the African Commission and Court are tied to the *African Charter on Human and Peoples' Rights*. The framework of the Charter consists of general obligations relating to the protection of human rights by the member States of the African Union, individual rights, freedoms, duties, and peoples' rights. Since a human rights treaty constitutes an integral framework for protecting human rights, all the human rights provisions contained in the Charter, including duties and peoples' rights, do apply to asylum seekers and refugees in given contexts. However, in a Study of this kind, emphasis is placed on those aspects of the Charter that have a direct bearing on the protection of refugees.

---

2 See AU Doc. AU/LEG/EXP/AFCHPR/PROT (III).

3 However, this Protocol has been ratified by only 26 Member States of the African Union, namely, Algeria, Burkina Faso, Burundi, Comoros, Congo, Côte d'Ivoire, Gabon, the Gambia, Ghana, Kenya, Libya, Lesotho, Mali, Malawi, Mozambique, Mauritania, Mauritius, Nigeria, Niger, Rwanda, South Africa, Sénégal, Tanzania, Togo, Tunisia and Uganda.

4 See Decision, Assembly/AU/Dec.213 (XII), on the abuse of the principle of Universal Jurisdiction, adopted in Addis Ababa, Ethiopia on 4th February 2009, by the 12th Ordinary Session of the Assembly of the African Union.

2. *The Duty to Protect*

Under Article 1, the Charter lays a duty on the States parties, in their capacity as Member States of the African Union, to recognize the rights, duties, and freedoms enshrined in the Charter. This duty requires the States parties to undertake to adopt legislative or other measures to give effect to these rights, duties, and freedoms. The duty is one of recognition of the applicable rights, freedoms and duties. Importantly, the duty descends from Membership of the African Union rather than the Charter itself. The implication is that all Member States of the African Union are under a duty to recognise the rights, duties, and freedoms established by the African Charter and to give effect to these rights, freedoms, and duties.

If the object of this duty is to give legal effect to the application of the African Charter within the national laws of African States as a means of promoting the protection of human rights at national level, then the failure to carry out this duty places the failing State in a posture of breach or violation of the African Charter. A serious legal consequence for breaching this and other obligations in the African Charter is to render the offending States liable to proceedings before the African Commission or Court when the breach itself results in an actual violation of human rights protected by the Charter. Against Zimbabwe the Commission held that an order of clemency which precluded the claimants from claiming redress in Zimbabwe breached of Article 1 of the African Charter.[5]

A breach of this nature touches upon state responsibility in international law. The responsibility for States which arises from the failure to discharge their obligations or to abide by them is overrides deficiencies in the relevant national law, national institutions and national courts. The African Commission has adopted the well-known principle that international treaty law prohibits States from relying on their national law as justification for their non-compliance with international duties or obligations. This means that national law is not an exclusive framework for treating asylum seekers and refugees, and reliance upon it is not an excuse to not carry out duties required internationally by human rights. Where these duties are concerned, it is irrelevant that the failure of a State to abide by them results from some inadequacy or other deficiency in national law or in the functioning of national institutions, including national courts or tribunals.

The duty to recognize human rights in the Charter is a wider aspect of the responsibility of States to perform their duties or obligations under international law. The African Commission and Court are the bodies before which African States parties to the Charter and the Protocol establishing the African Court are accountable in the way in which they treat human beings within their jurisdiction. The term 'jurisdiction' broadly connotes the power or competence of a State to prescribe law and enforce such law over its territory. It is clear that the concept of

[5] *Zimbabwe NGO Forum v Zimbabwe, Communication 245/2002*, Annex III, 21st Activity Report of the African Commission on Human and Peoples' Rights, 25–26 January 2007, EX.CL/322(X) at p. 54, para. 215.

jurisdiction lately has assumed wider implications in the application of human rights treaties to persons or property under the effective control of a State in its territory and beyond.

In so far as the application of international law is concerned, the Commission has taken the view that in interpreting and applying the Charter, it is guided by Articles 60 and 61 from which it can "draw inspiration from international law on human and peoples' rights" as reflected in the instruments of the AU and the UN as well as other international standard- setting treaties. This is because the Commission and the Court are obliged by the Charter to take into consideration other international conventions and African practices consistent with international norms and standards.

In the case of *Democratic Republic of Congo v Burundi, Rwanda and Uganda,*[6] the Commission applied instruments of international humanitarian law, namely, Part III of the *Geneva Convention Relative to the Protection of Civilian Persons in Time of War* 1949 and certain provisions of *Protocol 1 Additional to the Geneva Convention* to determine allegations of grave and massive violations of human and peoples' rights committed by the armed forces of the respondent states in eastern parts of the Democratic Republic of Congo. In the first decision of its kind, and addressing sexual violence in substance for the first time, the Commission held that the rape of women and girls in the eastern part of the Democratic Republic of the Congo was a violation of the African Charter on the basis of Articles 60 and 61, read together with the *International Convention on the Elimination of All Forms of Discrimination Against Women,* and Article 76 of *Additional Protocol* I, under which 'women shall be the object of special respect and shall be protected in particular against rape, forced prostitution and any form of indecent assault'.

It would appear that the Court would not have such broad and flexible latitude to apply general international law in its mandate. Under Article 7 of the *Protocol establishing the African Court on Human and Peoples' Rights,* the Court shall apply the provisions of the Charter and any other relevant human rights instruments *ratified* by the States appearing in any proceedings held by the Court. While this provision is somewhat limiting when compared to the broad reach of the Commission, it is nevertheless sufficiently broad in that the Court has the potential competence to apply those human rights instruments ratified by African Sates (and there are many) and which cannot be invoked by human rights courts elsewhere. Unlike its European or Inter-American counterpart, its competence is not tied to a single founding human rights instrument.

These flexible aspects of the African human rights system are unique legal arrangements offering the advantage of bringing within it a wide network of international agreements, declarations, and international human rights case law relevant to issues of human rights and refugees that could be applied by the Commission and the Court in their decisions and interpretation of the African Charter. 'Traditional' African hospitality to visitors in distress should also be

[6] *Communication 227/99*, Annex IV, 20th Activity Report at 111.

applied as a progressive aspect of African values and practice consistent with international obligations towards refugees.

Applicable instruments within the Charter include human rights instruments and specific refugee instruments such as the *AU Convention Governing the Specific Aspects of Refugee Problem in Africa* and the *United Nations Convention Relating to the Status of Refugees*, read together with the 1976 *Protocol* to that Convention. The former has previously been invoked by the Commission with respect to a complaint concerning the expulsion of Sierra-Leonese refugees from Guinea Conakry in 2000.[7] In this case, the African Commission decided that, by targeting refuges from Sierra-Leone for expulsion and other related measures, Guinea Conakry had violated Article 4 of the *AU Convention Governing the Specific Aspects of Refugee Problem in Africa*.[8]

In addition, there are sub-regional treaties establishing the Community of West African States (ECOWAS) 1974, the East African Community (EAC) 2000, and the Southern African Development Community (SADC) 1990, which could be applied under the framework of the African Charter. Conversely, these treaties also establish special courts or tribunals in which the African Charter on Human and Peoples' rights could be invoked generally or with regard to refugees specifically. The ECOWAS Court of Justice has held that the African Charter is the supreme law of ECOWAS.

3. *Human Rights and Refugee Protection*

Scholars, practitioners and advocates of refugee protection frequently encounter the problem that many States do not accept the use of human rights as part of the formal responsibility for protecting refugees. At national level, the vast majority of national Constitutions are framed or interpreted in ways that either exclude refugees from making use of human rights, or restrict the extent to which refugees may exercise constitutionally guaranteed rights. Consequently, the practice and theory of refugee law treated refugee protection separately from the protection of human rights. This began to change in the 1990's.

Underlying the difficulty of the use of human rights by refugees and asylum seekers to protect themselves is the attitude that being a refugee carries a stigma and that national institutions are prejudiced against refugees. There is the 'stereotype' that refugees are a bothersome category of individuals whose suffering does not deserve a certain quality of treatment or protection based on human rights.

---

7 *African Institute for Human Rights and Development (on behalf of Sierra Leonean refugees in Guinea) v Republic of Guinea, Communication 249/2002*, Annex II, African Union Executive Council, 20th Activity Report of the African Commission on Human and Peoples' Rights, 25–29th June 2006, EX.CL/279(IX), p. 132–142.

8 Under Article 4, 'Member States undertake to apply the provisions of this Convention to all refugees without discrimination as to race, religion, nationality, membership of a particular social group or political opinions.'

Yet the protection of human rights has always been concerned with redressing the suffering and ill-treatment of all human beings. The powerlessness brought about by the precarious status of refugees can be diminished by scholars, practitioners and advocates for refugee protection by using human rights as a strategic means of empowering refugees to deal with situations of deliberate neglect, inflicted hardships and helplessness.

A further obstacle to the use of human rights in the legal protection of refugees has been that standards and institutions for protecting refugees developed separately ahead of those of human rights. Even though the specific standards and institutions for the protection of refugees were grounded originally in human rights ideals, as the preamble to the Convention Relating to the Status of Refugees shows, such human rights ideals and standards became isolated by a narrow construction of refugee law. This despite the right to seek and enjoy asylum, established originally in Article 14 of the *Universal Declaration of Human Rights* in 1948.

The fact that this right was not included in subsequent international agreements on human rights led a number of scholars in refugee law to dismiss the right to seek and enjoy asylum as empty and of no real value. As a result of these and other factors, the intellectual and practical application of human rights to refugees has been a rear driven process fraught with resistance, uncertainty and even difficulty. Developments in the institutional protection of human rights are such that the time is ripe to break the mindset of refugee protection through scholarship, advocacy and targeted use of human rights.

3.1. *Human Rights and Refugee Protection*

The basic fact remains that individual and mass refugee out-flows result from violations of human rights of a varying scale and intensity. In this regard, human rights provide a two- pronged approach to the protection of the rights of refugees. First, unlike refugee law, human rights protection under the African Charter enables refugees to bring claims against their States of origin on the basis of continuing violations of their rights from the fact of persecution and flight to other States.

This was the case in *John D. Ouko v Kenya*.[9] The facts as found by the African Commission were that the complainant was a Students' Union leader at the University of Nairobi and he alleged that he was forced to flee Kenya due to his political opinions. Prior to his fleeing the country, he was arrested and detained without trial for 10 months in the basement cells of the Secret Service Department headquarters in Nairobi. The detention facility was a 'two by three metre' basement cell with a 250 watts electric bulb, which was left on throughout his ten months' detention. The complainant claimed that throughout his period of

---

9 *Communication 232/99, Compilation of Decisions on Communications of the African Commission on Human and Peoples' Rights*, p. 144.

detention, he was denied bathroom facilities and was subjected to both physical and mental torture.

He fled the country on 10th November 1997 to Uganda, where he initially sought political asylum but was denied it and he had to leave for the Democratic Republic of Congo (DRC) in March 1998 where he was recognized as a refugee. It is ironic that he was offered by refuge by a State that was in turmoil. He lodged a complaint against Kenya whilst a refugee residing in the Democratic Republic of the Congo, alleging violations of certain rights under the African Charter.

The African Commission decided that *the persecution and subsequent flight* of the complainant from Kenya, the country of origin, had violated human rights provisions in the African Charter, particularly Article 5 regarding respect for human dignity, protection from torture, inhuman and degrading treatment, Article 6 concerning liberty and security of the person, Article 9 in relation to freedom of expression, Article 10 on freedom of association, and Article 12 pertaining to freedom of movement and residence. Legal claims by refugees against their States of origin must be encouraged to establish the responsibility of those States for their failure to protect their nationals, or for authoring events causing their flight as refugees in third States. Such claims are also significantly helpful to protect property rights of refugees in the State of origin in the aftermath of their flight to other States in their search of safety.[10]

By focusing almost exclusively on the legal obligations of the receiving States, international refugee law fails to address this area of protection adequately. But this is an area where international human rights law makes an important difference to protection. The case of *Loizidou v Turkey*[11] demonstrates this well. The Applicant, *Loizidou*, belonged to a community of Kyrenian Cypriot refugees who had fled 'ethnic cleansing' in Northern Cyprus when Turkey invaded that territory in 1974 and had not been allowed to return there. She was part of an organised group of refugee women who took part in a 'walk back home' march and was thereupon arrested by Turkish authorities.

The case brought against Turkey before the European Court of Human Rights concerned denial of access to, and interference with, property rights of the Applicant in Northern Cyprus. Turkey claimed, amongst other things, that *Loizidou's* property had been irreversibly expropriated by virtue of certain laws passed by the 'Turkish Republic of Northern Cyprus' in 1985. The Court decided that the Applicant remained legal owner of the land in question, but since 1974 effectively lost all control, use and enjoyment of it, and that this was a continuing denial of access to property and amounted to an interference with her property rights.

Loizidou v Turkey is an example of a case that is appropriate to identify and bring before the African Commission or Court because its outcome had a wider

[10] See for example, International Conference on the Great Lakes Region, *Protocol on the Property Rights of Returning Persons* 2006.

[11] *Loizidou v Turkey* 23 EHRR 101.

impact on similarly deprived refugees. The decision became hugely important for *Loizidou* and the Kyrenian refugees who had not been able to go home and to their properties in Northern Cyprus since 1974.

In the second place, human rights enable refugees to bring claims for protection against the host, or receiving, country on which the focus of international refugee law lies. In this regard, human rights offer complementary protection where refugee law is deficient or offers no forum for complaints, and is unable to provide the specific type of legal protection that may be determined or obtained by means of a complaint to the African Commission or Court.

Encouragement to apply human rights to protect refugees stems from the positive response from human rights bodies to address refugee claims. Refugees themselves have resorted to the use of human rights when national legal systems fail to protect them legally. In addition, awareness of the plight of refugees has grown in the human rights movement, on the part of civil society, lawyers, academics, and activists. The movement's response to the plight of refugees has corresponded to the maturity and willingness of the human rights bodies to address refugee claims in the context of human rights at regional and international levels.

Explicit provisions on the right to seek and enjoy asylum in both the *American Convention on Human Rights* 1969[12] and the African *Charter on Human and Peoples Rights* 1981[13] have been invoked with notable success to protect refugee claims in the 1990's. This shows that the right to seek and enjoy asylum should no longer be regarded as empty of content; it has acquired substantive content and a real practical value that should be used to explore and promote complementary protection for refugees as human beings with human rights, where the legal protection of their rights is absent or ineffective at national level.

4. *Concluding Reflections*

Complaints alleging violations of human rights under the African Charter on Human and Peoples' Rights can only be brought to the African Commission or Court against States parties to the Charter. Is the State receiving asylum seekers and refugees a party to the African Charter on Human and Peoples' Rights? The ratification Chart in the Appendices to this Study is a helpful guide.

Further issues for reflection include: does the receiving State recognize the rights, duties, and freedoms, contained in the African Charter on Human and Peoples' Rights by providing for the Charter to be applied directly under its Constitution, legislation, other laws or by national courts? It is necessary to

12 See Article 22(7) which States that 'Every person has the right to seek and be granted asylum in a foreign territory, in accordance with the legislation of the State and international conventions, in the event he is being pursued for political offences or related common crimes'.

13 Under Article 12(3) of the Charter 'Every Individual shall have the right, when persecuted, to seek and obtain asylum in other States in accordance with the laws of those States and international conventions'.

examine the Index of the laws of the State concerned to help locate the Constitution, national legislation, other written laws, and assess all these accordingly, paying particular regard to the existence of the right to seek and enjoy asylum, other legislation or statutes concerning refugees.

If the application of the African Charter on Human and Peoples' Rights is provided for, then it is important to determine whether the actual treatment accorded to asylum seekers and refugees is consistent with the standards of the Charter. Where such treatment is not consistent with the Charter, there may be a case for considering possible violations of human rights of specific asylum seekers and refugees arising from a breach of the Charter in specific circumstances.

And where no provision exists for the direct or indirect application of the African Charter on Human and Peoples' Rights that strengthens the case for bringing individual complaints about human rights violations against the State concerned on account of the breach of a duty to give effect to the rights recognized in the Charter. In the case of those States that follow the civil law system, it is necessary to determine whether the Charter applies directly in national law even if there is not a specific law giving effect to it.

The pertinent questions would be: are there applicable international instruments and cases of international human rights law that are relevant and which could be applied? Are the regional and sub-regional instruments relevant to the specific problem at hand, and how could they be applied to provide protection to refugees? What is the official attitude of the Government towards refugees as shown in official statements? Ideally, a record of official pronouncements and acts towards refugees should be kept, regardless of whether they are positive or negative. Where relevant, these may be used as evidence in proceedings before the African Commission.

Is the official policy and attitude of the Government towards refugees based on human rights as laid out in the African Charter and other human rights instruments? Do constitutionally guaranteed rights apply to refugees and are refugees able to assert these rights before Government officials, Commissions on Human Rights, national courts and status determination Committees? These matters are crucial to determine what remedies, if any, are available to refugees at national level. The act of lodging complaints or commencing proceedings before the African Commission or Court should be a measure of last resort after determining that existing channels through which rights of refugees could be redressed at national level have either been exhausted, or are not available to refugees, or are absent altogether.

Is there any national legislation on refugees? If there isn't, on what basis are refugees protected? If there is any, does this legislation contain any human rights standards stipulated in the African Charter? If it does not, is such legislation compatible with human rights as protected at national level? It is advisable to check, in particular, whether this legislation is compatible with constitutionally guaranteed rights. How does this legislation measure up to the rights contained in the African Charter?

Does the legislation contain, or refer to specific standards for the protection of refugees in the *Convention Relating to the Status of Refugees* 1951, or the *AU Convention on Refugees* 1969, or both? These questions provide an important aspect of assessing the quality of treatment given to refugees and whether such treatment is compliant with human rights and with specific standards concerning refugee protection.

Chapter 4

The African Charter and the Protection of Refugees

1. *Sources*

In seeking to use the African Charter to protect refugees, it is important first to identify and those provisions that provide the foundation for protection. These are provisions that:

a. Establish positive duties for States to protect human rights. These duties can be identified from the mandatory language used, e.g., the State '*shall*', or 'every individual '*shall*'. This type of language is used typically in Articles 1 and 3 of the Charter. According to Article 1, 'The Member States of the Organization of African Unity parties to the present Charter *shall* recognize the rights, duties and freedoms enshrined in this Chapter and *shall* undertake to adopt legislative or other measures to give effect to them'. Under Article 3, 'Every individual shall be equal before the law';
b. Stipulate general guarantees underlying the protection of all the rights in the Charter, e.g., non-discrimination under Articles 2 and 18(3). Under Article 2: 'Every individual shall be entitled to the enjoyment of the rights and freedoms recognized and guaranteed in the present Charter without distinction of any kind such as race, ethnic group, color, sex, language, religion, political or any other opinion, national and social origin, fortune, birth or other status'. Article 18 (3) is of special importance to the protection of refugee women as well as refugee children. It reads: 'The State shall ensure the elimination of every

discrimination against women and also ensure the protection of the rights of the woman and the child as stipulated in international declarations and conventions'.

c. Set out specific individual rights that can be applied to provide protection in specific cases, e.g., life under Article 4: 'Every human being shall be entitled to respect for his life and the integrity of his person'; liberty under Article 6: 'Every individual shall have the right to liberty and to the security of his person'; to seek and obtain asylum under Article 12(3): 'Every individual shall have the right, when persecuted, to seek and obtain asylum in other States in accordance with laws of those States and international conventions'.

2. *Primary Duties for States*

The main duties laid down in Article 1 of the African Charter have been considered already from the general perspective of the responsibility of States for complying with international human rights obligations. It is now necessary to highlight the role of these duties in the protection of refugees under the Charter. The provisions of Article 1 of the Charter must be reiterated for this purpose:

> The Member States of the Organisation of African unity parties to the present Charter shall recognise the rights, duties and freedoms enshrined in this Charter and shall undertake to adopt legislative or other measures to give effect to them.

The Commission has interpreted this provision to mean that it establishes positive duties, i.e., duties requiring States to take action favourable to the protection of human rights.[1] The first is the duty to recognize the rights, duties and freedoms in the Charter, and the second is an undertaking to adopt legislative or other measures to give effect to these rights, duties, or freedoms. It has also described this duty as peremptory, meaning that it is binding on States parties in a way that is primary, paramount, overriding, and cannot be abrogated or departed from at all times. The Commission has reiterated that it is only if the States parties take these duties or obligations seriously that the human rights of persons can be protected.[2]

In emphasising the centrality of Article 1 to the legal protection of human rights under the Charter, the Commission has decided that a violation of any provision of the Charter automatically entails a violation of Article 1. 'If a State party to the Charter fails to recognise the provisions of the same (Article 1), there is no doubt that it is in violation of this Article. Its violation, therefore, goes to the root of the Charter'.[3]

1 *Legal Resources Foundation v Zambia, Communication 211/98, Compilation of Decisions*, p. 382, at pp. 392–393, para. 62.

2 Ibid.

3 *Sir Dawda K. Jawara v The Gambia, Communication 147/95 and 149/96, Compilation of Decisions* p. 108, at p. 115, para. 46. The suspension of the Bill of Rights and the application of the Charter was held by the Commission to be a breach of Article 1 of the Charter, para. 50.

This Statement has two implications for the protection of refugees. The first is that violations of human rights that compel individuals and masses to flee their States of origin to other States violate Article 1. In this sense, this Article could be relied upon by refugees as well as internally displaced persons to bring claims against their State of origin on grounds that the violation of their human rights alone is a breach of Article 1, and that the combined effect of these violations as a cause and consequence of their flight constitutes a continuing breach of Article 1 and other related rights.

It then becomes important to consider what the possible related rights of protection are. Under the Charter, these include arbitrary deprivation of the right to life (Article 4), in the event of death before or in the course of flight, torture, inhuman or degrading treatment (Article 5), deprivation of personal liberty (Article 6), freedom of movement and residence, including choice of place of residence (Article12), health (Article 16), property (14), family life (Article 18), education (Article 17), existence and internal self-determination (Article 20), peace and security (Article 23), equal enjoyment of the right to economic, social and cultural development with due regard to freedom and identity (Article 22).

Besides that, the State of origin would be acting in breach of the Article 1 duty to recognise or to give effect to the rights recognised in the Charter if it fails, or is unwilling, to provide protection to individuals and groups whose rights are violated by non-State actors, including rebel movements, as along as such individuals and groups are within the control of that State.[4]

The second implication is that the duties in Article 1 require the receiving States to recognize the rights, duties, and freedoms in the Charter with respect to refugees as human beings and to give effect to their protection in the framework of human rights. For this reason Article 1 is a very important baseline for the protection of human rights and for ensuring that African States treat and protect refugees in the context of the human rights recognised in the Charter. This point is worth emphasising because cases brought before the Commission on behalf of refugees failed to invoke or utilise Article 1.

In any case that is to be brought before the Commission, the first preliminary task is to examine whether and how, if at all, Article 1 of the Charter has been applied to refugees or other claimants by the State in question. A State party whose policy or action fails, or refuses, to recognize refugees as persons entitled to human rights, or excludes them from the protection of human rights under its law, would be violating Article 1 of the Charter.

3. *General Guarantees*

There are two general guarantees that can be used to protect any rights that refugees or other individuals are entitled to under the African Charter. These

[4] See C. Beyani, 'State Responsibility for Refugee Flows and Displaced Persons with Respect to the Country of Origin', *International Journal of Refugee Law*, Special Issue, Vo. 7 (1995).

guarantees take the form of the principles of non-discrimination and equality in Articles 2 and 3 of the Charter respectively. Article 2 provides that:

> Every individual shall be entitled to the enjoyment of the rights and freedoms recognised and guaranteed in the present Charter without distinction of any kind such as race, ethnic group, colour, sex, language, religion, political or any other opinion, national or social origin, fortune, birth or other status.

The guarantee to all individuals the enjoyment of rights and freedoms recognized in the Charter entails the application of all these rights and freedoms to refugees, as they would to all other human beings with equal force. In this way the Charter provides protection for everyone from discrimination on grounds such as race, ethnic group, colour, sex, language, religion, political or any other opinion, national or social origin, fortune, birth or other status. Discrimination generally can be identified and seen whenever the persons subjected to it have been treated or handled differently from other persons in similar situations on these and other grounds in a way not permitted or warranted by the Charter.

The Commission has applied the guarantees in Article 2 to acts of discrimination against nationals, non-nationals, and refugees. With respect to nationals, the Commission considered a complaint by the *Legal Resources Foundation v Zambia*[5] stating that the Zambian government had enacted into law a constitution that was discriminatory, divisive, and violated the rights of its citizens. The Commission noted that Article 2 of the Charter condemns discrimination on the basis of any of the grounds set out above and explained the importance of the right to be treated equally: 'It means that citizens should expect to be treated fairly and justly within the legal system and be assured of equal treatment before the law and equal enjoyment of the rights available to all other citizens. The right to equality is important for a second reason. Equality or lack of it affects the capacity of one to enjoy many other rights. For example, one who bears the burden of disadvantage because of one's place of birth or social origin suffers indignity as a human being and equal and proud citizen. He (she) may vote for others but has limitations when it comes to standing for office. In other words the country may be deprived of the leadership and resourcefulness such a person may bring to national life. Finally, the Commission should take note of the fact that in a growing number of African States, these forms of discrimination have caused violence and social and economic instability which has benefited no one. It has cast doubt on the legitimacy of national elections and the democratic credentials of States.'

In making this observation, the Commission captured precisely the circumstances that cause refugee out-flows in which discrimination is a tool in a pattern of measures calculated to oppress, exclude, and deprive individuals and, by definition, populations to which such individuals belong. To address and redress this phenomenon, it is vitally important that complaints concerning violations of

[5] *Compilation of Decisions*, p. 382, at p. 393, para. 63.

human rights within the scope of the Charter are also brought against the States from whose territories refugees originate.

With respect to non-nationals, the provisions on non-discrimination were applied by the Commission in the case of *Rencontre Africaine pour la Defense des Droits de l'Homme (RADDHO) v. Zambia,* already mentioned above, in which there was a mass expulsion of West African nationals from Zambia. In holding against Zambia, the Commission State d that the non-discrimination provision in Article 2 of the Charter imposes an obligation on African States to secure the rights protected in the Charter to all persons within their jurisdiction, nationals or non-nationals. It was clearly in breach of that provision that West African nationals constituted the majority of those expelled by Zambia.[6]

The application of non-discrimination with regard to refugees was dealt by the Commission in the complaint brought by *Organisation Mondiale Contre La Torture and Others against Rwanda*[7] in which the Commission found that the expulsion of Burundian refugees of a Hutu identity from Rwanda was a breach of non-discrimination under Article 2 of the Charter. This case shows that the guarantee of non-discrimination protects refugees from being discriminated because of their status as refugees (i.e., other status), or because of their identity (race, ethnic group, and colour), or because of who they are by virtue of sex or language, or because of what they believe in or say with respect to religion, political or any other opinion with respect to the enjoyment and protection of each and every right under the Charter.

In all, discrimination usually exists when individuals are treated differently without any reasonable or justifiable cause. The focal points for advocates to concentrate on in using the Charter are those areas in which refugees suffer prejudice and bad treatment mainly because they are refugees, (e.g., arrests, detention, harassment, female refugees) refugee women (e.g., sexual exploitation, sexual extortion, sexual assault, rape) and in the enjoyment of economic, social and cultural rights.

In any case where refugees are treated differently from other human beings or refugees, it is vital to find out why they are being treated in a different way from other human beings or refugees, and what the reasons for this difference are. The authorities must give reasonable justification for such treatment consistent with the requirements of the Charter. A most important factor is that the way refugees are treated differently must relate reasonably to why they are being treated differently and to their ability to enjoy their rights under the African Charter. All human rights under the Charter must be enjoyed or secured without discrimination.

On the question of equality, Article 3 of the Charter provides that:

1. *Every individual shall be equal before the law; and.*
2. *Every individual shall be entitled to equal protection of the law.*

The principle of equality and equal protection of the law offers additional protection on how individuals, including refugees, are treated whenever they come into

6 *Compilation*, pp. 369–370.
7 *Communication 27/89, Compilation*, p. 320.

contact with the legal and institutional system of the State in which they are. In this respect, refugees are to be treated and protected equally by any law applied to them by any administrative officials, institutions and courts regardless of whether such a law relates to human rights or not.

The principle enables the African Commission to rove and inquire into whether refugees have been treated and protected equally with respect to any law or right covered or not covered by the Charter itself. For example, the United Nations Human Rights Committee has used this principle to remedy the lack of equality and equal protection in the area economic social and cultural rights even if those rights are not normally within the remit of that Committee.[8]

On its part, the African Commission has explained that the 'right to equality is very important. It means that (individuals) should expect to be treated fairly and justly within the legal system and be assured of equal treatment before the law and equal enjoyment of the rights available to all other individuals. The right to equality is important for a second reason. Equality or lack of it affects the capacity of one to enjoy many other rights. For example, one who bears the burden of disadvantage because of one's place of birth or social origin suffers indignity as a human being'.

Non-discrimination and equality are related, and have similar and different uses.[9] Non-discrimination is used to guarantee the enjoyment and protection of the rights, duties and freedoms recognized in the Charter, and its use or application is limited to those rights. Equality and equal protection is used to guarantee the enjoyment and protection of the rights in the Charter and treatment under any national law, but its use or application goes beyond the rights, duties, and freedoms covered in the Charter. It can be applied from the Charter, but independently of it. However, both non-discrimination, and equality and equal protection may be limited in their application to refugees in the host State by Articles 13(1) and (2) which restrict the scope of enjoyment of the right to freely participate in government and public service, including the right to vote, to citizens only as shown above in *Legal Resources Foundation v Zambia*.

Article 18(3) and of the African Charter stipulates special standards for the elimination of discrimination against women. It obliges African States to eliminate every discrimination against women and to ensure the protection of the rights of women as stipulated in international declarations and conventions The latter include the International Convention on the Elimination of All Forms of Discrimination against Women 1979[10] as well as amongst others, the Protocol to the African Charter on Human and Peoples' Rights on the Rights of Women in Africa 2003.[11]

---

8 *Broeks v Netherlands,* Communication no. 172/1984, 2, *Selected Decisions*, p. 196.

9 A.Bayefsky, 'The Principle of Equality and Non-Discrimination in International Law 11 *Human Rights Law Journal* (1990) 1.

10 C. Beyani, 'Towards an Effective Guarantee of Women's Rights in the African Human Rights System' in R. Cook (ed.) *Human Rights of Women*, 285–306; H. Charleswoth and C. Chinkin, *The Boundaries of International Law: A Feminist Analysis* (Manchester, 2000); F. Banda, Women, Law and Human Rights: An African Perspective (Hart, Oxford, 2005).

11 Adopted by the 2nd Ordinary Session of the Assembly of the Union, Maputo, July 11–August 13, 2003, entered into force in November 2005.

In this context the African Charter protects refugee women from all forms of discrimination and all forms of physical, domestic, and sexual violence against them. Stereotype social attitudes and traditional practices that subordinate women to men generally, and specifically in refugee settlements are prohibited. In effect, the refugee protection system is permeated by these standards with regard to the entry and admission of female refugees, their treatment, food and water distribution systems, decision- making, and reproductive and sexual health.

The standards of the Charter, inclusive of international instruments applicable to women, can also be invoked against States of origin where the flight of refugee women is caused by any form of discrimination and violence against them. Despite these being obvious human rights protection issues, no complaint has so far been brought before the African system to redress their violation. The reason for this may lie in the problem of lopsided structural power relations that continue to dominate women and which constructively ignore, deny them, or fail to aid them to gain access to the African human rights system.

4. *Specific Individual Rights*

Refugees and forcibly displaced persons are likely to suffer violations of human rights at different points in the cycle of displacement or flight, entry and admission to the territory of the receiving State, status determination, conditions of life in the host States, and during voluntary repatriation. Claims by refugees alleging violations of human rights under the Charter are likely to arise from ill-treatment at different points of this cycle. Therefore, a pattern of protection corresponding to the cycle above must be worked out by identifying the provisions of human rights in the Charter that can be used throughout the cycle, with indications of how to use them at each point of the cycle.

Specific provisions essential to the protection of the human rights of refugees by receiving States under the African Charter include freedom of movement and residence, including the right to seek and enjoy asylum in Article 12, respect for life in Article 4, human dignity, including the prohibition of all forms of torture, cruel, inhuman and degrading treatment in Article 5, personal liberty in Article 6, fair trial and due process under Article 7, and family reunion in Article 18. The task for scholars, practitioners and advocates is to work out a pattern of protection based on such provisions and one which corresponds to the cycle of flight mentioned above.

It is obvious that the right to life under the African Charter affords protection against the arbitrary deprivation or taking of the lives of refugees to the same extent as any other persons. The words 'respect for life' in Article 4 connote a positive obligation on States to ensure respect for life and to prevent arbitrary loss of life. Therefore, States must put in place legal, policy, and institutional measures aimed at safe guarding the lives of refugees and protecting their lives from threats posed by agents of the State, non-State actors and private persons within the control or jurisdiction of the State. The failure or neglect to ensure such protection will breach Article 4 of the Charter in situations where the loss of the lives of refugees results from, or is attributable, to such failure or neglect by receiving States. In *Ken Saro-Wiwa's*[12] case, the African Commission took the view that the protection of the right to life in Article 4 also includes a duty for the State not to purposefully let a person die while in custody.

Article 4 also contains a 'negative' obligation for receiving States to refrain from the arbitrary killing of refugees by security forces or agents of the State. On this basis, the killing of refugees by security forces whilst quelling a riot, or during demonstrations, or internal disturbances, violates Article 4 of the Charter in that it is arbitrary. The word 'arbitrary' provides a guarantee against the taking of life not sanctioned or justified by national criminal law when examined against the framework of the Charter and international law in relation to human rights (e.g., fair trial) or armed conflict (e.g., killing of civilians).

It is useful to point out that in *Ken Saro-Wiwa,*[13] the African Commission held that because the trial which ordered the executions itself violated Article 7 on fair hearing, any subsequent implementation of sentences on the accused persons rendered the resulting deprivation of life arbitrary and in violation of Article 4. Finally, procedural obligations underlying Article 4 require States to investigate and punish any arbitrary killing, and to hold a public inquiry in the event of killing by security forces.

What follows below is a guide on how to use and apply some of the essential provisions of the Charter to qualitative aspects of refugee protection, taking into account the application of refugee law where relevant.

5. *Freedom of Movement, the Right to Seek and Obtain Asylum, and Protection from Expulsion under Article 12.*

Article12 of the African Charter relates to freedom of movement, the right to seek and obtain asylum, as provides protection from expulsion. The specific provisions of Article 12 are as follows:

(1) Every individual shall have the right to freedom of movement and residence within the borders of a State provided he abides by the law.
(2) Every individual shall have the right to leave any country including his own, and to return to his country. This right may only be subject to restrictions, provided for by law for the protection of national security, law and order, public health or morality.
(3) Every individual shall have the right, when persecuted, to seek and obtain asylum in other States in accordance with laws of those States and international conventions.

---

12 *Communications 137/94, 139/94, 154/96 and 161/97, International PEN, Constitutional Rights Project, Interights and Civil Liberties Organisation (On behalf of Ken Saro-wiwa Jnr) v Nigeria, Compilation of Decisions,* p. 230, at 245.

13 *Compilation of Decisions,* p. 230, at 244.

(4) A non-national legally admitted in a territory of a State Party to the present Charter may only be expelled from it by virtue of a decision taken in accordance with the law.
(5) The mass expulsion of non-nationals shall be prohibited. Mass expulsion shall be that which is aimed at national, racial, ethnic or religious groups.

5.1. *Freedom of Movement*

Freedom of movement and choice of place residence within the State of origin protects against forced displacement and flight from the State of origin to the receiving State.[14] Equally, the right to leave and return prohibits forced exile under Article 12(2). In the case of *Ouko v Kenya*, the African Commission held that the combined criteria of persecution and subsequent flight amount to a continuing violation of human rights under the Charter, inclusive of the right to leave and to return. The Commission further determined that the State of origin has a duty to facilitate safe return. However, the issue of safe return as such cannot be regarded as a self-standing. It must be viewed in the light of voluntary repatriation under Article 5 of the *Convention Governing the Specific Aspects of Refugee Problems in Africa*.

The relevant part of Article 5 reads:

1. The essentially voluntary character of repatriation shall be respected in all cases and no refugee shall be repatriated against his will.
2. The country of asylum, in collaboration with the country of origin, shall make adequate arrangements for the safe return of refugees who request repatriation.
3. The country of origin, on receiving back refugees, shall facilitate their resettlement and grant them the full rights and privileges of nationals of the country, and subject them to the same obligations.

These provisions are normally implemented by means of voluntary repatriation agreements signed between the State of origin, the host State and UNHCR. On the basis of the reasoning in *Ouko v Kenya*, repatriation agreements which do not satisfy the conditions stipulated in Article 5 of the *Convention Governing the Specific Aspects of Refugee Problems in Africa* may thus be challenged as a breach of the duty to ensure safe return under Article 12 of the African Charter.

Freedom of movement and residence within the receiving States provides an important scope for the treatment and protection of refugees. Both the 1951 Convention and the AU Convention restrict the freedom of movement and residence of refugees in order to designate places for refugee settlements and to ensure the safe location of refugees. Such restrictions may be challenged before the African Commission if they are so excessive as to deprive refugees of their freedom of movement within or outside the settlements and if they do not

14 See in general, C. Beyani, *Human Rights Standards and the Movement of People Within States* (Oxford, 2000).

achieve the objective of ensuring the safe location of refugees from the boundary of their country of origin. In any hearing of this issue before the African Commission, the receiving State would bear the burden of proving that restrictions on the movement and residence of refugees are necessary, with a legitimate aim, and are proportionate to the maintenance of public order, public security, and public health.

5.2. *The Right to Seek and Obtain Asylum*

The right to seek and obtain asylum in Article 12(3) clearly establishes the principal basis for the protection of refugees under the African Charter. The African Commission has Stated that 'this provision should be read as including a general protection of all those who are subject to persecution, that they may seek refuge in another State'. This approach by the Commission is strengthened by Article II(1) of the AU Refugee Convention which obliges member States to use their best efforts to receive refugees from other African States, as well as the non-refoulement provisions in Article II (3) which prohibit African States from rejecting or returning refugees at the frontier of the host or receiving States. The protection afforded to refugees here aims at enabling them to have access to safety and status determination procedures on the territory of the receiving State.

Decisions made by the Inter-American Commission can be used to interpret the scope of the right to seek and enjoy asylum under the African Charter. According to the Inter-American Commission, the right to seek asylum includes the possibility to advance a claim for asylum; preventing asylum seekers from doing so was a breach of this right such as, for example, in the case of the interdiction of Haitian refugees on the High Seas by the United States of America.[15]

According to the Inter-American Commission, the right to seek asylum and enjoy asylum has two elements. The first and most important is that of gaining entry and access to the territory of host State, including its status determination procedures, for the purpose of seeking asylum. The AU Convention strengthens this principle in Article II(3;) by prohibiting States from rejecting asylum seekers at the frontier or border. The 1951 Convention underlies the same principle under Article 31 by stating that asylum seekers should not be penalized for making direct illegal entry.

The second element concerns lawful admission through obtaining or enjoying asylum in accordance with in accordance with laws of those States and international conventions This element depends on whether the asylum seeker meets the criteria for refuge as set out in domestic law and international conventions, namely the AU Convention under which both group and individual eligibility to refugee status determination exists and the 1951 Convention under which individual eligibility to refugee status determination exits by practice. The African Commission does not apply domestic law or legislation on refugees. It has State

15 *Haitian Interdiction Case*, No. 10.675, 13 March 1997.

d its approach as follows: 'an international treaty body like the Commission has no jurisdiction in interpreting and applying domestic law. Instead a body like the Commission may examine a State's compliance with the treaty in this case the African Charter. In other words the point of the exercise is to interpret and apply the African Charter rather than to test the validity of domestic law for its own sake'.

Therefore, regard should be on the question whether the relevant domestic law complies with the Charter and international law on the issue of persecution. The decisions of the Commission show that persecution is established by reference to violated rights and subsequent flight. International law has several bases for constructing persecution as an international legal concept.

5.3. *Persecution*

In the case of *Tadic*,[16] the International Tribunal for the Prosecution of Persons Responsible for Serious violations of International Humanitarian Law Committed in the Territory of the Former Yugoslavia since 1991 decided that a necessary element of persecution is some form of discrimination that is intended to be, and results in, an infringement of an individual's fundamental rights on specific grounds such as race, religion or politics.

Under Article 7(2)(g) of the *Statute of the International Criminal Court*[17] adopted by the Diplomatic Conference in Rome on 17 July 1998, persecution is defined for the first time in an international instrument as the intentional and severe deprivation of fundamental rights contrary to international law by reason of the identity of the group or collectivity on political, racial, national, ethnic, cultural, religion, gender or other grounds that are universally recognized as impermissible under international law.[18]

The study by the International Law Commission on persecution in Article 18(e) of the *Draft Code of Crimes Against the Peace and Security of Mankind* 1996[19] views persecution as a denial of human rights and fundamental freedoms to which individuals are entitled without distinction or discrimination under the Charter of the United Nations 1945 and the International Covenant on Civil and Political Rights 1966. The element of persecution intersects international refugee law, which is based traditionally on a well-founded fear of persecution, and international criminal law. Evidence of persecution in claims for asylum as well as violations of human rights in the context of asylum or a pattern of systematic violations should have probative value in international criminal law. An effective human rights system should be able to detect such trends and provide protection from persecution.

---

16 Case No. IT-94-I-T, para. 697.
17 A/Conf.183/9, 17 July 1998. The Statute was adopted by 120 States in favour, 7 against, and 21 abstentions.
18 Ibid, Art. 7(1)(h).
19 *Report of the International Law Commission* 1996, A/51/10, pp. 9–120.

5.4. *The Prohibition of Expulsion*

Article 12(4) of the African Charter prohibits the expulsion of non-nationals without due process or recourse to legal procedures, while Article 12(5) prohibits the mass expulsion of non- nationals. Both of these provisions were interpreted by the African Commission in connection with the expulsion of Burundese refugees from Rwanda in a complaint brought by the *Organisation Mondiale Contre la Torture et al v. Rwanda*.[20] The Commission decided that the expulsion was as a breach of the right to seek and obtain asylum under Article 12 in general. With specific reference to Article 12(4), the Commission found that 'this provision should be read as including a general protection of all those who are subject to persecution, that they may seek refuge in another State' and that it prohibits the arbitrary expulsion of such persons from the country of asylum. The Commission concluded that Burundian refugees in this situation were expelled in violation of Articles 2 and 12 of the African Charter'.

The approach taken by the Commission reconciles the provisions of Article 12(4) with those of Article II(1) the AU Convention, which provide as follows:

1. Member States of the AU shall use their best endeavours consistent with their respective legislations to receive refugees and to secure the settlement of those refugees who, for well-founded reasons, are unable or unwilling to return to their country of origin or nationality.
2. The grant of asylum to refugees is a peaceful and humanitarian act and shall not be regarded as an unfriendly act by any Member State.
3. No person shall be subjected by a Member State to measures such as rejection at the frontier, return or expulsion, which would compel him to return to or remain in a territory where his life, physical integrity or liberty would be threatened for the reasons set out in Article I, paragraphs 1 and 2.

Apart from that, Article 12(4) may also be read to prohibit collective expulsions of non-nationals. In *Conka v Belgium*[21] the European Court of Human Rights held that collective expulsion is to be understood as any measure compelling aliens, as a group, to leave a country, except where such a measure is taken on the basis of a reasonable and objective examination of the particular case of each individual alien of the group. Accordingly the Court held that the collective expulsion of four Slovakian asylum seekers was unlawful under the *Fourth Protocol* to the *European Convention on Human Rights* 1950.

So far as the prohibition of the mass expulsion of non-nationals is concerned, the Commission found ample evidence in *Organisation Mondiale Contre la Torture et al v. Rwanda* that groups of Burundian refugees had been expelled by Rwanda on the basis of their nationality. According to the Commission, this constituted a clear violation of Article 12(5) under which 'mass expulsion shall be that which is aimed at national, racial, ethnic or religious groups'.

---

20 *Communications 27/89, 46/91, 99/93, Compilation of Decisions*, p. 320.

21 (2002) ECHR 14.

5.5. *Concluding Reflections*

Specific importance is attached to the protection of the right to life of asylum seekers, refugees, and internally displaced persons owing to their vulnerability generally. Are there adequate institutional and legal measures for protecting the lives of asylum seekers, refugees or internally displaced persons? What is the nature of such measures? Measures of protection may be found in the Penal Code, Criminal Justice Act, Criminal Procedure Code or Act, and the Police Act, if any. Is the exercise of such measures consistent with Article 4 (respect for life) of the African Charter?

The right to life carries positive and procedural obligations that require the State to investigate killing or the taking of life in general. If asylum seekers, refugees or internally displaced persons have been killed by private persons or non-State actors, has the State investigated the killing and taken steps to prosecute and punish the killers? If security forces have killed asylum seekers, refugees or internally displaced persons, has the State carried out an investigation and public inquiry into such deaths? Have relatives, or representatives of the deceased participated in the inquiry? Has the State taken steps to prosecute and punish the killers?

The right to seek and obtain asylum is of central importance to the protection of asylum seekers and refugees. Does the receiving State protect the right to seek and obtain asylum? What is the nature of such protection? Evidence of such protection may lie in legislation on refugees or asylum, or on foreign nationals. Is this legislation consistent with the right to seek and enjoy asylum under Article 12 of the Charter? Has the receiving State complied with the duty to not reject or return asylum seekers at the frontier or border? Have refugees been penalised for illegal entry into the receiving State? Has the receiving State determined or declared the status of asylum seekers?

The framework of human rights touches upon the responsibility of the State of origin for persecuting individuals. Is there a continuing violation of freedom of movement and residence that can be held against the State of origin by virtue of causing the persecution and subsequent flight of asylum seekers, refugees or internally displaced persons? Are any restrictions on freedom of movement and residence necessary, reasonable and justified on grounds of public order, public security, public health, or in order to protect refugees? Do camps or settlements for refugees or internally displaced persons deprive them of their liberty of movement and residence, or do they merely restrict such liberty, and if so, on what grounds? Are such camps necessary for the protection of the physical security of asylum seekers, refugees or internally displaced persons? Are they safely located?

In so far the Charter prohibits mass expulsion, are refugees being expelled individually, collectively, or on a mass basis? Do such expulsions meet the requirements of Article 12(3)(4)(5) of the Charter and Article II of the *AU Convention* with respect to the right to seek and obtain asylum, individual due process, and the prohibition on mass expulsions?

Voluntary repatriation is a return oriented solution for refugees to their country of origin. Crucially, refugees must not be coerced into returning. Have both the host State and the receiving State ensured the informed and voluntary repatriation of refugees in conditions of safe return?

6. *Human Dignity and the Prohibition of Torture, Inhuman, or Degrading Treatment*

The prohibition of torture, inhuman or degrading treatment is a major pillar for protecting human rights in accordance with human dignity, which entails respect for the worthiness of the human being. The prohibition of torture, inhuman and degrading treatment, and slavery, provides protection against severe ill-treatment and enslavement. It follows that human dignity and the prohibition of torture, inhuman or degrading treatment, and slavery, is of central importance to the protection of refugees.

Article 5 of the Charter formulates the applicable standards as follows:

> 'Every individual shall have the right to the respect of the dignity inherent in a human being and to the recognition of his legal status. All forms of exploitation and degradation of man particularly slavery, slave trade, torture, cruel, inhuman or degrading punishment and treatment shall be prohibited'.

A violation of Article 5 entitles the victim or survivor, including victims of sexual abuse, to seek and obtain asylum in third States. The threshold or level of ill-treatment prohibited by Article 5 covers beating, corporal punishment, torture, rape, sexual assault, sexual enslavement, and trafficking in women or men. Compliance with Article 5 is critical to the avoidance of refugee out-flows from States of origin. However, asylum seekers and refugees must not be subjected by receiving States to such ill-treatment or any other ill-treatment prohibited in Article 5 of the Charter.

In its entirety, the scope of the Article 5 prohibits States from expelling or returning refugees to States or places where they are likely to be subjected to prohibited forms of ill-treatment, particularly slavery, slave trade, torture, cruel, inhuman or degrading treatment. For this reason, States are obliged to comply strictly with the due process requirements of Article 12(4) before seeking to remove from their territories, refugees or persons seeking protection as refugees, to other States.

In this regard Article 5 expresses the principle of non-refoulement in the context of human rights under the African Charter. The classic statement of non-refoulement is to be found in Article 33[22] of the *United Nations Convention Relating*

---

22 1. No Contracting State shall expel or return ("refouler") a refugee in any manner whatsoever to the frontiers of territories where his life or freedom would be threatened on account of his race, religion, nationality, membership of a particular social group or political opinion.
2. The benefit of the present provision may not, however, be claimed by a refugee whom there are reasonable grounds for regarding as a danger to the security of the country in which he is, or who, having been convicted by a final judgement of a particularly serious crime, constitutes a danger to the community of that country.

to the Status of Refugees 1951. However the exception to non-refoulement under Article 33 of this Convention does not appear in the *AU Convention* on Refugees.[23] The absolute character of non-refoulement under the *AU Convention* on Refugees reflects the position of human rights on the application of non-refoulement, namely that the principle absolutely prohibits the expulsion, return, or extradition of a person to a State where there is a real risk of torture, or other cruel, inhuman or degrading treatment.

An early human rights case on this subject is that of *Mutombo v Switzerland*,[24] in which the United Nations Committee Against Torture held that the pending deportation of an asylum seeker to the Democratic Republic of the Congo (then Zaire) would violate Article 3[25] of the *Convention Against Torture*, which expresses the principle of non-refoulement.

In *Chahal v UK*,[26] the European Court of Human Rights upheld the absolute character of non-refoulement in the context of the prohibition against torture, inhuman or degrading treatment against assertions of national security by the United Kingdom. The Court held that Chahal could not be deported by the United Kingdom to India on grounds of national security as there was a real likelihood that he would be subjected to torture, inhuman or degrading treatment in Punjab. In coming to this conclusion, the Court contrasted the exception to non-refoulement under the *Convention Relating to the Status of Refugees* against the absolute character of the prohibition of torture, inhuman or degrading treatment. Similarly, the European Court of Human Rights also ruled against a deportation order issued by Austria against a refugee from Somalia after the refugee was convicted for a crime.[27]

In the absence of an express guarantee of a right to housing in the Charter, the Commission has based protection for housing-related rights on the Article 5 guarantee of human dignity, and the prohibition of torture, cruel, inhuman or degrading treatment. In Communication 93/97, *John K. Modise v. Botswana*,[28] the author was rendered Stateless by the respondent State, which cancelled his Botswana nationality and deported him to South Africa for political reasons. South Africa in turn deported

---

[23] 3. No person shall be subjected by a Member State to measures such as rejection at the frontier, return or expulsion, which would compel him to return to or remain in a territory where his life, physical integrity or liberty would be threatened for the reasons set out in Article I, paragraphs 1 and 2 (see paragraph 5.29 above).

[24] *Mutombo v Switzerland*, CAT/C/12/S/1993; see further *Agiza v Sweden*, CAT/C/34/D/233/2003 (decision of 24 May 2005).

[25] 1. No State Party shall expel, return ("refouler") or extradite a person to another State where there are substantial grounds for believing that he would be in danger of being subjected to torture.

2. For the purpose of determining whether there are such grounds, the competent authorities shall take into account all relevant considerations including, where applicable, the existence in the State concerned of a consistent pattern of gross, flagrant or mass violations of human rights.

[26] *Chahal v Uk* (1996) 23 EHRR 278; similar decision in *Saadi v Italy* 47 ILM (2008) 545.

[27] *Ahmed v Austria* 24 EHRR 278.

[28] *John K. Modise v. Botswana* (hereafter called *"the Modise case", Communication 97/93 (1996)*, *Compilation of Decisions*, p. 23.

him to the then Homeland of Bophuthatswana, which in turn deported him back to Botswana. Unable to resolve the question of where to keep the author, the authorities of the respondent State made him homeless over a long period on a specially created strip of territory called "no-man's land" along the South African border. The Commission found that such enforced homelessness was inhuman and degrading treatment that offended "the dignity of human beings" and thus violated Article 5.

With regard to the case brought before the Commission by the Malawi African Association and others,[29] it was alleged amongst other claims, that in September and October 1986 many villagers were arrested and tortured by the then Government of Mauritania. A common form of torture was known as "Jaguar" by which the victims' wrists were tied to their feet, and the victims were then suspended from a bar and thus kept upside down, sometimes over a fire, and beaten on the soles of their feet. Other methods of torture involved beating the victims, burning them with cigarette stubs or with a hot metal. Women were raped. Those held in custody were beaten, forced to make incriminating statements, and were denied sleep.

The conditions of detention were such that the prisoners were not fed; they were kept in chains, locked up in overpopulated cells lacking in hygiene and access to medical care. They were burnt and buried in sand and left to die a slow death. Electrical shocks were administered to their genital organs and they had weights tied on to them. Their heads were plunged into water to the point of suffocation; pepper was smeared on their eyes and some were permanently kept in small, dark or underground cells, which got very cold at night.

However, the government of Mauritania did not produce any argument to counter these facts. The Commission took the view that taken together or in isolation, these acts were proof of widespread utilisation of torture and of cruel, inhuman and degrading forms of treatment that violated Article 5 of the Charter. The fact that prisoners were left to die slow deaths equally constituted cruel, inhuman and degrading forms of treatment prohibited by article 5 of the Charter, and most likely also violated the right to life.

7. *Concluding Reflections*

Going by the foregoing analysis, substantive protection would require considering whether the asylum seeker or refugee has been subjected to severe ill-treatment such as rape, sexual assault, beating, corporal punishment, torture, e.g., by electric shock, slavery, trafficking, or any other intense degree of bad treatment that may amount to torture, inhuman or degrading treatment.

It should be determined who is responsible for subjecting asylum seekers or refugees to such treatment, in the State of origin, or in the receiving State? If the ill-treatment prohibited by Article 5 has not been perpetrated by the State, has the

29 *Communications 54/91, 61/91, 98/93, Compilation of Decisions*, p. 161.

State taken measures to prevent it and to punish the perpetrators? What sort of measures, if any, would have been taken to that end?

Importantly, has the receiving State complied with the duty of not rejecting or returning refugees at the frontier or border? Are refugees being expelled, deported, or returned, contrary to the absolute character of non-refoulement under the Charter and the AU Convention on Refugees?

There is a duty to not render persons stateless. Has the asylum seeker or refugee been denationalised by the State of origin, or denied adequate housing, or decent shelter by the receiving State?

8. *Fair Hearing and Due Process*

The right to fair hearing incorporates due process and entitlement to be heard by an independent, impartial, and competent body, in status determination, proceedings on deportation, or expulsion, or in any case where the cause of an asylum seeker or refugee is to be heard formally. It also incorporates the requirements of a fair trial in any case where an asylum seeker or refugee is put on trial for a criminal offence.

Article 7 of the Charter provides for this right as follows:

1. Every individual shall have the right to have his cause heard. This comprises: (a) the right to an appeal to competent national organs against acts of violating his fundamental rights as recognized and guaranteed by conventions, laws, regulations and customs in force; (b) the right to be presumed innocent until proved guilty by a competent court or tribunal; (c) the right to defence, including the right to be defended by counsel of his choice; (d) the right to be tried within a reasonable time by an impartial court or tribunal.
2. No one may be condemned for an act or omission which did not constitute a legally punishable offence at the time it was committed. No penalty may be inflicted for an offence for which no provision was made at the time it was committed. Punishment is personal and can be imposed only on the offender.

The terms of Article 7 relate to substantive fairness (how fairly has the claimant been treated) and procedural fairness (are there fair procedures in place). In its Resolution on Fair Trial adopted at its Eleventh Ordinary Session, in Tunis Tunisia, from 2 to 9 March 1992, the African Commission held that the right to fair trial includes, among other things, the right to be heard, the right of an arrested person to be informed at the time of arrest in a language he/she understands, of the reason for the arrest and to be informed promptly of any charges against them, the right of arrested or detained persons to be brought promptly before a judge or other officer authorised by law to exercise judicial power and be tried within a reasonable time or be released, the right to be presumed innocent until proven guilty by a competent court.[30]

[30] Communication 251/2002 (2005), *Lawyers for Human Rights v Swaziland*, para. 53.

Furthermore, the practice of the Commission shows that the right of the individual in Article 7 includes a positive duty on the part of the State to provide bodies or structures to enable this right to be exercised.[31] These bodies must, however, meet the criteria of impartiality, independence, and competence. In a case in which the complaint involved the creation of a Robbery and Firearms Tribunal under a Decree passed in Nigeria, the Commission held that the creation and composition of the Tribunal breached the requirements of impartiality and competence under Article 7 of the Charter because jurisdiction had been transferred from the normal courts to a tribunal composed of persons belonging to the executive branch of government that passed the Decree in question and the members of the Tribunal did not posses any legal expertise.[32]

The African Commission has yet to address specifically the question whether Article 7 of the Charter covers procedures for hearing asylum seekers in the course of determining their status as refugees or not. Such hearing is obviously inapplicable, if not irrelevant, to cases of group eligibility to refugee status arising from situations of mass out-flows. But it is clearly relevant to 'urban' asylum seekers who often undergo individual status determination procedures by virtue of their mode of entry.

Constitutive theory under which a treaty is approached as an integral whole would lean in favour of the application, within the framework of the Charter, of the right to a fair hearing under Article 7 to the right to seek and obtain asylum under Article 12(3) since both provisions appear within the same treaty. More concretely, the practice of the Commission on Article 7 would imply an obligation on the States parties to the Charter to establish institutions and fair procedures for status determination. Indeed many States in Africa have established eligibility or status determination Committees under refugee related legislation and the due process guarantees in Article 7 of the Charter would clearly apply to status determination procedures under such legislation or administrative hearings.

This conclusion is drawn from Article 26, which requires States parties to the Charter to allow the establishment and improvement of appropriate national institutions entrusted with the promotion and protection of the rights and freedoms guaranteed by the present Charter. According to the Commission,

> 'while Article 7 focuses on the individual's right to be heard, Article 26 speaks of the institutions which are essential to give meaning and content to that right. This Article clearly envisions, the protection of the Courts which have traditionally been the bastion of protection of the individual's rights against the abuses of state power.'[33]

The requirement by the Commission that the right of the individual in Article 7 includes a positive duty on the part of the State to provide the structures to enable

31 Communication 87/93, *Constitutional Rights Project (in respect of Zamani Lekwot & 6 Others) v. Nigeria*, Compilation of Decisions, p. 197.
32 *Communication* 60/91, Constitutional Rights Project v Nigeria.
33 Ibid, para. 38; see also *Communication* 129/9410.

the right to be exercised implies a duty on the State to extend legal assistance to refugees in the hearing of their cause or when charged with criminal offences. Fair procedures would also entail extending legal assistance, where necessary, to refugees in status determination processes. The decision of the Commission in *RADDHO v. Zambia* in which the Commission determined that the expulsion of West African nationals from Zambia was illegal because of the lack of due process and denial of legal aid fortifies the argument.

States are obliged to comply strictly with the standards of due process before removing refugees or persons seeking protection as refugees; the Commission has thus held the due process guarantees in Article 7 of the African Charter to be applicable to the involuntary removal of a refugee from a host State. 'By expelling refugees from Rwanda, without giving them the opportunity to be heard by the national judicial authorities, the government of Rwanda violated Article 7(1) of the Charter'.[34] This shows that the right to a fair hearing extends to the removal of asylum seekers and refugees, and it would be important to is such hearings to ensure that non-refoulement is not breached.

9. *Fair and Impartial Due Process*

Substantive and procedural requirements of the right to be heard fairly necessitate legal, procedural, and institutional guarantees of fairness. Do asylum seekers or refugees have access to, and the opportunity, to be heard fairly and within a reasonable time by, an independent, impartial and competent body, with regard to status determination (where applicable), deportation, expulsion, or exclusion from refugee protection? What is the composition of such bodies and who sits on them?

If the refugee or asylum seeker is subject to criminal proceedings, or proceedings which result in the imposition of a penalty, has s/he been presumed innocent until proven guilty by an independent, impartial and competent Court? Has s/he had access to a lawyer of her or his own choice? Has legal aid been made available to her or him to ensure the equality of arms?

10. *Personal Liberty*

The right to liberty and security of the person in Article 6 of the Charter applies to the treatment of asylum seekers and refugees when detained at the point of entry, or admission, to their stay, in the receiving State, including the circumstances of their lawful or unlawful departure to other States. Under Article 6:

> 'Every individual shall have the right to liberty and to the security of his person. No one may be deprived of his freedom except for reasons and conditions previously laid down by law. In particular, no one may be arbitrarily arrested or detained.'

---

34 *Organisation Mondiale Contre la Torture et al v. Rwanda, Compilation of Decisions, para. 35, p. 324.*

The importance of this provision lies in the fact that the deprivation of liberty is a key tool used by States to persecute individuals and to deter asylum seekers from exercising and enjoying the right to seek and obtain asylum. But the detention of persons on the basis of seeking asylum or on account of their status as refuges amounts to a breach of non-discrimination, equality and equal protection of the law under the Charter.

Under Article 31[35] of the 1951 Convention, the detention of asylum seekers in circumstances that deprive them their liberty, as in jail or detention centres, is unlawful. The Executive Committee of the United Nations High Commissioner for Refugees has held that this provision means that asylum seekers should not be penalized or exposed to any unfavourable treatment solely on the ground that their presence in the country is considered unlawful; they should not be subjected to restrictions on their movements other than those which are necessary in the interest of public health and public order, and that they should enjoy the fundamental civil rights internationally recognized, in particular those set out in the Universal Declaration of Human Rights.[36]

Restrictions that are necessary relate to the movement and residence of asylum seekers to ascertain their identity and determine their status, but such restrictions should be temporary, not prolonged, and should not amount to a deprivation of liberty under international human rights law. The difference between deprivation and restriction of liberty depends on the degree or closeness of confinement. Detention constitutes a deprivation of liberty while movement within a certain area but not outside it amounts to a restriction of movement.[37]

These views are reflected in the practice of the United Nations Human Rights Committee, which has held that the prolonged detention of an asylum seeker by Australia was unlawful under the *International Covenant on Civil and Political Rights*.[38] In *Amuur v France*[39] the holding of an asylum seeker at an airport alleged to be an international zone in France was held to be a breach of the right to personal liberty under Article 5 of the *European Convention on Human Rights*.

---

35 Article 31 reads:

1. The Contracting States shall not impose penalties, on account of their illegal entry or presence, on refugees who, coming directly from a territory where their life or freedom was threatened in the sense of article 1, enter or are present in their territory without authorization, provided they present themselves without delay to the authorities and show good cause for their illegal entry or presence.
2. The Contracting States shall not apply to the movements of such refugees restrictions other than those which are necessary and such restrictions shall only be applied until their status in the country is regularized or they obtain admission into another country. The Contracting States shall allow such refugees a reasonable period and all the necessary facilities to obtain admission into another country.

36 UNHCR, 'Protection of Asylum Seekers in Situations of Large Scale Influx,' *ExCom Conclusions* No. 22 (XXXII), 1981.

37 See generally, C. Beyani, *Human Rights Standards and the Movement of People within States* (Oxford, 2000).

38 *A v Australia*, Communication No. 560/1993.

39 *Judgement of the European Court of Human Rights*, 25th June 1996.

The African Commission has made decisions on the violation of personal liberty in the context of other rights such as torture.[40] It has also applied the *United Nations Body of Principles for the Protection of All Persons under Any Form of Detention or Imprisonment* 1988, particularly, Principles 1 and 6. Principle 1 provides that,

> 'All persons under any form of detention or imprisonment shall be treated in a humane manner and with respect for the inherent dignity of the human person.'

Principle 6 states that,

> 'No person under any form of detention or imprisonment shall be subjected to torture or to cruel, inhuman or degrading treatment or punishment. No circumstance whatever may be invoked as a justification for torture or other cruel, inhuman or degrading treatment or punishment.'

In a Communication by the *Malawi African Association and others*, which alleged that some detainees had been starved to death, left to die in severe weather without blankets or clothing, and deprived medical attention, the Commission found that starving prisoners and depriving them of blankets, clothing and health care violated Article 16 of the Charter.[41]

11. *Concluding Reflections*

The detention of asylum seekers is exceptional and must be justified as necessary and proportionate to a legitimate aim. The following questions are important to reflect on. Are asylum seekers and refugees being detained? What is the justification for detaining them? Are the reasons for such detention compatible with Article 6 of the African Charter? Is the detention of asylum seekers and refugees being used as a punitive measure, or as a means of deterring their entry? Have refugees been punished for illegal entry into the territory of the receiving State?

Is the movement and residence of asylum seekers merely being restricted to ascertain their identity? Do any such restrictions deprive asylum seekers of their personal liberty? Are asylum seekers being subjected to torture, inhuman and degrading treatment, including slavery, whilst in detention or in general?

40 See for example, *Ouko v Kenya*.

41 *Communications 54/91, 61/91, 98/93, Compilation of Decisions*, para. 122, p. 186.

Chapter 5

Access to Justice: The Right of Asylum Seekers and Refugees to Lodge Individual Complaints

1. *Complaints before the African Commission*

When the African Commission on Human and Peoples' Rights was created in 1987, its specific mandate under Article 30 of the Charter was to 'promote human and peoples' rights' and to ensure 'their protection in Africa.' Unquestionably, the institutional set up of the Commission is purposefully geared towards resolving problems or disputes arising from the violation of human rights within Africa.

The functions of the Commission are set out in Article 45 of the Charter. One such function is to receive, consider and decide on specific complaints from States or non-State entities, such as individuals or non-governmental organisations alleging violations of provisions of or rights guaranteed by the African Charter.[1] Non-governmental organisations can therefore lodge complaints to the Commission on behalf of refugees in accordance with the procedures governing individual complaints that the Commission has laid down. It is mainly due to this flexibility of the procedures of the Charter on legal standing that claims for protection by asylum seekers and refugees have been lodged before the Commission. The activism of non-governmental organisations has thus been crucial in enabling refugees to have access to justice under the African Charter.

---

1 Articles 45(2), 47, & 55.

2. *Complying with the Procedure for Communications*

Cases alleging any violation of any of the rights in the Charter by a State Party to the African Charter may be transmitted to the African Commission by complaints (petition) or Communications. Knowledge and familiarity of the procedures of the African Commission is a vital step for scholars, advocates, and practitioners towards seizing the jurisdiction of the Commission through Communications or complaints. The Secretariat of the Commission receives, processes and prepares Communications for consideration by the Commission.[2]

There are two stages pertaining to Communications in the procedure used by the Commission. The first is admissibility, a stage at which the Commission considers whether a case is one which it ought to admit to a hearing or not. The second is the merits phase. Thus, in keeping with standard procedures, a case that passes the admissibility phase proceeds to the merits or hearing phase.

2.1. *Admissibility Requirements*

The purpose of the admissibility phase is to determine whether a Communication has passed all the conditions prescribed by Article 56[3] of the African Charter in order to be considered or heard by the Commission. These conditions are cumulative and a Communication that fails any of these conditions will be dismissed by the Commission as inadmissible without any further consideration of the issues it raises.[4] Consequently technicalities underlying the admissibility of complaints may sometimes stand in the way of substantive justice, but they have to be seen to be an important part of orderly conduct, which is imposed by process and procedure in the functioning of human rights bodies in international human rights law.

---

[2] The Secretariat is located in Banjul, Gambia and is headed by the Commission's Secretary. The contact address of the Commission is provided in the appendix.

[3] 'Communications relating to human and peoples' rights received by the Commission, shall be considered if they:

1. Indicate their authors even if the latter request anonymity,
2. Are compatible with the Charter of the Organization of African Unity or with the present Charter,
3. Are not written in disparaging or insulting language directed against the State concerned and its institutions or to the Organization of African Unity,
4. Are not based exclusively on news discriminated through the mass media,
5. Are sent after exhausting local remedies, if any, unless it is obvious that this procedure is unduly prolonged,
6. Are submitted within a reasonable period from the time local remedies are exhausted or from the date the Commission is seized of the matter, and
7. Do not deal with cases which have been settled by these States involved in accordance with the principles of the Charter of the United Nations, or the Charter of the Organization of African Unity or the provisions of the present Charter.'

[4] *Communication* 304/2005 – *FIDH, National Human Rights Organization (ONDH) and Rencontre Africaine pour la Defense des Droits de l'Homme (RADDHO) / Senegal.*

In real terms, the main goal of the Communications procedure before the Commission is to initiate a dialogue in good faith, which would result in an amicable resolution between the complainant and the State concerned so as to remedy the injustice that informs the complaint.[5] It follows that a Communication will only be admissible if it is brought against a State that has ratified the Charter. Since the African Charter is applicable only to African States, the Commission will not consider or receive cases brought against non-African States, e.g., those that have been brought alleging the mistreatment of African immigrants and refugees outside Africa. Similarly, the Commission will not receive Communications against entities that are not States. It has, in the past, rejected a case purportedly brought against a former Secretary-General of the AU.[6]

2.2. *Communication Must Relate to Violations Occurring after a State Ratified Charter*

The Commission will only receive allegations against a State for violations committed after the State has ratified the Commission. The Commission may, nevertheless, receive and consider a case about violations occurring before a State ratified the Charter if it takes the view that the violations are continuing. The legal and factual circumstances in which continuing violations can be examined by the Commission are important to note.

These were considered by the African Commission during the admissibility of a complaint brought by *Louis Emgba Mekongo v. Cameroon,*[7] a Cameroonian businessman. The applicant alleged that he was a victim of several violations of human rights arising from interferences with his property and person between 1979 and 1983. His case first came before the domestic courts in Cameroon in 1979 before the African Charter was adopted in 1981. The case was still pending in those courts when he lodged his Communication to the Commission in 1991. Cameroon had by then ratified the African Charter on 20 June 1989, ten years after the violations first began. The Commission held that the failure of the Cameroonian courts to dispose of the case after nearly 12 years of litigation kept the case alive, making it a case of continuing violation and declared that the case was admissible to a full hearing before the Commission.

2.3. *Communication Should Indicate the Names and Contact Addresses of the Authors*

It is important a Communication or complaint must say on the face of it who is initiating it, whether an individual or group, including the names and addresses of

[5] *World Organization Against Torture, Lawyers' Committee for Human Rights, Jehova's Witness Inter-African Union for Human Rights v Zaire,* Communications 25/89, 47/90, 56/91, and 100/93.
[6] *Mohammed El-Nekheily* v *AU,* Communication 12/88.
[7] *Communication 59/91,* Compilation of Decisions, p.61.

such persons. Communications should not be anonymous; they should indicate the name of the victim and contain clear statements of the nature of the violations alleged, including particulars of the acts from which such violations are alleged to result from.

Normally, the complaint or Communication is initiated by "the Author". But the African system is sufficiently flexible so that the Author of a Communication does not need to be a direct victim or survivor of any of the violations contained in the Communication; nor should an Author be related to the victim or survivor, or have their authority to lodge a complaint on their behalf.[8] It is sufficient that the Author, such as an academic, a lawyer or a non-governmental organisation, is interested in protecting or defending human rights and justice in relation to the victim. This immensely broadens the scope for access to justice. There is special protection for Authors of complaints too. An Author who is uncomfortable with having their identity disclosed is permitted to request the Commission to protect their anonymity and the Commission does not call for the identification of the victims.[9] Quite unique, this is a flexible and progressive aspect of the Charter under which victims alleging sexual violence, for instance, could request anonymity and receive protection in the course of the proceedings as a matter of human rights.

2.4. *Communications Should Be Compatible with both the AU Constitutive Act and the African Charter*

A Communication should be based on the provisions of the African Charter and should not seek remedies that are incompatible with the basic commitments contained in the *Constitutive Act of the African Union* 2000.[10] To that extent, the obligations assumed by African States under the *Constitutive Act* of the African Union would appear to circumscribe the scope of available remedies. In addition, Communications should not be written in insulting language nor based exclusively on materials sourced from the media. The requirement that Communications should not be written in insulting language (Article 56(3) of the Charter) can be justifiably criticised because it introduces an element of arbitrariness into the decision as to whether or not Communications should be admissible. For instance, in the case of *Ligue Camerounaise des Droits de l'Homme vs. Cameroon*,[11] the Commission condemned as insulting language used in reference to President Paul Biya of Cameroon, that 'Paul Biya must respond to crimes against humanity,' '30 years of the criminal neo-colonial regime incarnated by the duo Ahidjio/Biya,' 'regime of torturers', and 'government barbarisms.'

[8] See *Communications* 54/91, 61/91, 98/93, 164/97 to 196/97, 210/98: *Malawi African Association, Amnesty International, Mrs. Sarr Diop, InterAfrican Human Rights Union and RADDHO, Widows and Entitled Persons Association, Mauritanian Human Rights Association vs. Mauritania.*

[9] *Communication* 304/2005 – *FIDH, National Human Rights Organization* (*ONDH*) *and Rencontre Africaine pour la Defense des Droits de l'Homme* (*RADDHO*) / *Senegal.*

[10] See *Communication 75/92, Compilation of Decisions*, p. 359, *Katangese Peoples' Congress v. Zaire.*

[11] *Communication* 65/92.

However, it is trite that Communications should describe in basic detail the acts complained of, when and where they occurred, and who perpetrated them. As much as possible, the violations alleged should allege facts known to or reported to the Authors. It is the practice of the Commission that Communications should not be based exclusively on media reports although they can be supported or substantiated from such reports.

2.5. *Communications Should Be Sent after Exhausting Local Remedies Unless It Is Obvious That the Pursuit of Such Remedies Will Be Unduly Prolonged*

An important and risky requirement at the admissibility phase precludes the admissibility of Communications sent by Authors or on behalf of victims that have not exhausted domestic remedies. The exhaustion of domestic remedies is a general requirement of international law with respect to both the diplomatic protection of nationals abroad and human rights based claims. In the context of the African Charter, the exhaustion of domestic remedies provides the States Parties to the Charter the first opportunity to consider claims alleging violations of human rights for which they may be responsible. Where domestic remedies exist, victims save the time, money and trauma that would otherwise be invested in seeking regional remedies. So it is important to utilise domestic remedies wherever these are available.

However, Complainants are not bound to exhaust domestic remedies that are unduly prolonged. This means that domestic remedies must be available, effective and sufficient for the violations alleged. Going by the practice of the Commission, "a remedy is *available* if the petitioner can pursue it without impediment; it is deemed *effective* if it offers a prospect of success; and it is found *sufficient* if it is capable of redressing the complaint".[12] The Commission fully elaborated its approach to these principles in *Anuak Justice Council v Ethiopia*[13] as follows:

> In the jurisprudence of this Commission, three major criteria could be deduced in determining the rule on the exhaustion of local remedies, namely: that the remedy must be available, effective and sufficient. According to this Commission, a remedy is considered to be available if the petitioner can pursue it without impediments or if he can make use of it in the circumstances of his case. The word "available" means "readily obtainable; accessible"; or "attainable, reachable; on call, on hand, ready, present; ... convenient, at one's service, at one's command, at one's disposal, at one's beck and call." In other words, "remedies, the availability of which is not evident, cannot be invoked by the State to the detriment of the complainant."

[12] *Communications 147 & 149/95, Compilation of Decisions, para 32, Sir Dauda K Jawara v. The Gambia.*
[13] *Communication 299/05,* paras 51–52.

> A remedy will be deemed to be effective if it offers a prospect of success. If its success is not sufficiently certain, it will not meet the requirements of availability and effectiveness. The word "effective" has been defined to mean "adequate to accomplish a purpose; producing the intended or expected result," or "functioning, useful, serviceable, operative, in order; practical, current, actual, real, valid." Lastly, a remedy will be found to be sufficient if it is capable of redressing the complaint. It will be deemed insufficient if, for example, the applicant cannot turn to the judiciary of his country because of a generalized fear for his life "or even those of his relatives." This Commission has also declared a remedy to be insufficient because its pursuit depended on extrajudicial considerations, such as discretion or some extraordinary power vested in an executive state official. The word "sufficient" literally means "adequate for the purpose; enough"; or "ample, abundant; ... satisfactory."

To its credit, the Commission has never held 'the requirement of exhaustion of local remedies to apply literally in cases where it is impractical or undesirable for the individual complainant to seize domestic courts in the cases of each individual complainant. This is the case where there are a large number of individual victims. Due to the seriousness of the human rights situation as well as the great numbers of people involved, such remedies as might theoretically exist in the domestic courts are, as a practical matter, unavailable or, in the words of the Charter, unduly prolonged.'[14] These exceptions apply very much to refugees and internally displaced persons. Very often, the circumstances of the violations against such persons entail that they are unable to exhaust domestic remedies and would, therefore, enable the Commission to exempt them from the strict requirements to do so. That would be the case where, as the Commission has pointed out above, an applicant cannot turn to the judiciary of their country because of a generalized fear for their life or even those of his relatives. This applies squarely to refugees and internally displaced persons.

2.6. *Communications Should Be Submitted Soon after the Exhaustion of Domestic Remedies*

It is best to initiate Communications at the earliest opportunity after the Authors or their advisers conclude that there are no domestic remedies or that domestic remedies have been exhausted. The advantages for this are that the pursuit of remedies is maintained, the loss of time and the continuing trauma experienced by the victims is minimised, and the Commission is able to provide an early resolution of any case before it. Sometimes, cases linger for too long before domestic courts. In such cases, it is advisable to proceed to the Commission so that it can determine whether delays in the domestic proceedings are compatible with the Charter.

---

[14] *Communication 25/89 etc, Compilation of Decisions,* p. 364, *para* 37, *Free Legal Assistance Group et al v. Zaire.*

2.7. *Communications Should Not Be Submitted to both the African Commission and Another International Tribunal at the Same Time or after Being Decided by Another International Body*

Many States accept more than one international human rights supervisory mechanism by being parties to the respective treaties This means that victims in many cases would have an option as to which international body to submit their cases to. Just as it is forbidden in domestic proceedings to submit the same case to different courts at the same time, international procedures do not permit the same case to be submitted to different human rights bodies at the same time.

A case will not be admissible if it is lodged to the African Commission or Court and another international human rights body, such as the United Nations Human Rights Committee. Where the Commission finds this to be the case, it usually gives the Authors the option of withdrawing the case from one of the bodies or suspending the proceedings before the African Commission, pending the outcome of such a case before another body. However, the consideration of a case by an international NGO, such as Amnesty International or Human Rights Watch, or by an inter-governmental body like the Commonwealth, the AU or the Human Rights Council of the United Nations, would not preclude the African Commission from considering it.

2.8. *Provisional or Interim Measures*

The necessity to file a Communication or complaint to the Commission may be so urgent that if the parties wait until the Commission reaches a decision on the actual complaint or merits, the reason for bringing the case in the first place will be defeated, or meaningless. This would be the case where, for instance, the Communication concerns a person who has been sentenced to death at the end of all domestic appeal procedures, or where an asylum seeker or refugee faces deportation or expulsion.

In such instances, the Authors can request the Commission to issue or indicate provisional or interim measures under Rule 111 of the *Commission's Rules of Procedure*. Provisional measures in international law have the same effect as interim injunctions in domestic proceedings and have the effect of restraining States from doing anything that may affect the case before the Commission reaches a final decision. Interim measure can be requested and granted at any time between the initiation of the Communication and a final decision on it. Where a State disregards provisional measures, the Commission is entitled to submit the matter to the African Court of Human Rights, but the jurisdiction of the Court to determine the matter would depend on whether the State concerned is a party to the Protocol establishing the Court, and whether such a State has also accepted the jurisdiction of the Court.

2.9. *Procedure on Admissibility*

After receiving a Communication, the Commission is required to bring it to the attention of the State against whom the Communication is brought. Both parties are given three months to forward their observations on the admissibility of the Communication. Before deciding on admissibility, the Commission also offers both the Author and the Respondent State an opportunity to be heard orally in support of their respective positions. The admissibility procedure is therefore adversarial, and not inquisitorial in form and manner.

2.10. *The Merits Phase*

If the Commission found that a Communication met all the admissibility requirements, it would then declare a Communication formally admissible. Thereafter it gives both parties an opportunity to submit their arguments on the merits of the Communication. The Respondent State has up to three months to respond to the substance of the allegations by the Author and the Author would usually be entitled to reply in writing to make a response to the Respondent State. Thereafter, the Commission issues hearing notices inviting the parties to address it orally in support of the merits of their respective positions. The Commission then reaches its decision after hearing both sides. The decision is communicated to the parties.

All decisions reached by the Commission on Communications or cases are transmitted to the Council of Ministers of the AU and, through them, to the Summit of the Assembly of Heads of State and Government of the AU. The Council of Ministers and the Assembly of Heads of State normally endorse the findings of the Commission. However, the Assembly of Heads of State embargoed the Commission's report on Zimbabwe, which the Commission issued after its 19th Session.

2.11. *Identifying Cases That Are Appropriate for Consideration by the Commission*

The procedures listed above provide a guide to identifying the type of cases that may be brought before the African Commission. The primary question to ask is whether the facts as narrated by the asylum seeker or refugee and verified by an advocate or NGO disclose a possible violation of human and peoples' rights contained in the Charter, particularly those covered in Part One of this Study. Secondly, it is important to consider whether the case at hand is appropriate to bring before the Commission. In other words, is the case likely to advance or erode the protection of refugees or internally displaced persons or others?

When assessing this issue, it is important to examine and apply those cases that the African Commission has decided already and which raise similar or related, or different, issues altogether. All cases referred to in this Study are clearly relevant to issues of asylum, the expulsion, deportation, and detention of asylum seekers and refugees as well as to the admissibility of Communications. However, there may be future cases which may raise different legal issues altogether and concerning which the Charter has to be treated as a living instrument. The basic guide is that it is advisable to identify cases that establish a strong case of the violation of the human rights of an asylum seeker or refugee and which advances the quality of protection either by itself, or in relation to other refugees or persons whose situation or plight is similar.

2.12. *Observations on Preparing a Case to Be Brought to the Commission*

There is not a hard and fast rule on how to prepare a case for consideration by the Commission or Court. But any preparation will be guided by an understanding of the procedural requirements of the forum on which the case will argued, in this case the African Commission or Court, application of the provisions of the law of the African Charter on which it is based, and identification of the facts relevant to those provisions.

A basic chronological lead may be offered by way suggestion. First of all, the obligation of African States to guarantee the protection of human rights under Article 1 of the Charter, which underlies the Charter as a whole, should be sought to be invoked overall. Secondly, the provisions on non-discrimination in Article 2 would come into play whenever there appears be to be a difference of treatment handed down to asylum seekers, refugees, or internally displaced persons, without a legitimate aim. Thirdly, the guarantee of equal protection of the law in Article 4 is an inescapable basis of protection implicating any law under which questionable action has been taken against asylum seekers and refugees. In the fourth place, the relation of the provisions on asylum in Article 12 to the particular facts, such as denial of asylum, deportation or expulsion, is a substantive requirement of assessing the legality of treatment extended to asylum seekers and refugees.

A crucial factor here turns on the quality of evidence assembled to support the facts as narrated by the claimant. More detailed care should be taken to test how dependable and reliable the evidence is. In the fifth place, it is advisable to argue a case by reference to a number of related provisions, e.g., those relating to the right to life or torture, inhuman and degrading treatment, that are captured by the facts alleged to have violated the rights of an asylum seeker or refugee. Last but not least, related or comparative international human rights case law, such as that indicated in this Study, should be used where it is applicable to support the legal validity of the claim made, based on the mandate of the African Commission to take into account wider aspects of international law under Article 60 of the Charter.

3. *Concluding Reflections*

Despite the fact that the African Commission has been in existence since 1987, not that many asylum seekers, refugees, lawyers, NGO, and scholars for that matter, are aware of its role in protecting human rights. There is a lack of intellectual and practical familiarity with its basic framework, competence, and procedures. Establishing a base of knowledge about the Commission generally and with respect to the specialised field of the right to enjoy and obtain asylum is still an important task thirty years after it was created. What more should be done to sensitise asylum seekers, refugees, lawyers, NGO, and scholars on the role of the Commission under the African Charter on Human and Peoples' Rights? Is there familiarity with the procedures of the Commission regarding individual Communications or complaints?

Is the State that is the potential subject of a Communication a Party to the African Charter on Human and Peoples' Rights? Did the alleged violations occur after the State complained against ratified the Charter? If the alleged violations occurred before the State complained against ratified the Charter, have such violations continued after the State in question has ratified the Charter?

Does the Communication indicate the names and contact addresses of the Authors? Does the Author want to protect their name or contact address from disclosure? Is the Communication sufficiently detailed in terms of the acts complained of, when and where they occurred, and who perpetrated them? Have local remedies been exhausted, or is it obvious that the pursuit of such remedies will be unduly prolonged?

Has the Communication been submitted soon after the exhaustion of domestic remedies? Has the Communication been submitted to a human rights body other than the African Commission or Court? Are provisional measures appropriate to secure immediate protection from deportation, expulsion, detention, or death penalty?

Is a potential case likely to bear a significant and positive impact on the protection of the human rights of refugees or asylum seekers? Do the facts of such a case disclose a possible violation of human rights the Charter? Have the allegations of such facts been verified or corroborated? What are the relevant provisions under which the claim for protection can be suitably framed?

4. *The African Human Rights Court*

The Protocol establishing an African Court of Human and Peoples Rights (the African Human Rights Court) was adopted by the then Organisation of African Unity in 1998 and entered into force in 2000 under the auspices of the newly established African Union. Shortly thereafter, the African Union took the decision to merge the African Human Rights Court with the African Court of Justice. The first Judges of the Court were elected at a Summit of the Heads of State and Government of the African Union ironically held in Sudan in January 2006.

The African Human Rights Court is intended to add strength to the protection of human rights in Africa. Under Article 2 of the Protocol establishing it, the Court shall complement the protective mandate of the African Commission. It will be a full-time body and its decisions will be binding on the States that ratify the Protocol establishing it. Under Article 3 of the Protocol, the jurisdiction of the Court shall extend to all cases and disputes submitted to it concerning the interpretation and application of the Charter, the Protocol itself and any other relevant human rights instrument ratified by the States concerned. Disputes regarding the jurisdiction of the Court shall be decided by the Court in the framework of its competence under Protocol establishing the Court.

The Court will complement the activities of the Commission and build on the Commission's existing jurisprudence or case law. Under Article 6 of the Protocol, the Court may consider cases or transfer cases to the Commission, but its decisions on the admissibility will be based on Article 56 of the Charter, which means that it will be guided by the practice of the Commission as explained above. For this reason, the Court may request the opinion of the Commission on the issue of admissibility.

Cases may be submitted to the Court by the Commission; a State party which previously lodged a complaint to the Commission, or a State party against which a complaint was lodged before the Commission; a State party whose citizen is a victim of human rights violation; an interested third State party, who may be permitted to join the proceedings upon making a request to the Court and African Intergovernmental Organizations. In addition, the Court may grant standing to relevant Non Governmental organizations (NGOs) with observer status before the Commission as well as and individuals, to institute cases directly before it, in accordance with Article 34 (6) of the Protocol establishing the Court. This provision expresses the usual rejoinder that a State shall make a declaration accepting the competence of the Court to receive cases under this Protocol. The Court shall not receive any petition involving a State Party which has not made such as declaration.

Chapter 6

Protection Techniques

1. *Introduction*

Refuges often lack a constituency of political support in the countries in which they seek protection. For this reason, the international protection of refugees is linked to civil society historically, at least since the International Committee of the Red Cross took the initiative in 1921 to request the League of Nations to convene an international conference to consider the plight of refugees who had then been denationalised by the Soviet Union. Most claims brought by refugees before the European Court of Human Rights are initiated by civil society.

In Africa too, particular responsibilities for creating awareness and support for the protection concerns of refugees lie on civil society. There is a clear growth in civil society in Africa, represented by a chorus of non-governmental organisations paying special attention to the problem of protection and assistance to refugees. Today, no one can seriously dispute the fact that civil society, from the point of view of human rights, is an active participant in the institutional system of protection and assistance. Civil society is the bearer of moral public conscience on other issues as well, such as democracy, governance, and economic and social development. Civil society has not only the potential for generating public awareness and appreciation of the problem of refugees, but it also does provide leverage to the existing structures of protection at national, regional and international levels.

Because refugees lack support and the means to protect their rights when violated, promotion of their rights, advocacy and action by NGOs, legal practitioners, and enlightened scholars is vital to the protection of their rights. A good functional strategy is to establish an association of scholars, advocates, and civil society for the purpose of advancing the cause of protecting the rights of refugees. The aim should be to enhance links of protection within and between the sub-regions East, North, Southern, and West Africa, based on a partnership with active academic institutions and practitioners.

The focal point of the duty to promote human rights lies in advocacy about the utility of the African Commission and Court to protect the human rights of asylum seekers and refugees by following up on the compliance of States with the decisions of the African Commission. Following up on State reports to the African Commission and the UN treaty bodies and the implementation of their recommendations on improving refugee and human rights protection is a standard technique required by the international system of human rights. The problem is that a perennial gap in the protection of human rights exists between the recommendations made by the African Commission and the UN Treaty bodies in their Concluding Reflections and follow-up on the implementation of such recommendations at national level. Parliamentary scrutiny over executive action or inaction in foreign affairs (e.g., failure to compliance with human rights treaties) accompanied by pertinent oversight by civil society are among the ways in which this lacuna may be filled.

The general aim is to sustain the ideas and momentum of protection by exercising freedom of association and assembly through intellectual partners drawn from individual scholars, academic institutions, civil society, as well as those responsible for policy protection by States in Africa, the AU, OHCHR, and UNHCR.

A strong motivation underpinning the development of this Study has been the need to forge, build and strengthen knowledge and alliances in scholarship and civil society around refugee protection, not only at the national level but also sub-regionally and regionally. The magnitude and complexity of the protection challenges faced by refugees and asylum-seekers, as well as the regional and international dynamic involved, require that collective work and effort is necessary if there is to be any impact at all.

A regional mechanism such as the African Commission or Court is a natural fulcrum around which such cooperation can turn. As noted already, taking a case to the African Commission can provide a valuable additional source of protection for refugees and asylum-seekers where domestic remedies fail or are absent, but it can also be a lengthy and time-consuming process and requires a level of sustained commitment over time. There is the potential danger that a case brought by an asylum seeker or refugee against a receiving State whose attitude towards the 'rule of law' and access to justice is inimical to legal claims by refugees may bring additional risk to the claimant. Where such a risk exists, potential or actual claimants may require additional measures of protection, such as being evacuated from the offending State in order to lodge their claims from the territory of a third State.

2. *A Collaborative Approach*

The advantages of a collaborative approach to research by scholars, practitioners, civil society, and asylum seekers and refugees themselves, lie is assembling the relevant protection material, pooling protection experiences, writing, and drawing on this, amongst other things, to compile and sustain a case before the Commission. These are fairly self- evident; they stretch from the inception of a case right through the implementation phase of any decision. It is useful to think strategically about identifying and lodging complaints in those areas where a Commission or Court decision could spread a 'domino' effect not only to the individual or group concerned, but also to refugees throughout a country or region. As one participant noted, "A case on behalf of one is a case on behalf of many."

Indeed, many of the concerns which were expressed by researchers in one region, were held in common with researches in other regions of Africa. A case in point is the lack of identity documents, which was cited again and again as constituting a particular problem for refugees and asylum-seekers, increasing their susceptibility to being harassed and arbitrarily detained by law enforcement officials. Restrictions on freedom of movement, arbitrary detention, sub-standard camp conditions were others. Ideally, all affected asylum seekers and refugees could benefit from substantive protection that strategically targets and focuses the attention of the Commission on any one of these areas. A decision in one case could precipitate momentum that can be seized upon and used by as a 'precedent' to effect legal change throughout the African region. In this way a multiple or magnifying effect can be generated by any decision of the African Commission or Court.

Cooperation between scholars and practitioners in States of origin and those in receiving States, for instance, may underscore a vital element in assembling those facts that will be so critical to the success of any Communication. In *Rencontre Africaine pour la Defense des Droits de l'Homme* [*RADDHO*] *vs Zambia*, RADDHO called on the expertise of Zambian scholars, lawyers, and a former Zambia based regional organization, AFRONET, to provide expert testimony on the circumstances surrounding the deportation of some 517 West African nationals from Zambia. In addition, where a pattern of abuses is detected, the quantum of abuse can be harnessed to strengthen the factual basis for any one Communication or may indeed be brought together as a joint or consolidated Communication against any one State.

In addition to assistance in assembling the factual basis for a solid Communication, linkages can also help to connect advocates who have little experience in taking a case to the Commission with others, either within the advocacy community or amongst legal practitioners and academics who may have acquired expertise over time and can mentor and advise others in the process.

Regional coalition work at the decision and compliance stage is particularly important and represents those areas where there is a compounded failure to fully capitalize on the opportunities presented by a Commission decision. Whilst mechanisms to ensure compliance with decisions of the Commission are weak, much can be achieved by national Parliaments and civil society in terms of implementation, by mobilizing and harnessing their efforts to spotlight the issue of State compliance with Commission decisions. This follow- up needs to be systematic and sustained and may need to take place at a variety of levels.

The duty to ensure human rights entails advocacy and partnerships targeted at the State directly affected by a decision of the Commission or Court is obviously a priority, but coalition work within the region is also important to ensure that the maximum number of States take note of a decision of the Commission where appropriate. Other than that, reaching out to other African States is a means of mobilizing one of the most effective levers for implementation – peer pressure based on the principle that the protection of human rights is in the interest of all States in and outside Africa. The Commission and Court are, after all, institutions created by African States themselves and decisions of the Commission are ultimately adopted by the African Union, adding to their weight as a force for change in the field of human rights and not vice-versa.

Thus, follow up lobbying and profiling of these decisions at regional fora, such as meetings of the African Union and regional organizations, such as ECOWAS, SADC, IGAD and others, as well as international meetings such as those of the UNHCR Executive Committee, are useful as a method of driving home the responsibility of States for complying with the decisions of the Commission. The utilization of occasions such as African Refugee Day [June 10] and African Human Rights Day [27 October] to advance the cause of human rights and raise the issue of unimplemented decisions of the Commission might also be ideas worth exploring.

Whilst compliance is the hurdle at which most Commission oriented strategies fall, there are signs that this is changing and that States are taking the decisions of the Commission more seriously than before. After the Commission decided against Botswana in the case of *Modise*, the Government of Botswana willingly opened negotiations over appropriate remedies for the complainant. Despite the 'doom' and 'gloom' that often accompanies the issue of compliance in human rights, the implementation of decisions by human rights bodies is not altogether elusive. Whilst the Commission itself could do more to develop more effective systems of following up on its decisions, scholars, practitioners and civil society must be equally diligent in ensuring that this aspect of the process is taken seriously by States.

It is useful to recall that a successful Communication – 'winning' as it were – before the Commission or Court, is not the only way in which to reap the rewards of a Commission oriented strategy. In the words of one advocate, whose case was ultimately unsuccessful before the Commission, 'victory is not what it appears to be.'[1] The advocate concerned – himself a Mauritanian refugee then residing in

1 Narrated by Adjouma Cissokho of Mauritania.

Senegal – noted that the very process of compiling and submitting a Communication to the Commission brought its own rewards and succeeded in highlighting the concerns of Mauritanian refugees, alerting other advocates to the issue and bringing the matter to the attention of the Senegalese government, which ultimately began a dialogue with the complainants.

At the various workshops, participants expressed views about the valuable role to be played in coalition work around refugee protection and in particular with respect to the African Commission or Court. Scholars, national human rights groups and refugee organizations were clearly identified as falling in the first line of importance in such a coalition. In the absence of any formal supervisory mechanism for the UN and AU Refugee Conventions, human rights and refugee NGOs can play an important role in highlighting practices that are contrary to these instruments and in bringing pressure for change. Moreover, academics and national human rights organisations almost by default, find themselves playing a front line role, addressing the material, legal and physical security needs of refugees and asylum-seekers who have found no remedy for their situation at a domestic level or in approaching UNHCR. A realistically-assessed Commission-targeted strategy may expand their options, both to meet the immediate needs of the claimants but also in terms of trying to promote more human rights-based approaches to refugee protection.

However, participants at the workshops were also keen to acknowledge and include the perspective of sister organizations working in the field of humanitarian relief. The role of relief and assistance agencies in the protection arena is a critical one that should be encouraged and supported. Not only are relief agencies often the first on the scene of any humanitarian crisis, but they also often have unique access to information and the populations which they serve. Effective cooperation on protection with the relief community can multiply the number of 'eyes and ears' of the protection community.

Moreover, the relief and assistance components of civil society are important conduits for early warning of impending crises. Whilst relief agencies may not be willing to commence a Communication, they may provide the critical first hand account of human rights violations and practices that could ultimately form the foundation for a Complaint to the Commission or Court where appropriate.

More generally, it is important to note that whilst the focus at many of the workshops was understandably on national and regional linkages between scholars, national and international civil society, their networks could also be important partners in any Commission or Court oriented strategy, whether it be in initiating individual complaints, or presenting the relevant evidence. This is particularly useful to counter xenophobic diatribes coined in the language of 'irregular movements' of asylum seekers, 'effective protection' and its antecedent of establishing regional transit centres for processing the claims of asylum seekers. Academics, as well as legal practitioners were identified as important partners in any Commission or Court oriented coalition, potentially contributing legal expertise and research to the development and argument of a Communication before the

Commission. The media also has an important role to play to highlight pertinent protection issues and reporting at key junctures, such as when an individual complaint is brought before the Commission.

All participants noted that refugees and asylum seekers are themselves important players in any concerted effort focused on ensuring that they can have access to the African system in order to protect their human rights. A number of the Communications considered by the Commission have been brought by refugees themselves, either individually or through self help groups. Whilst refugee communities are at varying degrees of organization and pro-activeness, it is critical that at a minimum they should be aware of their human rights under the African Charter and the possibility of recourse to the African Commission or Court. This underscores the importance of education about human rights protection under the African Charter on Human and Peoples' Rights.

Finally, other important bodies to take into account in any Commission oriented strategy include National Human Rights Commissions, such as those in Ghana, Kenya, South Africa, Uganda and Zambia [to name a few] which would have a natural interest in the human rights protection of refugees at national level. For this reason, the former Vice Chairperson of the South African Human Rights Commission was an active participant in the workshops at which the preparation of this Study was discussed. It is critical not to assume that the UNHCR or UNHCHR has knowledge of decisions of the Commission or that it will act on them, so targeting their participation must be an important part of protection measures under the African Charter.

3. *Mutuality*

With States taking cues from one another in the evolution and shaping of their refugee laws, policies and practice, it is imperative that scholars and practitioners also work in tandem in shaping appropriate intellectual and functional responses. Although problems may differ in their specificities from individual to individual and from place to place, the framework provided by human rights law has a universal application to them. In the final analysis, developing those institutions and mechanisms which African States themselves have established, and nurturing their ability to address the plight of refugees, would add significantly to the regional protection of refugees and asylum seekers in Africa.

4. *Concluding Reflections*

The human rights based approach to the protection of asylum seekers and refugees based on the right to seek and enjoy asylum is rooted in a broader purposes for which the United Nations was established under Article 1(3) of its Charter in order 'to achieve international co-operation in solving international problems of an economic, social, cultural, or humanitarian character, and in promoting and encouraging respect for human rights and for fundamental freedoms for all without distinction as to race, sex, language, or religion.' The duty to promote human rights and ensure their fulfillment is not only for States and the United Nations as an organization. It is incumbent upon all those others who live under the banner of the United Nations, as individuals, scholars or academics, or civil society. What collaborative approaches are necessary to achieve co-operation in promoting and encouraging respect for human rights beyond States and the United Nations? Is mutuality one way to achieve co-operation in solving the humanitarian character of refugee protection by means of human rights? What have we done individually and collectively to respond to the plight of those for whom human rights is a virtue to their salvation?

Chapter 7

Case Studies

1. *Introduction*

This part of the Study outlines case studies on the use of human rights to protect asylum seekers and refugees under the *African Charter on Human and Peoples' Rights*. The case studies were an integral part of the preparation of this Study in so far as the application of human rights to the situation of refugees and asylum seekers is concerned in substantive and educational terms. Case studies also represented real dimensions about how to protect the rights of refugees in East Africa, West Africa, and Southern Africa. They were outlined by the participants themselves in separate regional workshops in light of the difficulties they faced in their efforts to protect refugees. As detailed in this Chapter, the case studies are to be used for teaching, educational, and training purposes.

One general case study encapsulates the common legal and political issues of human rights throughout Africa, with issues identified, and approaches to these issues outlined. This case study also served as a basis for the study of the regional case studies during teaching or training sessions.

2. *The General Case Study*

Chaotica and Nadir are neighbouring States in East Africa. They have both signed and ratified the *African Charter on Human and Peoples' Rights* 1981, the two major refugee conventions, the *AU Convention Governing Specific Aspects of Refugee*

Problems in Africa 1969 and the *UN Convention Relating to the Status of Refugees* 1951, the *International Covenant on Civil and Political Rights* 1966 and the *International Covenant on Economic, Social and Cultural Rights* 1966. They have also ratified the *Convention on the Elimination of All Forms of Discrimination against Women* 1979.

For the last 40 years since independence, the State of Nadir has witnessed internal conflict of varying intensities. A decade ago, a coup in Nadir led to the take over by a dictatorial regime dominated by a minority group within the country. Large numbers of the largest ethnic group in the country fled. Chaotica has been host to a group of several hundred thousand refugees from Nadir for the last 10 years.

By and large they are hosted in large camps, in rural areas along the border with Nadir. The camps have recently been the subject of a newspaper series in "The East African," which profiled widespread malnutrition amongst the refugee population, a high maternal mortality rate and a high mortality rate amongst children under the age of five. The camp residents are subject to a number of restrictions including, needing to seek permission from the Ministry of Home Affairs in order to leave the camp. Permission will only be granted in certain exceptional situations, such as where there is a need for urgent medical care. It normally takes at least 5 days to process the request and to receive the necessary documentation in order to leave the camp. In answering a Parliamentary question as to the reasons for these measures, the Minister noted, "We simply don't want these people to mix with the local population."

The host population believes that the refugees are stealing their jobs and that they are the cause of increased levels of crime [including sexual offences] in the area as well as high rates of sickness and contagion. For a number of years, tensions have been building between the host and refugee populations and there have been a number of attacks on the camp residents by unknown assailants. Approximately 20 people are estimated to have died in these attacks. There have however been no investigations of these crimes, or inquests into the killings and certainly no prosecution of any offenders. After a recent theft of a local resident's shop, the tension exploded into a massive invasion of the camp by local mobs who torched the camp; some 300 residents of the camps are unaccounted for. Several were killed. Many more were injured. A number of female camp residents were sexually assaulted.

Following these events, the President announces on national television that the refugees must voluntarily return home. The conflict in Nadir has continued unabated and the country is now controlled by a number of rebel factions. The government has control of the capital city and its environs and it is to this area that the refugees are being returned through rebel held territory. UNHCR, feeling that it is unable to provide the refugees with any degree of protection in Chaotica, makes arrangements for their bus trips back to Nadir. During the first set of bus journeys, a number of buses were stopped by armed elements in Nadir and a number of refugees disappeared.

However, a small group of about 500 refugees managed to avoid return to Nadir by hiding and making their way to Chaotica City over a number of weeks. By this time international horror at the disappearances of refugees in Nadir causes the President of Chaotica to agree to screen this residual population. The screening will be conducted by security police, under the auspices of the Ministry of Defence. There will be a right to appeal to the Minister, who is also an army general. This process can take up to 3 years. Pending the decision, asylum seekers are not entitled to documentation; however they have a right to work, if they can present appropriate documentation. They are frequently harassed and detained on account of this lack of proper documentation.

Midway through the process of applying for asylum in Chaotica, a family of refugees, including parents and 4 children, decides that the uncertainty and deprivation of life in Chaotica has become intolerable and decides to relocate to the Republic of Utopia. They arrive without any documentation and present themselves at the border post where they declare that they would like to seek asylum in Utopia. However, they are immediately arrested for attempting to enter Utopia illegally and are detained. The parents are detained in separate facilities and the children, aged between 3–17 are placed together in a separate facility from the parents. The authorities inform them that the family cannot apply for asylum in Utopia, due to the fact that they had received protection in Chaotica. The authorities further inform the family that they are in the process of making arrangements to return them and would give them a choice of either Chaotica or Nadir. As the advocacy officer of NGO Refugee Services, you have been approached by a leader of the Association of Nadiran exiles with a request for advice and assistance. What advice would you give her or him?

3. *Issues in the General Case Study*

Right to Life – possible violation by Chaotica. A number of refugees have been killed in attacks and there has been no investigation or inquiry into these deaths. The government seems to condone or acquiesce in the killings. Article 4 of the Charter provides that every person has the right to life and protection from the arbitrary deprivation of right. The killing of refugees in the circumstances of this case is clearly arbitrary.

Right to Seek and Enjoy Asylum. Under Article 12(3) – Every individual has the right, when persecuted, to seek and obtain asylum in other States in accordance with laws of those States and international conventions. That Chaotica has asked the refugees to 'voluntarily repatriate' amounts in fact forced or coerced repatriation. In addition, Utopia has denied the family that fled to its territory the right to seek and enjoy asylum. It has threatened to deport them immediately. This raises the issue of non-refoulement.

Principle of Non-Refoulement. Article 12(3) provides for the right to seek and enjoy asylum in the event of persecution. Chaotica's call for the refugees to voluntarily repatriate to Nadir yet the conflict there has not abated is a breach of the right to seek and enjoy asylum. It also effectively amounts to forced repatriation, contrary to the principle of non-refoulement under Article 5 of the Charter and Article II of the AU Refugee Convention, read together with Article 33(1) of the UN Refugee Convention.

Lack of Legislation to Protect the Refugees Rights. Under article 1 of the African Charter, member States are obliged to "...recognize the rights, duties and freedoms enshrined in [the] Charter and [to] undertake to adopt legislative or other measures to give effect to them." The lack of such legislation is a breach of Article 1 of the African Charter. A consequence of this lack of legislation to protect the rights of refugees is that Chaotica seems to be making *ad hoc* decisions about refugees influenced by the pressure of the situation rather than guided by an appropriate legal framework for the protection of refugees.

Right to Liberty and Freedom of Movement. Chaotica's refugee camps appear to be detention centres. Refugees do not enjoy the freedom to work, as they do not have freedom of movement. The State official indicated that they are confined in the camps to prevent them from mingling with the locals. This is in violation of Articles 6 and 12 which provide for the right of liberty and security and the freedom of movement, respectively. The confinement of refugees to refugee camps deprives them of their personal liberty rather than restricting their freedom of movement.

UNHCR's Role. The agency needs to take seriously its mandate of refugee protection and not to aid or abet the government's violation of the principle of non-refoulement.

Right to Health. Refugees in Chaotica do not enjoy the right to health. Infant and maternal mortality rates are high, malnutrition is widespread and urgent medical attention can be only be enjoyed with permission from the authorities to leave the camp. Processing this permission takes inordinately long. The government of Chaotica is failing to fulfil the right of refugees to health under Article 16 of the Charter. Underlying the right to health are the requirements of access to health care and services, availability and affordability of such services.

Domestic Remedies Are Not Available. The attacks on the refugee camps, the resultant killings, the raping of women and the disappearance of 300 camp residents have remained un-addressed by the government. The government has not investigated any crimes committed against the refugees. This is indicative of the unavailability of local remedies for the refugees. In addition, the rape of women is contrary to human dignity and the prohibition of torture, inhuman and degrading treatment under Article 5 of the Charter.

4. *Other Issues That May Be Raised before the Commission*

Breach of the Principle of Safe Location of Refugees. The refugee camps in Chaotica are situated along the border with Nadir, their State of origin. This raises the issue of the safe location of refugees and the question whether refugees' freedom of movement and residence could be restricted to safe places away from the border under Article 12. Conditions in the refugee camp may be regarded as inhuman and degrading, contrary to Article 5, and Article 16 on the right to health.

Failure of Chaotica to Investigate Attacks and Sexual Assault. This may violate Chaoticas' obligation to recognise and give effect to human rights under the Charter. Furthermore, Article 3 of the Charter provides that all persons are equal before the law and are entitled to equal protection under the law. Clearly refugees do not seem to enjoy equal protection under the law in Chaotica.

Mob Invasion of the Camp. Under Article 4, which protects the right to life, the government of Chaotica has a positive obligation to prevent arbitrary deprivation of the lives of refugees and to ensure that their right to life is protected by Chaotica, the host country.

Sexual Offences. Chaotica has a responsibility to ensure the protection of the human rights of women according to international obligations as specified under Article 18, including CEDAW, and in particular to prevent discrimination against women, and remove such discrimination in the civil, political, economic and social fields; and prevent and protect women from gender based violence, especially sexual violence, as elaborated by General Recommendation 19 by CEDAW.

State Responsibility for Refoulement. It is necessary to establish who was responsible for the forced the movement of refugees by bus back to Nadir. UNHCR has to make clear its objection to what is effectively the refoulement of the refugees to Nadir. In the event that Chaotica had no choice but to return the refugees, it must be clearly established that its government would take full responsibility for any violations of human rights occurring during the enforced departure and return of refugees to Nadir as such refugees were under its jurisdiction or effective control. Chaotica is obliged to ensure the safe return and voluntary repatriation of refugees to Nadir. The forcible return of refugees to Nadir is a breach of the requirement of voluntary repatriation.

Screening of the Refugees. The issue is the legal purpose for which such screening is to be undertaken, namely to determine the identity of the asylum seekers and their eligibility to protection, and to register their names. Further questions are why is the military involved in this exercise? Why is the Minister for Defence, who is an army general, the final body of appeal? He does not legally represent an independent and impartial body in any hearing of the cause of refugees, contrary to Article 7 of the Charter.

5. *Jurisprudence of the African Commission Specific to the Case Study*

Shortly after this case study was formulated, an identical case was decided by the African Commission on Human and Peoples' Rights on a confidential basis in 2004. However, the decision of the Commission was only published in 2006 after being adopted officially by the Executive Council of the African Union. Until then, the details of the case were not known but they bear a remarkable resemblance to the case study presented above. This shows the extent to which research leading to the preparation of the Study was grounded empirically. The full text of the case is as follows.

African Institute for Human Rights and Development (on behalf of Sierra Leonean refugees in Guinea) v Republic of Guinea[1]

Summary of Facts

1. It is alleged by the Complainant that on 9th September 2000, Guinean President Lansana Conté proclaimed over the national Radio that Sierra Leonean refugees in Guinea should be arrested, searched and confined to refugee camps. His speech incited soldiers and civilians alike to engage in mass discrimination against Sierra Leonean refugees in violation of Article 2 of the African Charter.
2. The Complainant alleged that the discrimination occasioned by President Conté speech manifested itself primarily in at least five ways:
3. First, widespread looting and extortion occurred in the wake of President Conté's speech. Guinean soldiers evicted Sierra Leoneans from their homes and refugee camps. The soldiers further looted the homes, confiscated food, personal property and money from refugees at checkpoints. They also extorted large sums of money from detained refugees. These items were never returned to the refugees.
4. Second, the speech motivated soldiers and civilians to rise up against Sierra Leonean refugees inside and outside of the refugee camps. The resulting physical violence ranged from beatings, rapes, to shootings. Countless refugees died in these attacks, and many have scars as permanent reminders of their time in Guinea.
5. Third, after President Conté's speech, Guinean soldiers targeted Sierra Leonean refugees for arrest and detention without any just cause. Soldiers at checkpoints would inspect refugees for supposed rebel scars, calloused hands from carrying a gun, speaking Krio (the local language in Sierra Leone), or carrying a refugee card. However, the refugees had scars from tribal markings rather than the rebels and calloused hands from farming not carrying a gun. These false identifications were used to then detain refugees for hours and days for no other reason than being "a rebel" based upon being Sierra Leonean.
6. Fourth, the speech instigated widespread rape of Sierra Leonean women in Guinea. Furthermore, Guinean soldiers subjected men and women to

---

[1] *Communication 249/2002*, decision adopted at the 36th Ordinary Session of the African Commission held from 23 November to 7 December 2004 in Dakar, Senegal, and published in 2006. See African Union Executive Council, *20th Activity Report of the African Commission on Human and Peoples' Rights*, Ninth Ordinary Session, 25–29th June 2006, EX.CL/279(IX), pp 132–142.

humiliating strip searches. These searches were conducted sometimes several times a day and in front of large groups of people and on-looking soldiers.

7. Finally, Sierra Leonean refugees were forced to decide whether they were to be harassed, tortured and die in Guinea, or return to Sierra Leone in the midst of civil war where they would face an equally harsh fate. Thousands chose to flee back to their native Sierra Leone in response to the Guinean mistreatment. Furthermore, Guinean soldiers collected refugees, bussed them to Conakry seaport, and physically put them on the ferry forcing their return to Sierra Leone. The Guinean government was therefore not providing refuge and protection required by law, reported the Complainant.

Complaint

8. The Complainant alleges that Articles 2, 4, 5, 12(5) and 14 of the African Charter on Human and Peoples' Rights have been violated.

Procedure

9. The communication dated 17th April 2002, was submitted by the Institute for Human Rights and Development in Africa on behalf of the Sierra Leonean refugees.
10. On 18th April 2002, a letter was sent to acknowledge receipt and inform the Complainant that the communication would be scheduled for consideration at its 31st session.
11. At the 31st Ordinary Session held from 2–16 May 2002 in Pretoria, South Africa, the Commission decided to be seized of the case and requested the parties to submit their observations on the admissibility of the case.
12. On 29th May 2002, the Secretariat of the African Commission informed the parties of the decision of the African Commission.
13. On 24th June 2002, the Complainant forwarded to the Secretariat of the African Commission its written submission on the admissibility of the case, a copy was sent to the Respondent State by post on 16 August 2002.
14. By letters dated 28 November 2002, 17 January 2003 and 20 March 2003, the Secretariat wrote to the government requesting it to react to this complaint. Up to the holding of the 33rd Ordinary session in Niamey, Niger, from 15–29 May 2003, the Secretariat had not received any feedback from the Respondent State.
15. At the 33rd Ordinary Session the African Commission declared this communication admissible, and the parties were requested to forward their written submission on the merits.
16. On 18th June 2003, the Secretariat informed the parties of the above decision and requested them to transmit their brief on the merits to the Secretariat within a period of 3 months, the Note Verbal to the Respondent State was hand delivered.

17. On 29th August 2003, the Complainant forwarded its written submission on the merits of the case. On 22 September 2003, the Secretariat of the African Commission forwarded the written submission from the Complainant to the Respondent State
18. On 9th October 2003, the Secretariat of the African Commission received a Note Verbale from the Respondent State stating that they had not received the written submission from the Complainant.
19. By note Verbale dated 14th October 2003, the Secretariat of the African Commission forwarded once again the written submission from the Complainant to the Respondent State by DHL.
20. During its 34th Ordinary Session held in Banjul, The Gambia from the 6th to 20th November 2003, the African Commission heard the oral presentations on admissibility of the parties concerned and decided to postpone consideration on the merits of the case to its 35th Ordinary Session. By note verbale dated 4 December 2003, and by letter bearing the same date both parties were accordingly informed of the commission's decision.
21. The Commission instructed the Secretariat to have the comments of the Complainant translated into French and have the translation sent to the Respondent State to enable it submit its written comments on the merits of the communication.
22. These submissions on the merits of the case submitted by the Complainant were translated into French and sent to the Respondent State by Note Verbale on the 11th December 2003. The Respondent State was also informed that the communication would be considered on the merits at the Commission's 35th ordinary session.
23. By Note verbale dated 26 December 2003, the Secretariat received an acknowledgement from the Respondent State to its note verbale of 11 December 2003 noting that the Respondent State will forward its submission on admissibility within three months.
24. By note verbale dated 9 March 2004 the Secretariat reminded the Respondent State to forward its submission on admissibility noting further that the communication will be considered at the 35th ordinary session to be held in Dakar, Senegal from 3–17 May, 2004.
25. The Respondent State sent its reaction as to the merits of the communication to the Secretariat of the Commission on the 5th April 2004.
26. At the 35th Ordinary session, the Respondent State was not represented due to the change of the venue. At the 35th Ordinary Session, the Commission heard oral submissions from complainants and testimonies from witnesses on the merits of the communication.
27. By note verbale dated 18 June 2004 the Secretariat of the African Commission informed the State of its decision taken at the 35th ordinary session and by letter of the same date informed the complainant accordingly.
28. At its 36th Ordinary Session held from 23 November to 7 December 2004 in Dakar, Senegal, the African Commission considered this communication and decided to deliver its decision on the merits.

LAW

Admissibility

29. The admissibility of communications brought pursuant to Article 55 of the African Charter is governed by the condition stipulated in Article 56 of the Charter. This Article lays down seven (7) conditions for admissibility.
30. The African Commission requires that all these conditions be fulfilled for a communication to be declared admissible. Regarding the present communication, the two parties do not dispute that Article 56 (1, 2, 3, 4, 6 and 7) have been fulfilled, and the only article that is in dispute is Article 56(5) of the African Charter.
31. Article 56(5) requires the exhaustion of local remedies as a condition of the presentation of a complaint before the Commission is premised on the principle that the Respondent State must first have an opportunity to redress by its own means within the framework of its own domestic legal system, the wrong alleged to have been done to the individual.
32. Concerning the matter of exhausting local remedies, a principle endorsed by the African Charter as well as customary international law, the Complainant argues that any attempt by Sierra Leonean refugees to seek local remedies would be futile for (3) three reasons:
33. First, the persistent threat of further persecution from state officials has fostered an ongoing situation in which refugees are in constant danger of reprisals and punishment. When the authorities tasked with providing protection are the same individuals persecuting victims an atmosphere in which domestic remedies are available is compromised. Furthermore according to the precedent set by the African Commission in *Communication 147/95 and 149/96 Sir Dawda K. Jawara / the Gambia*, the need to exhaust domestic remedies is not necessarily required if the Complainant is in a life-threatening situation that makes domestic remedies unavailable.
34. Second, the impractical number of potential plaintiffs makes it difficult for domestic courts to provide an effective avenue of recourse. In September of 2000, Guinea hosted nearly 300,000 refugees from Sierra Leone. Given the mass scale of crimes committed against Sierra Leonean refugees – 5,000 detentions, mob violence by Guinean security forces, widespread looting – the domestic courts would be severely overburdened if even a slight majority of victims chose to pursue legal redress in Guinea. Consequently, the requirement to exhaust domestic remedies is impractical.
35. Finally, exhausting local remedies would require Sierra Leonean victims to return to Guinea, the country in which they suffered persecution, a situation that is both impractical and unadvisable. According to precedent set by the Commission in *Communication 71/92 Rencontre Africaine pour la Défense des Droits de l'Homme / Zambie*, victims of persecution are not necessarily required to return to the place where they suffered persecution to exhaust local remedies.

36. In this present case, Sierra Leonean refugees forced to flee Guinea after suffering harassment, eviction, looting, extortion, arbitrary arrests, unjustified detentions, beatings and rapes. Would it be required to return to the same country in which they suffered persecution? Consequently, the requirement to exhaust local remedies is inapplicable.

For these reasons, the communication is declared admissible.

Merits

37. In interpreting and applying the African Charter, the African Commission relies on its jurisprudence and, as provided by Articles 60 and 61 of the African Charter, on appropriate and relevant international and regional human rights instruments, principles and standards.
38. The African Commission is therefore amenable to legal arguments that are supported by appropriate and relevant international and regional human rights principles, norms and standards.
39. The Petitioners have enclosed several affidavits from Sierra Leonean refugees who suffered widespread human rights abuses including harassment, evictions, looting, extortion, arbitrary arrests, beatings, rapes and killings while seeking refuge in the Republic of Guinea.
40. These accounts are based on interviews obtained from collaboration between the Institute for Human Rights and Development in African and Campaign for Good Governance, a Sierra Leonean NGO. Lawyers from both organisations interviewed and recorded statements from refugees who had returned to Sierra Leone from Guinea. For the most part, the depiction of events is substantiated by reports from Human Rights Watch and Amnesty International who have documented the situation of Sierra Leonean refugees in Guinea during the period in question.
41. The Republic of Guinea has ratified several regional and international human rights instruments which include the African Charter, the OAU Convention on the Specific Aspects of Refugee Problems in Africa, the International Covenant on Civil and Political Rights, the UN Convention Against Torture, and the 1951 UN Convention on the Status of Refugees, together with its 1967 Optional Protocol.
42. While the efforts of the Guinean authorities to host refugees are commendable, the allegations that the government instigated and directly discriminated against Sierra Leonean refugees present a picture of serious human rights abuses which contravene the African Charter and the other international human rights instruments to which Guinea is a party.
43. The statements made under oath by several refugees indicate that their refugee camps were direct targets and taken together with accounts of numerous other abuses, constitute tangible evidence that the Sierra-Leonean refugees in this situation had been targeted on the basis of their nationality and had been

forced to return to Sierra Leone where their lives and liberty were under threat from the on-going war.

44. In view of the circumstances, the Complainant alleges that the situation which prevailed in Guinea in September 2000 manifestly violates Article 12 (5) of the African Charter which sets forth that:

"The mass expulsion of strangers is prohibited. Mass expulsion is that which targets national, racial, ethnic or religious groups as a whole".

45. Among the Articles and other legal instruments to which the Respondent State is a party and by which it is bound to protect all persons against discrimination can be noted: Article 4 of the OAU Convention on the Specific Aspects of Refugees, Article 26 of the International Covenant on Civil and Political Rights and Article 3 of the 1951 United Nations Convention on the Status of Refugees.
46. The Complainants allege that in his speech of the 9th September 2000, delivered on radio in *Susu* language, President Conte incited soldiers and civilians to engage in large scale discriminatory acts against Sierra-Leonean refugees, the consequences of which had been that these persons were the direct victims of harassment, deportations, looting, stealing, beatings, rapes, arbitrary arrests and assassinations. It is further alleged that the President made no effort to distinguish between refugees and rebels and that the Government is therefore directly responsible for the violation of this fundamental precept of international law: Non-discrimination.
47. The Complainants also allege that the Respondent State violated the principle of non-refoulement under which no person should be returned by force to his home country where his liberty and life would be under threat.
48. The Complainants contend that President Conte's speech not only made thousands of Sierra-Leonean refugees flee Guinea and return to the dangers posed by the civil war, but it also clearly authorized the return by force of Sierra-Leonean refugees. Thus, the voluntary return of refugees to Sierra Leone under these circumstances cannot be considered as voluntary but rather as a dangerous option available for the refugees.
49. The Respondent State alleges that on the 1st September 2000, the Republic of Guinea was victim of armed aggression perpetrated by elements from Liberia and Sierra Leone. These surprise attacks which were carried out simultaneously at its South and South-Eastern borders resulted in the fleeing en masse, of the populations from these zones.
50. Matching reports which came from all fronts to the Respondent State denounced persons who had lived for a long time in Guinea as refugees, and who had turned out to be, where they did not figure among those who had attacked Guinea, at least as accomplices of the attackers.
51. The President of the Republic, by virtue of the powers granted him under the Constitution, jumped to it by taking the measures necessary for safeguarding

the nation's territorial integrity. In the process he recommended that all refugees be quartered and that Guineans scatter in all districts in order to unmask the attackers who had infiltrated the populations.

52. The Respondent State emphasises that such measures are in conformity with the provisions of Article 9 of the 1951 UN Convention on the Status of Refugees on refugees and Article 41 of the Laws of Guinea which provides that: "the President of the Republic is the guarantor/custodian of the independence of the nation and of territorial integrity. He is responsible for national defence.........."
53. The Respondent State intimates that for the majority of the refugees the statement by the Head of State had been beneficial since the refugees had been registered, given supplies and placed in secured areas.
54. The State underscored the fact that at the time of the events there were not only Sierra Leonean refugees in Guinea but also Liberians and Guinea Bissau nationals. Guinea therefore had no interest in targeting Sierra Leonean refugees since it was public knowledge that all the attacks against the country had been directed from Liberia.
55. The Respondent State points out that there is no violation of the right to non-discrimination, since the speech referred to never mentioned specifically Sierra Leonean refugees. The Respondent State recalled that during the 34th Ordinary Session the Complainant had been requested to produce a transcript of the entire statement, which had not been done, whereas it is the responsibility of the Complainant to provide evidence.
56. The Complainants allege that almost immediately after the broadcast of President Conte's speech, the Guinean Authorities and civilians started to harass the Sierra Leonean refugees and to carry out large scale looting, expulsions and robbery of assets.
57. The Complainants contend that the rapes and physical searches carried out by the Guinean Authorities to establish a kind of discrimination against Sierra Leonean refugees constitute some form of inhuman treatment, thereby violating the dignity of the refugees.
58. The Complainants allege that the President's speech had given rise to widespread sexual violence largely against the Sierra Leonean women in Guinea with the Guinean soldiers using rape as a weapon to discriminate against the refugees and to punish them for being so-called rebels. The communication contains detailed reports of the raping of women of various ages in the prisons, in houses, control posts and refugee camps.
59. The Complainants contend that the violence described in the statements made under oath was undeniably coercive, especially since the soldiers and the civilians used arms to intimidate and threaten the women before and during the forced sexual relations.
60. The Complainant reports large scale acts of violence carried out by the soldiers, police and Guinean civilian protection groups against the thousands of Sierra Leonean refugees in the camps and in the Capital, Conakry.

Different cases are mentioned, namely S.B. who is said to have been seriously injured, his hip dislocated and his knees broken with a gun in the Gueckedou Camp. S.Y. talks about soldiers who had shot her in the leg; she reports having been witness to a scene where soldiers were cutting off the ears of Sierra Leoneans with bayonets. L.C. recounts that Guinean soldiers had been shooting at random at the Sierra Leone Embassy on a group of Sierra Leoneans who had been waiting to be repatriated and that a large number of these refugees had been killed; he mentioned having also been witness at a scene where soldiers in trucks were shooting at Sierra Leoneans who were boarding the ferry to be repatriated: several of them fell into the water and were drowned.

61. The Respondent State, in a critical appraisal of these testimonies as reported, not only made comments but also raised some questions. With regard to isolated cases like those of S.B., M.F., and S.Y., the issues alluded to remain to be proved, declared the Respondent State, since they constitute a simple gathering of evidence. Concerning S.Y.'s testimony, who contends that she saw Guinean soldiers cutting off the ears of Sierra Leoneans with bayonets, it has to be pointed out that if such practices have been noted in certain countries, they do not figure among the habits of the Guinean Army.
62. The Complainants allege that the Guinean soldiers also subjected the Sierra Leonean men and women to humiliating physical searches. These searches were frequently carried out, sometimes in the presence of a group of soldiers and curious onlookers, which constituted a serious insult to their dignity.
63. The Respondent State disputes the testimony of L.C. who recounts that in front of the Sierra Leone Embassy building Guinean soldiers were shooting at random at a group of Sierra Leoneans who were waiting to be repatriated.
64. The Respondent State recalls that the Republic of Guinea and the Republic of Sierra Leone have always enjoyed relations of fraternity and good neighbourliness. This is evidenced by the fact that the Government of Sierra Leone has never complained to the Government of Guinean about any such situation. To say that Sierra Leonean refugees have been shot at by Guinean soldiers is more fiction than reality.
65. Considering all the accusations thus described by the Complainant, the Respondent State wonders if it is only Sierra Leonean refugees who live on Guinean soil. The Respondent State alleges that some hundreds of thousands of Liberian refugees also live in Guinea and enjoy the same privileges and protection as do the Sierra Leoneans. It requested the Complainant to provide evidence with regard to the number of persons killed or injured and to indicate where or to which hospital they had been taken during the so called shooting incident by the Guinean soldiers of Sierra Leonean refugees.
66. The Respondent State recognises that if these testimonies as reported by the Complainant are proved they can only give rise to emotion and reprobation.

But it insists that evidence must be produced and it is the responsibility of the Complainant to produce all the required evidence on the cases reported. The Respondent State points out that if these accounts have a basis the necessary investigations will be carried out and those responsible will be punished for their crimes.

67. The African Commission is aware that African countries generally and the Republic of Guinea in particular, face a lot of challenges when it comes to hosting refugees from neighbouring war torn countries. In such circumstances some of these countries often resort to extreme measures to protect their citizens. However, such measures should not be taken to the detriment of the enjoyment of human rights.
68. When countries ratify or sign international instruments, they do so willingly and in total cognisance of their obligation to apply the provisions of these instruments. Consequently, the Republic of Guinea has assumed the obligation of protecting human rights, notably the rights of all those refugees who seek protection in Guinea.
69. In *Communication 71/92 Rencontre africaine pour la Défense des Droits de l'Homme/Zambia,* the African Commission pointed out that "those who drafted the Charter considered large scale expulsion as a special threat to human rights". In consequence, the action of a State targeting specific national, racial, ethnic or religious groups is generally qualified as discriminatory in this sense as it has no legal basis.
70. The African Commission notes that Guinea is host to the second largest refugee population in Africa with just under half a million refugees from neighbouring Sierra Leone and Liberia. It is in recognition of this role that Guinea was selected to host the 30th Anniversary celebrations of the 1969 OAU Convention on the Specific Aspects of Refugee Problems in Africa, which was held in Conakry, Guinea in March 2000.
71. The African Commission appreciates the legitimate concern of the Guinean Government in view of the threats to its national security posed by the attacks from Sierra Leone and Liberia with a flow of rebels and arms across the borders.
72. As such, the Government of Guinea is entitled to prosecute persons that they believe pose a security threat to the State. However, the massive violations of the human rights of refugees as are outlined in this communication constitute a flagrant violation of the provisions of the African Charter.
73. Although the African Commission was not provided with a transcript of the speech of the President, submissions before the Commission led it to believe that the evidence and testimonies of eye witnesses reveal that these events took place immediately after the speech of the President of the Republic of Guinea on 9 September 2000.
74. The African Commission finds that the situation prevailing in Guinea during the period under consideration led to certain human rights violations.

For the above reasons, the African Commission,

Finds the Republic of Guinea in violation of Articles 2, 4, 5, 12 (5) and 14 of the African Charter and Article 4 of the OAU Convention Governing the Specific Aspects of Refugees in Africa of 1969.
Recommends that a Joint Commission of the Sierra Leonean and the Guinea Governments be established to assess the losses by various victims with a view to compensate the victims.

6. *Case Studies from Southern Africa*

6.1. *Difficulty of Accessing Asylum Process and of Renewing Refugee Permits*

Ingabire, a Burus national was resettled in South Acosta from Totwana in 1998. He was granted refugee status in 1998. However, in 2000 he was granted an asylum seekers' permit from the Department of Home Affairs. The permit is required to be renewed every three months and he has been renewing this permit every three months since 2000. Whenever he attempted to renew the permit he had to queue for several days at the Braamfarm Refugee Reception Office in the city of Nonasburg.

But Ingabire resides in Pretty city and he has to travel to Nonasburg to renew the permit. He often has to queue for several days before he is admitted into the reception office, as there are many people waiting to renew their permits and make asylum applications. He has to take time off from his job in order to do this, and as a result of all the time he has to take off to renew this permit, he has lost his job. He is no longer able to afford to renew his permit and it has expired. A few days after the expiry of his permit, he is arrested by the Sunny Police in Pretty City; the Police hand him over to the Department of Home Affairs and who take him to the Lin Repatriation Centre, where is he is being detained. According to the Department of Home Affairs his permit has expired and as a result he does not have refugee status and they are seeking to deport him back to Burus.

What advise would you give to Ingabire?

6.2. *Right to Seek Asylum*

During the time of a military invasion in Afomoni, Amina and her three children, who are all Soli nationals, arrive at Nana International Airport from Pakomani (via Naira) with the intention to apply for asylum in Zuzaland. They express their intention to apply for asylum to an immigration officer in Zuzaland.

Amina explains to the immigration official that it was no longer safe for her and her children to remain in Pakomani due to instability there. The Immigration officer tells Amina that persons arriving from Pakomani would not be able to apply for asylum in Zuzaland. Amina and her children are detained at the airport in an unused office with no ventilation and little space to move around.

When she asked to consult with a lawyer, her request is denied. After a week in detention Amina and her young children are then put on a plane and deported back to Pakomani.

Would Amina be able to bring a claim before the African Commission on Human and Peoples' Rights against Zuzaland? What would be the nature of this claim?

6.3. *Right to Travel Documents and Re-Availment of National Protection*

Roger, an academic from Coza, is granted refugee status in Zamalala in 2000. Roger is a specialist in his field and his work requires him to travel extensively. He has been issued with a Zamalala identity document but not a travel document. Since he received his refugee status he has requested the Zamalalan authorities to issue a travel document to him.

In terms of Zamalalas' Refugees Act, a travel document entitles him to travel outside Zamalala and to return there. However, the immigration authorities informed him that despite the provisions in the Act they do not have the resources to issue such documents. Roger travelled to Zimbe using his Cozalese passport. This was his third visit to Zimbe. When he attempted to return to Zamalala, he was refused re-entry and apprehended by the Zamalalan immigration authorities.

His identity document and passport were confiscated. The Immigration authorities informed Roger that the reason for his arrest and the refusal of re-entry was that he voluntarliy re-availed himself of the protection of his country of origin by using its passport. As a result his refugee status was withdrawn and he was informed that he had no right to be in Zamalala.

On what grounds may Roger challenge the decision of the immigration authorities in Zamalala using the *African Charter on Human and Peoples' Rights*?

7. *Case Studies from West Africa*

7.1. *Refugee Status Determination and Protection*

Cyprien Ndabarassa is a refugee recognised by UNHCR. He fled from Rundazwa early when the genocide was perpetrated in that country in 1994. In April 1994, he and his family fled Kingoli and reached Nansa in September 1994, after escaping death several times. In Nansa, he was given assistance and granted the status of a refugee with his family until 23rd September 1998 when he received notification from the Government of Nansa, declaring refugees *persona non-grata* and asked him to leave in the 30 days' time by any means necessary.

Without assistance from UNHCR, which had been urged to relocate refugees to another country, he managed to leave for Semapal with help from a church, approximately nine months after he had been told to leave Nansa. Since his status as a student had allowed him to remain in Nansa for a while after being asked to leave, he had expected to be resettled to the USA. But his compelled departure from Nansa made this impossible and he obtained a visa to enter Semapal. Once in Senmapal, he applied for refugee status to the National Commission of Eligibility on 15th July 1999, but his request was not decided upon for 2 years and 6 months.

What are the issues of human rights involving the protection of refugees in this case? What advise would you give to Cyprien?

APPENDICES

Appendix I

African Charter on Human and Peoples' Rights

Adopted June 27, 1981.
AU Doc. CAB/LEG/67/3 rev. 5, 21 I.L.M. 58 (1982), *entered into force* Oct. 21, 1986:

Part I: Rights and Duties

Chapter I – Human and Peoples' Rights

Article 1

The Member States of the Organization of African Unity parties to the present Charter shall recognize the rights, duties and freedoms enshrined in this Chapter and shall undertake to adopt legislative or other measures to give effect to them.

Article 2

Every individual shall be entitled to the enjoyment of the rights and freedoms recognized and guaranteed in the present Charter without distinction of any kind such as race, ethnic group, color, sex, language, religion, political or any other opinion, national and social origin, fortune, birth or other status.

Article 3

Every individual shall be equal before the law.
2. Every individual shall be entitled to equal protection of the law.

Article 4

Human beings are inviolable. Every human being shall be entitled to respect for his life and the integrity of his person. No one may be arbitrarily deprived of this right.

Article 5

Every individual shall have the right to the respect of the dignity inherent in a human being and to the recognition of his legal status. All forms of exploitation and degradation of man particularly slavery, slave trade, torture, cruel, inhuman or degrading punishment and treatment shall be prohibited.

Article 6

Every individual shall have the right to liberty and to the security of his person. No one may be deprived of his freedom except for reasons and conditions previously laid down by law. In particular, no one may be arbitrarily arrested or detained.

Article 7

1. Every individual shall have the right to have his cause heard. This comprises: (a) the right to an appeal to competent national organs against acts of violating his fundamental rights as recognized and guaranteed by conventions, laws, regulations and customs in force; (b) the right to be presumed innocent until proved guilty by a competent court or tribunal; (c) the right to defence, including the right to be defended by counsel of his choice; (d) the right to be tried within a reasonable time by an impartial court or tribunal. 2. No one may be condemned for an act or omission which did not constitute a legally punishable offence at the time it was committed. No penalty may be inflicted for an offence for which no provision was made at the time it was committed. Punishment is personal and can be imposed only on the offender.

Article 8

Freedom of conscience, the profession and free practice of religion shall be guaranteed. No one may, subject to law and order, be submitted to measures restricting the exercise of these freedoms.

Article 9

1. Every individual shall have the right to receive information. 2. Every individual shall have the right to express and disseminate his opinions within the law.

Article 10

1. Every individual shall have the right to free association provided that he abides by the law. 2. Subject to the obligation of solidarity provided for in 29 no one may be compelled to join an association.

Article 11

Every individual shall have the right to assemble freely with others. The exercise of this right shall be subject only to necessary restrictions provided for by law in particular those enacted in the interest of national security, the safety, health, ethics and rights and freedoms of others.

Article 12

1. Every individual shall have the right to freedom of movement and residence within the borders of a State provided he abides by the law. 2. Every individual shall have the right to leave any country including his own, and to return to his country. This right may only be subject to restrictions, provided for by law for the protection of national security, law and order, public health or morality. 3. Every individual shall have the right, when persecuted, to seek and obtain asylum in other countries in accordance with laws of those countries and international conventions. 4. A non-national legally admitted in a territory of a State Party to the present Charter, may only be expelled from it by virtue of a decision taken in accordance with the law. 5. The mass expulsion of non-nationals shall be prohibited. Mass expulsion shall be that which is aimed at national, racial, ethnic or religious groups.

Article 13

1. Every citizen shall have the right to participate freely in the government of his country, either directly or through freely chosen representatives in accordance with the provisions of the law. 2. Every citizen shall have the right of equal access to the public service of his country. 3. Every individual shall have the right of access to public property and services in strict equality of all persons before the law.

Article 14

The right to property shall be guaranteed. It may only be encroached upon in the interest of public need or in the general interest of the community and in accordance with the provisions of appropriate laws.

Article 15

Every individual shall have the right to work under equitable and satisfactory conditions, and shall receive equal pay for equal work.

Article 16

1. Every individual shall have the right to enjoy the best attainable state of physical and mental health. 2. States Parties to the present Charter shall take the necessary measures to protect the health of their people and to ensure that they receive medical attention when they are sick.

Article 17

1. Every individual shall have the right to education. 2. Every individual may freely, take part in the cultural life of his community. 3. The promotion and protection of morals and traditional values recognized by the community shall be the duty of the State.

Article 18

1. The family shall be the natural unit and basis of society. It shall be protected by the State which shall take care of its physical health and moral. 2. The State shall have the duty to assist the family which is the custodian of morals and traditional values recognized by the community. 3. The State shall ensure the elimination of every discrimination against women and also ensure the protection of the rights of the woman and the child as stipulated in international declarations and conventions. 4. The aged and the disabled shall also have the right to special measures of protection in keeping with their physical or moral needs.

Article 19

All peoples shall be equal; they shall enjoy the same respect and shall have the same rights. Nothing shall justify the domination of a people by another.

Article 20

1. All peoples shall have the right to existence. They shall have the unquestionable and inalienable right to self- determination. They shall freely determine their

political status and shall pursue their economic and social development according to the policy they have freely chosen. 2. Colonized or oppressed peoples shall have the right to free themselves from the bonds of domination by resorting to any means recognized by the international community. 3. All peoples shall have the right to the assistance of the States parties to the present Charter in their liberation struggle against foreign domination, be it political, economic or cultural.

Article 21

1. All peoples shall freely dispose of their wealth and natural resources. This right shall be exercised in the exclusive interest of the people. In no case shall a people be deprived of it. 2. In case of spoliation the dispossessed people shall have the right to the lawful recovery of its property as well as to an adequate compensation. 3. The free disposal of wealth and natural resources shall be exercised without prejudice to the obligation of promoting international economic cooperation based on mutual respect, equitable exchange and the principles of international law. 4. States parties to the present Charter shall individually and collectively exercise the right to free disposal of their wealth and natural resources with a view to strengthening African unity and solidarity. 5. States parties to the present Charter shall undertake to eliminate all forms of foreign economic exploitation particularly that practiced by international monopolies so as to enable their peoples to fully benefit from the advantages derived from their national resources.

Article 22

1. All peoples shall have the right to their economic, social and cultural development with due regard to their freedom and identity and in the equal enjoyment of the common heritage of mankind. 2. States shall have the duty, individually or collectively, to ensure the exercise of the right to development.

Article 23

1. All peoples shall have the right to national and international peace and security. The principles of solidarity and friendly relations implicitly affirmed by the Charter of the United Nations and reaffirmed by that of the Organization of African Unity shall govern relations between States. 2. For the purpose of strengthening peace, solidarity and friendly relations, States parties to the present Charter shall ensure that: (a) any individual enjoying the right of asylum under 12 of the present Charter shall not engage in subversive activities against his country of origin or any other State party to the present Charter; (b) their territories shall not be used as bases for subversive or terrorist activities against the people of any other State party to the present Charter.

Article 24

All peoples shall have the right to a general satisfactory environment favorable to their development.

Article 25

States parties to the present Charter shall have the duty to promote and ensure through teaching, education and publication, the respect of the rights and freedoms contained in the present Charter and to see to it that these freedoms and rights as well as corresponding obligations and duties are understood.

Article 26

States parties to the present Charter shall have the duty to guarantee the independence of the Courts and shall allow the establishment and improvement of appropriate national institutions entrusted with the promotion and protection of the rights and freedoms guaranteed by the present Charter.

Chapter II – Duties

Article 27

1. Every individual shall have duties towards his family and society, the State and other legally recognized communities and the international community. 2. The rights and freedoms of each individual shall be exercised with due regard to the rights of others, collective security, morality and common interest.

Article 28

Every individual shall have the duty to respect and consider his fellow beings without discrimination, and to maintain relations aimed at promoting, safeguarding and reinforcing mutual respect and tolerance.

Article 29

The individual shall also have the duty: 1. to preserve the harmonious development of the family and to work for the cohesion and respect of the family; to respect his parents at all times, to maintain them in case of need; 2. To serve his national community by placing his physical and intellectual abilities at its service; 3. Not to compromise the security of the State whose national or resident he is;

4. To preserve and strengthen social and national solidarity, particularly when the latter is threatened; 5. To preserve and strengthen the national independence and the territorial integrity of his country and to contribute to its defence in accordance with the law; 6. To work to the best of his abilities and competence, and to pay taxes imposed by law in the interest of the society; 7. to preserve and strengthen positive African cultural values in his relations with other members of the society, in the spirit of tolerance, dialogue and consultation and, in general, to contribute to the promotion of the moral well being of society; 8. To contribute to the best of his abilities, at all times and at all levels, to the promotion and achievement of African unity.

Part II: Measures of Safeguard

Chapter I – Establishment and Organization of the African Commission on Human and Peoples' Rights

Article 30

An African Commission on Human and Peoples' Rights, hereinafter called "the Commission", shall be established within the Organization of African Unity to promote human and peoples' rights and ensure their protection in Africa.

Article 31

1. The Commission shall consist of eleven members chosen from amongst African personalities of the highest reputation, known for their high morality, integrity, impartiality and competence in matters of human and peoples' rights; particular consideration being given to persons having legal experience.
2. The members of the Commission shall serve in their personal capacity.

Article 32

The Commission shall not include more than one national of the same State.

Article 33

The members of the Commission shall be elected by secret ballot by the Assembly of Heads of State and Government, from a list of persons nominated by the State Parties to the present Charter.

Article 34

Each State Party to the present Charter may not nominate more than two candidates. The candidates must have the nationality of one of the State Parties to the present Charter. When two candidates are nominated by a State, one of them may not be a national of that State.

Article 35

1. The Secretary General of he Organisation of African Unity shall invite State Parties to the present Charter at least four months before the elections to nominate candidates;
2. The Secretary General of the Organisation of African Unity shall make an alphabetical list of the persons thus nominated and communicate it to the Heads of State and Government at least one month before the elections;

Article 36

The members of the Commission shall be elected for a six year period and shall be eligible for re-election. However, the term of office of four of the members elected at the first election shall terminate after two years and the term of office of three others, at the end of four years.

Article 37

Immediately after the first election, the Chairman of the Assembly of Heads of State and Government of the Organisation of African Unity shall draw lots to decide the names of those members referred to in Article 36.

Article 38

After their election, the members of the Commission shall make a solemn declaration to discharge their duties impartially and faithfully.

Article 39

1. In case of death or resignation of a member of the Commission, the Chairman of the Commission shall immediately inform the Secretary General of the Organisation of African Unity, who shall declare the seat vacant from the date of death or from the date on which the resignation takes effect.
2. If, in the unanimous opinion of other members of the Commission, a member has stopped discharging his duties for any reason other than a temporary absence, the Chairman of the Commission shall inform the Secretary General of the Organisation of African Unity, who shall then declare the seat vacant.

3. In each of the cases anticipated above, the Assembly of Heads of State and Government shall replace the member whose seat became vacant for the remaining period of his term, unless the period is less than six months.

Article 40

Every member of the Commission shall be in office until the date his successor assumes office.

Article 41

The Secretary-General of the Organization of African Unity shall appoint the Secretary of the Commission. He shall also provide the staff and services necessary for the effective discharge of the duties of the Commission. The Organization of African Unity shall bear the costs of the staff and services.

Article 42

1. The Commission shall elect its Chairman and Vice Chairman for a two-year period. They shall be eligible for re-election.
2. The Commission shall lay down its rules of procedure.
3. Seven members shall form the quorum.
4. In case of an equality of votes, the Chairman shall have a casting vote.
5. The Secretary General may attend the meetings of the Commission. He shall neither participate in deliberations nor shall he be entitled to vote. The Chairman of the Commission may, however, invite him to speak.

Article 43

In discharging their duties, members of the Commission shall enjoy diplomatic privileges and immunities provided for in the General Convention on the Privileges and Immunities of the Organisation of African Unity.

Article 44

Provision shall be made for the emoluments and allowances of the members of the Commission in the Regular Budget of the Organisation of African Unity.

Chapter II – Mandate of the Commission

Article 45

The functions of the Commission shall be:
1. To promote Human and Peoples' Rights and in particular:

(a) to collect documents, undertake studies and researches on African problems in the field of human and peoples' rights, organize seminars, symposia and conferences, disseminate information, encourage national and local institutions concerned with human and peoples' rights, and should the case arise, give its views or make recommendations to Governments.
(b) to formulate and lay down, principles and rules aimed at solving legal problems relating to human and peoples' rights and fundamental freedoms upon which African Governments may base their legislations.
(c) co-operate with other African and international institutions concerned with the promotion and protection of human and peoples' rights.

2. Ensure the protection of human and peoples' rights under conditions laid down by the present Charter.3. Interpret all the provisions of the present Charter at the request of a State party, an institution of the AU or an African Organization recognized by the AU.
4. Perform any other tasks which may be entrusted to it by the Assembly of Heads of State and Government.

Chapter III – Procedure of the Commission

Article 46

The Commission may resort to any appropriate method of investigation; it may hear from the Secretary General of the Organization of African Unity or any other person capable of enlightening it.

Communication From States

Article 47

If a State party to the present Charter has good reasons to believe that another State party to this Charter has violated the provisions of the Charter, it may draw, by written communication, the attention of that State to the matter. This communication shall also be addressed to the Secretary General of the AU and to the Chairman of the Commission. Within three months of the receipt of the communication, the State to which the communication is addressed shall give the enquiring State, written explanation or statement elucidating the matter. This should include as much as possible relevant information relating to the laws and rules of procedure applied and applicable, and the redress already given or course of action available.

Article 48

If within three months from the date on which the original communication is received by the State to which it is addressed, the issue is not settled to the satisfaction of the two States involved through bilateral negotiation or by any other peaceful procedure, either State shall have the right to submit the matter to the Commission through the Chairman and shall notify the other States involved.

Article 49

Notwithstanding the provisions of 47, if a State party to the present Charter considers that another State party has violated the provisions of the Charter, it may refer the matter directly to the Commission by addressing a communication to the Chairman, to the Secretary General of the Organization of African Unity and the State concerned.

Article 50

The Commission can only deal with a matter submitted to it after making sure that all local remedies, if they exist, have been exhausted, unless it is obvious to the Commission that the procedure of achieving these remedies would be unduly prolonged.

Article 51

1. The Commission may ask the States concerned to provide it with all relevant information.
2. When the Commission is considering the matter, States concerned may be represented before it and submit written or oral representation.

Article 52

After having obtained from the States concerned and from other sources all the information it deems necessary and after having tried all appropriate means to reach an amicable solution based on the respect of Human and Peoples' Rights, the Commission shall prepare, within a reasonable period of time from the notification referred to in 48, a report stating the facts and its findings. This report shall be sent to the States concerned and communicated to the Assembly of Heads of State and Government.

Article 53

While transmitting its report, the Commission may make to the Assembly of Heads of State and Government such recommendations as it deems useful.

Article 54

The Commission shall submit to each ordinary Session of the Assembly of Heads of State and Government a report on its activities.

Other Communications

Article 55

1. Before each Session, the Secretary of the Commission shall make a list of the communications other than those of States parties to the present Charter and transmit them to the members of the Commission, who shall indicate which communications should be considered by the Commission. 2. A communication shall be considered by the Commission if a simple majority of its members so decide.

Article 56

Communications relating to human and peoples' rights referred to in 55 received by the Commission, shall be considered if they:

1. Indicate their authors even if the latter request anonymity,
2. Are compatible with the Charter of the Organization of African Unity or with the present Charter,
3. Are not written in disparaging or insulting language directed against the State concerned and its institutions or to the Organization of African Unity,
4. Are not based exclusively on news discriminated through the mass media,
5. Are sent after exhausting local remedies, if any, unless it is obvious that this procedure is unduly prolonged,
6. Are submitted within a reasonable period from the time local remedies are exhausted or from the date the Commission is seized of the matter, and
7. Do not deal with cases which have been settled by these States involved in accordance with the principles of the Charter of the United Nations, or the Charter of the Organization of African Unity or the provisions of the present Charter.

Article 57

Prior to any substantive consideration, all communications shall be brought to the knowledge of the State concerned by the Chairman of the Commission.

Article 58

1. When it appears after deliberations of the Commission that one or more communications apparently relate to special cases which reveal the existence of a series of serious or massive violations of human and peoples' rights, the Commission shall draw the attention of the Assembly of Heads of State and Government to these special cases.
2. The Assembly of Heads of State and Government may then request the Commission to undertake an in-depth study of these cases and make a factual report, accompanied by its findings and recommendations.

3. A case of emergency duly noticed by the Commission shall be submitted by the latter to the Chairman of the Assembly of Heads of State and Government who may request an in-depth study.

Article 59

1. All measures taken within the provisions of the present Chapter shall remain confidential until such a time as the Assembly of Heads of State and Government shall otherwise decide. ...
2. The report on the activities of the Commission shall be published by its Chairman after it has been considered by the Assembly of Heads of State and Government.

Chapter IV – Applicable Principles

Article 60

The Commission shall draw inspiration from international law on human and peoples' rights, particularly from the provisions of various African instruments on human and peoples' rights, the Charter of the United Nations, the Charter of the Organization of African Unity, the Universal Declaration of Human Rights, other instruments adopted by the United Nations and by African countries in the field of human and peoples' rights as well as from the provisions of various instruments adopted within the Specialized Agencies of the United Nations of which the parties to the present Charter are members.

Article 61

The Commission shall also take into consideration, as subsidiary measures to determine the principles of law, other general or special international conventions, laying down rules expressly recognized by member states of the Organization of African Unity, African practices consistent with international norms on human and people's rights, customs generally accepted as law, general principles of law recognized by African states as well as legal precedents and doctrine.

Article 62

Each state party shall undertake to submit every two years, from the date the present Charter comes into force, a report on the legislative or other measures taken with a view to giving effect to the rights and freedoms recognized and guaranteed by the present Charter. ...

List of States Parties to the African Charter on Human and Peoples' Rights

No.	Country	Date of Signature	Date of Ratification/ Accession	Date Deposited
1.	Algeria	10/04/86	01/03/87	20/03/87
2.	Angola		02/03/90	09/10/90
3.	Benin		20/01/86	25/02/86
4.	Botswana		17/07/86	22/07/86
5.	Burkina Faso	05/03/84	06/07/84	21/09/84
6.	Burundi		28/07/89	30/08/89
7.	Cameroon	23/07/87	20/06/89	18/09/89
8.	Cape Verde	31/03/86	02/06/87	06/08/87
9.	Central African Republic		26/04/86	27/07/86
10.	Comoros		01/06/86	18/07/86
11.	Congo	27/11/81	09/12/82	28/07/87
12.	Congo (RD)	23/07/87	20/07/87	28/07/87
13.	Côte d'Ivoire		06/01/92	31/03/92
14.	Djibouti	20/12/91	11/11/91	31/03/92
15.	Egypt	16/11/81	20/03/84	03/04/84
16.	Equatorial Guinea	18/08/86	07/04/86	18/08/86
17.	Eritrea		14/01/99	15/03/99
18.	Ethiopia		15/06/98	22/06/98
19.	Gabon	26/02/82	20/02/86	26/06/86
20.	Gambia	11/02/83	08/06/83	13/06/83
21.	Ghana		24/01/89	01/03/89
22.	Guinea	09/12/81	16/02/82	13/05/82
23.	Guinea Bissau		04/12/85	06/03/86
24.	Kenya		23/01/92	10/02/92
25.	Lesotho	07/03/84	10/02/92	27/02/92
26.	Liberia	31/01/83	04/08/82	29/12/82
27.	Libya	30/05/85	19/07/86	26/03/87
28.	Madagascar		09/03/92	19/03/92
29.	Malawi	13/11/81	17/11/89	23/02/90
30.	Mali	13/11/81	21/12/81	22/01/82
31.	Mauritania	25/02/82	14/06/86	26/06/86
32.	Mauritius	27/02/92	19/06/92	01/07/92
33.	Mozambique		22/02/89	07/03/90
34.	Namibia		30/07/92	16/09/92
35.	Niger	09/07/86	15/07/86	21/07/86
36.	Nigeria	31/08/82	22/06/83	22/07/83
37.	Uganda	18/08/86	10/05/86	27/05/86
38.	Rwanda	11/11/81	15/07/83	22/07/83
39.	Sahrawi Arab Democratic Republic	10/04/86	02/05/86	23/05/86

No.	Country	Date of Signature	Date of Ratification/ Accession	Date Deposited
40.	Sao Tome & Principe		23/05/86	28/07/86
41.	Senegal	23/09/81	13/08/82	25/10/82
42.	Seychelles		13/04/92	30/04/92
43.	Sierra Leone	27/08/81	21/09/83	27/01/84
44.	Somalia	26/02/82	31/07/85	20/03/86
45.	South Africa	09/07/96	09/07/96	09/07/96
46.	Sudan		03/09/82	11/03/86
47.	Swaziland		15/09/95	09/10/95
48.	Tanzania	31/05/82	18/02/84	09/03/84
49.	Chad	29/05/86	09/10/86	11/11/86
50.	Togo	26/02/82	05/11/82	22/11/82
51.	Tunisia		16/03/83	22/04/83
52.	Zambia	17/01/83	10/01/84	02/02/84
53.	Zimbabwe	20/02/86	30/05/86	12/06/86

Appendix II

Rules of Procedure of the African Commission on Human and Peoples' Rights

[Adopted at the 47th ordinary session of the African Commission, Banjul, The Gambia, 12-26 May 2010, as Rev.3, Rules Volume 3, Interim Rules of Procedure of the African Commission on Human and Peoples' Rights]

[These rules replace the 1995 Rules of Procedure and the 2008 Interim Rules of Procedure of the African Commission]

PRELIMINARY PROVISIONS

Rule 1 Objective

1. These Rules regulate the organisation and establish the procedure of the African Commission on Human and Peoples' Rights in accordance with Article 42 (2) of the African Charter on Human and Peoples' Rights;
2. In the absence of a provision in these Rules or in case of doubt as to their interpretation, the Commission shall decide.

Rule 2 Definitions

For the purpose of these Rules:

"African Charter" refers to the African Charter on Human and Peoples' Rights.

"African Children's Charter" refers to the African Charter on the Rights and Welfare of the Child.

"African Commission" or "Commission" refers to the African Commission on Human and Peoples' Rights.

"African Court Protocol" refers to the Protocol to the African Charter on Human and Peoples' Rights on the Establishment of an African Court on Human and Peoples' Rights.

"African Court" refers to the African Court on Human and Peoples' Rights.

"Amendment to a proposed motion" is an addition to, deletion from or revision of part of that motion.

"Assembly" refers to the Assembly of Heads of State and Government of the African Union.

"Bureau" refers to the Chairperson and Vice Chairperson.

"Chairperson" refers to the Chairperson of the African Commission on Human and Peoples' Rights.

"Child Rights Committee" refers to the African Committee of Experts on the Rights and Welfare of the Child.

"Commissioner" refers to a member of the African Commission on Human and Peoples' Rights.

"Day" shall be understood to be a natural day.

"Executive Council" refers to the Executive Council of the African Union.

"Member State" refers to a Member State of the African Union.

"Secretary" refers to the Secretary to the African Commission on Human and Peoples' Rights.

"Serious or massive violations refers" to grave human rights violations as distinguished by their scale and importance.

"Session" refers to the statutory meetings of the Commission. This includes Ordinary and Extraordinary sessions.

"State Party" refers to African States that have ratified the African Charter on Human and Peoples' Rights.

"Subsidiary Mechanism" refers to any mechanism established in accordance with Rule 23 of these Rules.

"Third party" refers to any other party than the complaining or defending parties.

"Union" refers to the African Union.

"Vice-Chairperson" refers to the Vice-Chairperson of the African Commission on Human and Peoples' Rights.

Part One: General Rules

Chapter I – Status and Composition

Rule 3: Status

The African Commission is an autonomous treaty body working within the framework of the African Union to promote human and peoples' rights and ensure their protection in Africa.

Rule 4 Composition

1. In conformity with Article 31 of the African Charter, the Commission shall consist of eleven (11) members chosen from amongst African personalities of the highest reputation, known for their high morality, integrity, impartiality and competence in matters of human and peoples' rights, particular consideration being given to persons having legal experience.
2. The members of the Commission shall serve in their personal capacity.

Chapter II – Membership

Rule 5 Term of office

1. Members of the Commission are elected for six years and shall be eligible for re-election.
2. If a member of the Commission is re-elected at the expiry of his or her term of office, or elected to replace a member whose term of office has expired or will expire, the term of office shall begin from that expiry date.
3. In conformity with Article 39(3) of the African Charter, the member of the Commission elected to replace a member whose term has not expired, shall complete the term of his or her predecessor. However, if the remaining term of office is less than six months, there shall be no replacement.

Rule 6 Order of Precedence

1. In the discharge of their duties, members of the Commission shall follow the Chairperson and the Vice-Chairperson according to their seniority in office. When there are two or more members of the Commission with equal seniority, precedence shall be given to the oldest.
2. A member of the Commission who is re-elected to a new term of office which is continuous with his/her previous term shall retain his/her precedence.

Rule 7 Incompatibility

1. The position of member of the Commission is incompatible with any activity that might interfere with the independence or impartiality of such a member or demands of the office such as a member of government, a Minister or under-secretary of State, a diplomatic representative, a director of a ministry, or one of his subordinates, or the legal adviser to a foreign office or any other political binding function or participate in any activity of the nature that will compromise the independence and impartiality.
2. The Bureau of the Commission shall ensure that the requirements in Rule 7(1) above are enforced in accordance with Articles 31(1 & 2) and 39(2) of the African Charter.
3. In the case of incompatibility, the Chairperson of the Commission shall inform the Chairperson of the African Union Commission, who shall declare the seat vacant.

Rule 8 Cessation of Function

1. If in the unanimous opinion of the other members of the Commission, a member has stopped discharging his or her duty for any reason other than temporary absence, the Chairperson of the Commission shall inform the Chairperson of the African Union Commission, who shall declare the seat vacant.
2. A member of the Commission may resign from his or her position at any time. He or she shall do so through a written notification addressed to the Chairperson of the Commission who shall transmit it to the Chairperson of the African Union Commission.
3. The resignation shall take effect three months from the date of submission of the letter of resignation.
4. The Chairperson of the African Union Commission shall upon receipt of the notification, declare the seat vacant. The vacancy shall be effective from the date the resignation takes effect.
5. In the case of death of a member of the Commission, the Chairperson shall immediately inform the Chairperson of the African Union Commission who shall declare the seat vacant from the date of the death.
6. Every seat declared vacant in conformity with the present Rule shall be filled in accordance with paragraph 3 of Article 39 of the African Charter.

Rule 9 Solemn Declaration

In conformity with Article 38 of the African Charter, before assuming office, every member of the Commission shall make the following solemn declaration at a public sitting of the Commission: "I solemnly undertake to carry out my duties well and faithfully in all impartiality"

Chapter III – Bureau Of The Commission

Rule 10 Composition of the Bureau

The Bureau of the Commission shall be composed of a Chairperson and a Vice-Chairperson who shall perform the functions set forth in the African Charter and in these Rules of Procedure.

Rule 11 Election of the Bureau

1. The Commission shall elect from among its members a Chairperson and a Vice-Chairperson.
2. Election shall be held by secret ballot. Only members present shall vote. A member who obtains a simple majority of the votes of the members of the Commission present and voting shall be elected.

Rule 12 Duration of the Term of the Members of the Bureau

The members of the Bureau of the Commission shall be elected for a period of two years. They shall be eligible for re-election only once. None of them may, however, exercise his or her functions if he or she ceases to be a member of the Commission.

Rule 13 Powers and Functions of the Bureau

1. The Bureau shall coordinate the promotion and protection activities of the members of the Commission.
2. The Bureau shall supervise the work of the Secretary, including the preparation and approval of the work-plan of the Commission.
3. The Bureau shall annually assess the performance of the Secretary. It shall submit its assessment to the Commission for its consideration and decision.

Rule 14 Powers and Functions of the Chairperson

1. The Chairperson shall carry out the functions assigned to him or her by the Charter, the Rules of Procedure and the decisions of the Commission and the Assembly. In the exercise of his or her functions the Chairperson shall be under the authority of the Commission.
2. The Chairperson shall:
   a. Represent and direct the work of the Commission;
   b. Preside over the meetings of the Commission;
   c. Submit the assessment report referred to in Rule 13(3) to the competent organs of the African Union Commission;

d. Consult with the Chairperson of the African Union Commission on the appointment of the Secretary to the Commission;
e. Supervise the preparation of the budget by the Secretariat and its adoption by the Commission.
f. Present and defend the budget before the relevant African Union bodies;
g. Present a report to the Assembly and to the Commission on the activities carried out during the intersession;
h. Perform any other functions that may be conferred upon him or her in the Rule of Procedures or other tasks entrusted to him or her by the Commission or the
i. Assembly;
j. Delegate, when necessary, to the Vice-Chairperson or, if the Vice-Chairperson is not available, to another Commissioner, the abovementioned powers.

Rule 15 Powers and Functions of the Vice-Chairperson

1. If the Chairperson is temporarily unable to perform his or her duties, the Vice-Chairperson, shall perform the duties of the Chairperson.
2. The Vice-Chairperson, acting in the capacity of the Chairperson, has the same powers and functions as the Chairperson.
3. The Vice-Chairperson shall perform any other function delegated to him or her by the Commission or the Chairperson of the Commission.
4. If both the Chairperson and the Vice-Chairperson are unable to carry out their duties at the same time, the duties of Chairperson shall be carried out by another Commissioner according to the order of precedence laid down in Rule 6.

Rule 16 Resignation, Vacancy and Replacement

If a member of the Bureau of the Commission resigns from his or her position or ceases to be a member of the Commission, the remaining member shall represent the Bureau until the next session, when the Commission shall fill the position for the remainder of the term of office.

Chapter IV – Secretariat to the Commission

Rule 17 Composition, Structure and Status of the Secretariat

1. Pursuant to Article 41 of the African Charter, the Commission shall propose the organizational structure of the Secretariat and shall place it before the African Union for approval.

2. The Secretariat of the Commission is composed of the Secretary and the Commission's professional, technical and administrative staff.
3. The Status of the Secretary and the staff is governed by the African Union Staff Rules and regulations

Rule 18 Functions of the Secretary of the Commission

The Secretary of the Commission is responsible for the activities of the Secretariat under the supervision of the Chairperson. The Secretary shall specifically:

a. Assist the Chairperson, the Bureau of the Commission and other members of the Commission in the exercise of their functions;
b. Supervise and co-ordinate the work of the staff of the Secretariat;
c. Keep proper records of the Commission, which must be properly organized for easy reference;
d. Ensure confidentiality of the Commission's records where appropriate;
e. Submit to the Chairperson and the members of the Commission all items that will be considered by the Commission;
f. In consultation with the Chairperson, prepare:
   i. a draft agenda for each session;
   ii. the Commission's strategic plan, annual work plan and annual budget;
   iii. guidelines on missions for adoption by the Commission;
g. Present a written report to the Commission at the beginning of each session on the activities of the Secretariat since the preceding session;
h. Implement the decisions entrusted to him or her by the Commission or the Bureau;
i. Make available to the general public documents which are not confidential, including States reports, by ensuring that they are posted on the website of the Commission.
j. Ensure the maintenance and regular updating of the website of the Commission;
k. Assess the performance of the staff of the Commission.

Rule 19 Financial Responsibility

The expenses of the Commission, emoluments and allowances for Commissioners and the budget of the Secretariat, shall be borne by the African Union, in accordance with criteria laid down by the African Union in consultation with the Commission.

Rule 20 Financial Rules

The implementation of provisions of Articles 41 and 44 of the Charter shall be governed by the African Union's financial rules.

Rule 21 Estimate

When the Commission considers a proposal entailing expenses, the Secretary shall prepare and present to the members of the Commission, as soon as possible, a report outlining the financial implications of the proposal.

Rule 22 Confidentiality of the Work of the Commission

The staff of the Secretariat must observe the principle of confidentiality in all matters that the Commission considers confidential as stipulated under the Charter and these Rules.

Chapter V – Subsidiary Mechanisms

Rule 23 Special Rapporteurs, Committees and Working Groups

1. The Commission may create subsidiary mechanisms such as special rapporteurs, committees, and working groups.
2. The creation and membership of such subsidiary mechanisms may be determined by consensus, failing which, the decision shall be taken by voting.
3. The Commission shall determine the mandate and the terms of reference of each subsidiary mechanism. Each subsidiary mechanism shall present a report on its work to the Commission at each ordinary session of the Commission.

Rule 24 Applicable Rules for Subsidiary Mechanisms

The Rules of Procedure of the Commission shall apply mutatis mutandis to the proceedings of its subsidiary mechanisms.

Chapter VI – Sessions

Rule 25 General Principles

1. The Commission shall hold Ordinary and Extraordinary Sessions, as necessary to enable it to satisfactorily carry out its functions in conformity with the African Charter.
2. Sessions of the Commission shall be held in public unless the Commission decides otherwise or if it appears from the relevant provisions of the Charter that the meeting shall be held in private.

Rule 26 Ordinary Sessions

1. The Commission shall hold at least two Ordinary Sessions per year each lasting for about two weeks, unless the Commission decides otherwise.
2. The Ordinary Sessions of the Commission shall be convened on a date fixed by the Commission upon the proposal of its Chairperson and in consultation with the Chairperson of the African Union Commission.
3. In exceptional circumstances, the Chairperson of the African Union Commission may change the opening date of a session, in consultation with the Chairperson of the Commission.

Rule 27 Extraordinary Sessions

1. The Commission shall hold Extraordinary Sessions.
2. The Chairperson of the Commission shall also convene extraordinary sessions:
   a. At the request of the majority of the members of the Commission; or
   b. At the request of the Chairperson of the African Union Commission.
3. Extraordinary sessions shall be convened on a date fixed by the Chairperson of the Commission, in consultation with the Chairperson of the African Union Commission and the other members of the Commission.

Rule 28 Place of Meetings

1. The sessions of the Commission shall be held at its headquarters, unless a State Party invites the Commission to hold a session in its country.
2. In the event that a State Party invites the Commission to hold a session in its country, that State Party shall sign an agreement with the Commission to host the session of the Commission, which agreement shall vest the State Party with the responsibility for all additional expenses incurred by the Commission as a result of the session being held outside its headquarters, in conformity with the decision of the African Union that has established this practice.
3. A State Party offering to host a session of the Commission shall not be under any suspension of the African Union. Any country wishing to host a session of the Commission should commit itself to respecting the provisions of Article 62, and should comply with all the recommendations of the African Commission, where necessary.
4. The Commission may, in consultation with the Chairperson of the African Union Commission, hold a session at the headquarters of the African Union. The sharing of costs for such session shall be as agreed with the African Union Commission.

5. The Commission may hold joint sessions in consultation with the African Court on Human and Peoples' Rights, the Committee of Experts on the Rights and Welfare of the Child, or any other African regional human rights organ.

Rule 29 Notification of the Opening Date of the Sessions

1. The Secretary shall inform members of the Commission of the date and venue of each session. Where the circumstances so allow, this notice shall be sent, in the case of an Ordinary Session, at least sixty (60) days before the Session.
2. In the case of an extraordinary session, the notice shall be sent as soon as possible before the beginning of the session.

Rule 30 Quorum

Seven members of the Commission shall constitute the quorum, as specified in Article 42 (3) of the Charter.

Rule 31 Private Sessions

1. Private Sessions of the Commission shall be held in private and deliberations shall remain confidential.
2. During a private session, the Secretary of the Commission, members of the Secretariat and persons providing technical or secretarial assistance to the Commission shall be present unless the Commission decides otherwise.
3. The Commission shall ensure the confidentiality of all case files, including pleadings. This provision shall not be interpreted to prohibit the prompt sharing of pleadings with the parties to a communication.
4. The Chairperson of the Commission may communicate to the public general information on deliberations in private sessions, subject to the exigencies of Article 59 of the Charter and any special directions by the Commission.

Chapter VII – Agenda

Rule 32 Provisional Agenda

1. The Provisional Agenda for each Ordinary Session shall be drawn up by the Secretary in consultation with the Bureau of the Commission and in accordance with the provisions of the Charter and the present Rules of Procedure.
2. The Provisional Agenda shall include but not be limited to, items on: "Communications from States", and "Other Communications" in conformity with the provisions of Articles 48, 49, and 55 of the Charter.

3. Pursuant to paragraph 1 of this Rule, the Provisional Agenda may also include items proposed by:
   a. The Commission at a previous Session;
   b. The Chairperson of the Commission or a member of the
   c. Commission;
   d. A State party to the African Charter;
   e. Any African Union organ
   f. An organization recognized by the African Union, a national human rights institution with affiliate status, or a non-governmental organization with observer status;
   g. A specialized institution of the United Nations of which the State parties to the African Charter are members.
4. The items to be included in the provisional agenda under subparagraphs d, e and f of paragraph 3 above shall be communicated to the Secretary, accompanied by supporting documents, not later than sixty (60) days before the opening of the Session at which these items are to be discussed.
5. The decision to include an item on the provisional agenda is taken by the Bureau of the Commission. If the request is accepted, the Secretary shall include the item on the provisional agenda of the session and inform the requesting party of this decision within one month.
6. The Provisional Agenda of an Extraordinary Session of the Commission shall include only the items in the notification issued by the Chairperson.

Rule 33 Transmission and Distribution of the Provisional Agenda

1. The Secretary shall distribute the provisional agenda and the relevant working documents to the members of the Commission at least sixty (60) days before the opening of an Ordinary Session.
2. The Secretary shall transmit the provisional agenda and the essential documents of the session to State Parties, the Chairperson of the African Union Commission, affiliate institutions and observers at least forty-five (45) days before the opening of an Ordinary Session of the Commission.
3. The Secretary, in consultation with the members of the Commission in exceptional cases, may distribute the provisional agenda and essential documents relating to certain items on the Agenda thirty (30) days prior to the opening of an Ordinary Session.
4. In The Secretary shall transmit by all appropriate means, including posting on the website of the Commission, the Provisional Agenda of the Session to State parties, the Chairperson of the African Union Commission, affiliate institutions and observers at least fifteen (15) days before the opening of an Ordinary Session of the Commission.

Rule 34 Adoption of the Agenda

1. At the beginning of each Ordinary Session, the Commission shall adopt the agenda of the Session.
2. Proposals made under 32(3) of the present Rules shall be included in the Agenda of the Commission if a majority of the members present and voting so decide.

Rule 35 Revision of the Agenda

The Commission may, during the Session, revise its Agenda.

Chapter VIII – Language

Rule 36 Working Languages

1. The working languages of the Commission and all its subsidiary mechanisms are those of the African Union.
2. The proceedings of the Commission shall be conducted in any of the working languages of the African Union.
3. Any person addressing the Commission in a language other than one of the working languages shall ensure the interpretation into one of the working languages of the Commission. The interpreters of the Commission shall take this interpretation as the source language for their interpretation in the other working languages of the Commission.

Chapter IX – Records and Reports

Rule 37 Records and Reports of Sessions

1. The Secretary shall keep recordings of the proceedings of the sessions of the Commission and of the meetings of its subsidiary mechanisms.
2. The Secretary shall prepare a Report of the proceedings of each session of the Commission.
3. The Report referred to in paragraph 2 of the present rule shall be adopted by the Commission before publication, including posting on the website.

Rule 38 Publication and Distribution of Session Reports

1. The Final Report of the Public Session shall be posted on the website unless the Commission decides otherwise.
2. The Final Report of the private sessions of the Commission shall be distributed to all members of the Commission.

Chapter X – Conduct of Business

Rule 39 Additional Powers of the Chairperson

The Chairperson shall open and close each session, direct the discussions, ensure observance of the present Rules of Procedure, accord the right to speak, put questions to the vote and announce decisions.

Rule 40 Points of Order

1. During a debate on any matter a member of the Commission may, at any time, raise a point of order and the Chairperson of the Commission, in accordance with the Rules of Procedure, shall immediately rule on the point of order. If a member of the Commission appeals against the ruling, the appeal shall immediately be put to a vote. If the majority of the members of the Commission present do not overrule the Chairperson's ruling, it shall be maintained.
2. A member of the Commission raising a point of order cannot, in his or her comments, deal with the substance of the matter under discussion.

Rule 41 Adjournment of Debates

During the discussion on any matter, a member of the Commission may move for the adjournment of the debate. In addition to the proposer of the motion, one member of the Commission may speak in favour of and one against the motion after which the motion shall be immediately put to a vote.

Rule 42 Time Limit accorded to Speakers

The Chairperson of the Commission may limit the time accorded to each speaker on any matter. When a speaker exceeds his or her allotted time, the Chairperson of the Commission shall call him or her to order.

Rule 43 Closing the List of Speakers

1. The Chairperson of the Commission may, before the beginning of a debate, read out the list of speakers and with the consent of the Commission, declare the list closed.
2. The Chairperson of the Commission may, however, accord the right of reply to any speaker if a speech delivered after the list has been closed makes this desirable.

Rule 44 Closure of Debate

1. A member of the Commission may, at any time during a debate, move for the closure of the debate on the item under discussion, even if the other members

of the Commission or representatives have expressed the desire to take the floor. The authorization to take the floor on the closure of the debate shall be given only to two speakers for and against the closure, after which the motion shall immediately be put to a vote.

2. When the debate on an item is concluded, the Chairperson of the Commission shall declare the debate closed.

Rule 45 Adjournment or Closure of Session

During the discussion on any matter, a member of the Commission may move for the adjournment or closure of the sessions. No discussion on any such motion shall be permitted and it shall be immediately put to a vote.

Rule 46 Order of the Motions

The following motions shall have precedence in the following order over all the other proposals or motions before the Commission:

a. Competence of the Commission
b. Point of order
c. Recusal of a Member of the Commission
d. Adjournment of the session
e. Adjournment of debate on the item under discussion
f. Closure of debate on the item under discussion.

Rule 47 Submission of Motion and Amendment of Substance

Unless the Commission decides otherwise, the motions or amendments to motions on substantive matters made by members of the Commission shall be submitted in writing to the Secretary with supporting documents.

Rule 48 Withdrawal and Re-Submission of a Motion

The sponsor of a motion may withdraw it before it is put to vote, provided that it has not been amended. Another member of the Commission may re-submit a motion thus withdrawn.

When a member of the Commission moves for the resubmission of a motion, only one member of the Commission may speak in favour of and one against the motion, after which it shall immediately be put to a vote.

Rule 49 Oral Interventions

1. No one may take the floor at a meeting of the Commission without the authorization of the Chairperson of the Commission. The Chairperson of the Commission shall grant the floor to speakers in the order in which it has been requested.

2. Oral intervention shall deal solely with the matter under discussion by the Commission and the Chairperson of the Commission shall call to order any speaker whose remarks are irrelevant.
3. The Chairperson of the Commission may limit the time accorded to speakers as well as the number of interventions in accordance with the present Rules of Procedure. The time limit for each speaker shall be determined by the Chairperson.

Rule 50 Right of Reply

1. A right of reply may be granted by the Chairperson of the Commission to any member of the Commission or representative of a State Party who requests it.
2. A member of the Commission or representative of a State Party must, while exercising this right, respect the time limit fixed by the Chairperson for reply and take the floor preferably at the end of the sitting at which this right has been requested.
3. The right of reply shall be limited to one reply per party and all parties shall have the same length of time to reply.

Chapter XI – Voting

Rule 51 Right to Vote

1. Decisions of the Commission may be taken by consensus, failing which the decision shall be taken by voting.
2. However, if a member so requests, a proposal or motion to put a motion to a vote, shall be put to a vote.
3. Each member of the Commission shall have one vote. In the case of a tie in votes, the Chairperson of the Commission shall have a casting vote.

Rule 52 Required Majority

1. Except as otherwise provided by the African Charter or the present Rules of Procedure, decisions of the Commission shall be taken by a simple majority of the members present and voting.
2. For the purpose of the Rules of Procedure, the expression "members present and voting" shall mean members voting for or against. The members who shall abstain from voting shall be considered as non-voting members.

Rule 53 Method of Voting

1. Subject to the provisions of Rule 56 of the present Rule, the Commission, unless it otherwise decides, shall vote by show of hands, but any member may request

a roll-call vote, which shall be taken in alphabetical order of the names of the members of the Commission.

2. In all the votes by roll-call each member shall reply "yes", "no" or "abstention". The vote of each member participating in the ballot shall be recorded in the minutes.
3. The Commission may decide to hold a secret ballot.

Rule 54 Explanation of Vote

Members may make brief statements only for the purpose of explaining their vote, before the beginning of the vote or once the vote has been taken.

Rule 55 Rules to be Observed While Voting

A vote shall not be interrupted except if a member raises a point of order related to the manner in which the voting is being done.

Rule 56 Elections

Elections shall be held by secret ballot unless the election is for a post for which only one candidate has been proposed and that candidate has been agreed upon by the members of the Commission.

Chapter XII – Motions and Proposals

Rule 57 Division of Motions

Proposals may be separated if a member so requests. The parts of proposals or amendments that have been adopted shall later be put to a vote as a whole. If all the operative parts of a proposal have been rejected, the proposal shall be considered to have been rejected as a whole.

Rule 58 Order of Voting on Proposals

1. If two or more proposals are made on the same matter, the Commission, unless it decides otherwise, shall vote on these proposals in the order in which they were submitted.
2. After each vote, the Commission may decide whether it shall put the next proposal to a vote.
3. However, motions which are not on the substance of a proposal shall be voted upon before the said proposals.

Chapter XIII – Reports of the Commission

Rule 59 Activity Reports

1. The Commission shall submit an Activity Report of its promotion, protection and other activities to each Ordinary Session of the Assembly
2. The content of the Activity Report of the Commission shall be determined by the Commission.
3. Once the Activity Report is considered and adopted by the Assembly, the Secretary shall publish, including posting on the website, transmit it to State Parties, African Union organs, National Human Rights Institutions and Civil Society Organizations.

Rule 60 Mission Reports

1. Upon completion of a Mission, the Secretary shall, within thirty (30) days, draft the mission report in conformity with the Commission's Guidelines on Mission Reports.
2. The Secretary shall send the draft mission report to all the members of the Commission's delegation who shall submit their comments within Thirty (30) days.
3. In the case of a mission for promotion activities, the Secretary shall, after the mission report has been commented upon by the members of the delegation referred to in paragraph 2 of the present Rule, submit the Report to the Commission for consideration and adoption at its next session.
4. The adopted mission report shall be sent to the State Party concerned for its comments, to be given within sixty (60) days from the day of receipt of the report. After sixty days, the report shall be adopted with the comments of the state, if any.
5. In the case of a mission for protection activities, the mission report shall be sent to the members of the delegation referred to in paragraph 2 of this Rule, as well as to other concerned parties, including any party to a communication that was a subject of the mission. The Commission shall consider the comments of these parties when finalizing the Report, especially with regard to any proposal for amicable settlement.
6. The report as well as the comments from the State Party concerned, and other concerned parties, where applicable, shall be annexed to the Activity Report of the Commission to the Assembly.

Rule 61 Distribution of Reports and Other Official Documents

1. Reports, decisions, session documents and all other official documents of the Commission and its subsidiary mechanisms shall be documents for general distribution unless the Commission decides otherwise. Upon their adoption by

the Commission, reports shall be published in accordance with Article 59(2) of the Charter.

2. Reports and additional information submitted by States Parties under Article 62 of the African Charter shall be documents for general distribution in the official languages of the African Union and shall be posted on the Commission's website as soon as they are received at the Secretariat of the Commission;
3. The Secretary shall ensure the publication of the Commission's Activity report and post it on the website of the Commission after adoption by the Assembly.

Chapter XIV – Relationships With State Parties, Intergovernmental Institutions, National Human Rights Institutions, Non-Governmental Organisations, And Other Partners

Rule 62 General Principle

The Commission may invite any organisation or persons capable of enlightening it to participate in its sessions without voting rights.

Rules 63 Discussions on Human Rights Situations

1. In conformity with Rule 32(3) of the present Rules of Procedure, any State Party, African Union organ, specialized agency or body of the United Nations or other organisation recognized by the African Union, national human rights institution with affiliate status, or non-governmental organisation with observer status may request that the African Commission include in its agenda for an ordinary session a discussion on any human rights issue. Such a request shall be made sixty (60) days in advance of the session at which the discussion is to take place.
2. Where the discussion requires the presence of other partners and parties, the requesting party shall indicate as such in the documents that it presents to the Commission pursuant to Article 34(2). If the Bureau of the Commission decides that the participation of additional partners and parties is necessary, it shall invite them to attend and transmit to them all relevant documentation and information received on the proposed discussion from the requesting party.

Rule 64 Participation of States Parties

1. The Commission or its subsidiary mechanisms may invite any State Party to participate in the discussion of any issue that shall be of particular interest to that State.
2. A State thus invited shall have no voting right, but may submit proposals which may be put to a vote at the request of any member of the commission or of the subsidiary mechanism concerned.

Rule 65 Participation of Specialized Agencies, Intergovernmental Organizations and United Nations Bodies

1. Specialized agencies, intergovernmental organisations and United Nations bodies may take part in the public sessions of the Commission.
2. The Commission may permit representatives of these bodies to make oral or written statements to the Commission when the implementation of the African Charter in areas falling within the scope of their activities is being considered.
3. Pursuant to Articles 45(1) and 46 of the African Charter, the Commission may invite these bodies to submit reports on the implementation of the African Charter in areas of common concern.
4. The Commission may take part in the activities of specialized agencies, intergovernmental organisations and United Nations bodies and agree through an MOU on areas of common concern.

Rule 66 Donors

1. Subject to Article 41 of the Charter, the Commission may negotiate financial agreements with donors. These financial agreements shall be signed by the Secretary after approval by the Bureau. Original copies of such agreements shall be kept at the Secretariat of the Commission.
2. The Commission shall inform the African Union Commission of any proposal to accept funds from any donor including details of the amount of money to be provided, the project or projects for which the funds are sought and any condition of receipt of such funding.
3. Such agreements shall specify expected outcomes, monitoring and evaluation of the project funded by the donor.
4. The Secretary shall prepare and submit reports on the implementation of the agreement to the Commission at each ordinary session.
5. Donors may be invited to attend sessions of the Commission.

Rule 67 National Human Rights Institutions

1. National human rights institutions established by States Parties and functioning according to internationally and regionally recognized norms and standards may be granted affiliate status with the Commission.
2. National Human Rights Institutions having affiliate status with the Commission shall enjoy the rights and perform the duties stipulated in the Resolution on the Granting of Affiliate Status to National Human Rights Institutions in Africa.
3. The African Commission shall grant affiliate status to only one National Human Rights Institution in each State Party.
4. The African Commission may invite other National Human Rights Institutions that do not meet the criteria provided in paragraphs 1 and 2 of the present rule to attend its sessions as observers.

Rule 68 Non-governmental Organisations

1. Non-governmental organisations working in the field of human rights in Africa may be granted observer status with the Commission.
2. Non-governmental organisations shall enjoy the rights and perform the duties stipulated in the Resolution on the Granting of Observer Status to Non-Governmental Organizations of the African Commission.
3. Non-Governmental organisations with observer status with the Commission shall fulfil their obligations stipulated under the Resolution referred to in paragraph 2 of the present Rule.

Part Two: Promotion Activities

Chapter I – General Provisions

Rule 69 Program of Promotion Activities

The Commission shall adopt and carry out a program of promotion activities to give effect to its mandate under the African Charter, i accordance with Article 45(1).

Rule 70 Promotion Missions

1. The Commission shall carry out promotion missions, to States Parties.
2. Promotion missions shall be governed by the Commission's Guidelines for Missions as well as the Format for Pre-mission Reports.
3. For each promotion mission, the Commission shall develop terms of reference bearing in mind the human rights situation in the country.

Rule 71 Other Promotion Activities

1. The Commission shall undertake promotion activities other than promotion missions, including seminars, conferences, symposia etc.
2. These activities shall be undertaken either on its own or in collaboration with partners.
3. Where the Commission receives an invitation from a partner to participate in any promotion activity, the Secretary shall inform the Bureau immediately, and the latter will advise the Secretary of the proper course of action.

Rule 72 Activity Reports of Commissioners

At each Ordinary Session, each member of the Commission shall submit a written report of his or her inter-session promotion activities.

Chapter II – The State Reporting Procedure under Article 62 of the Charter

Rule 73 Contents of State Reports

1. Pursuant to Article 62 of the African Charter and other relevant legal instruments which supplement them, including the Protocol to the African Charter on the Rights of Women in Africa in its Article 26, States parties shall submit reports in accordance with the guidelines of the Commission, on the measures they have taken to give effect to the provisions of the African Charter and on the progress they have made. Reports shall indicate the challenges, if any, affecting the implementation of the African Charter and its relevant protocols.
2. The Secretary to the Commission shall send to States Parties the Guidelines on State reports.

Rule 74 Transmission of State Reports

1. Upon receipt of a State Report, the Secretary shall upload the Report on the Commission's website and indicate when the Report will be examined by the Commission.
2. Institutions, organizations or any interested party wishing to contribute to the examination of the Report and the human rights situation in the country concerned, shall send their contributions, including shadow reports, to the Secretary at least 60 days prior to the examination of the Report.
3. The Secretary may also invite specific institutions to submit information relating to the state report within a time limit that he/she may specify.

Rule 75 Consideration of Reports

1. The Chairperson of the Commission shall, through the Secretary inform States Parties of the opening date and venue of the Session at which their respective reports shall be considered.
2. States Parties shall be represented in the sessions of the Commission at which their reports is to be considered.
3. Representatives of State Parties shall respond to the questions prepared by the Commission, and questions of the members of the Commission and provide when necessary, any other information requested during or after the session.
4. If a State Party fails to send a representative to the session of the Commission at which its report is to be examined, consideration of the report shall be rescheduled for the next session. If, at the said session, the concerned State Party, after due notification, fails to send a representative, the Commission shall consider the state report.
5. During the consideration of the state report submitted by a State Party in accordance with Article 62 of the Charter, the Commission shall explore all

the pertinent information relating to the human rights situation in the State concerned, including statements and shadow reports from NGOs.

Rule 76 Non-submission of Reports

1. The Commission shall, at the beginning of each year, inform the States Parties which are not up to date with their obligations under Article 62 of the deadlines of their submission of their reports and the date at which they are expected to comply.
2. At the beginning of each ordinary session, the Secretary shall inform the Commission of all cases of non-submission of reports or of additional information requested by the Commission. In such cases, the Chairperson of the Commission may send a reminder, through the Secretary, to the State Party concerned;
3. The activity report of the Commission shall point out the status of initial and periodic report of States Parties.

Rule 77 Concluding Observations

1. The Commission shall, after consideration of the report of a State Party, formulate concluding observations.
2. The concluding observations of the Commission shall comply with the Guidelines of the Commission on Concluding Observations.
3. The Concluding Observations shall be transmitted to the State Party concerned within thirty (30) days after the session at which the Concluding Observations were adopted. They shall form part of the Commission's activity report and be posted on the website of the Commission after the adoption of the Activity Report.

Rule 78 Follow up of Implementation of Concluding Observations of State Reports

1. In the Concluding Observations, the Commission shall specify, if necessary, the issues that require urgent attention on the part of the State Party. The date of the presentation of the next periodic report by the State Party should be included in the Concluding Observation.
2. The Members of the Commission shall ensure the follow up on the implementation of the recommendations from the Concluding Observations within the framework of their promotion activities to the States Parties concerned.
3. The Commission shall also transmit to the Assembly the observations mentioned in Rule 77(1), with copies of the reports it has received from the States Parties as well as the comments supplied by the latter, if any.

Part Three: Protection Activities

Chapter I – Matters of Emergency

Rule 79 Decision on Matters of Emergency

1. The Commission shall treat a situation as a matter of emergency under Article 58(3) of the African Charter, when:
   a. it is one of serious or massive human rights violations;
   b. it presents the danger of irreparable harm or requires urgent action to avoid irreparable damage
2. When a situation of emergency arises during a session of the Commission, the decision to treat it as such shall be taken by the Commission.
3. When a situation arises during the Commission's inter-session period, the decision to treat it as a matter of emergency shall be taken by the Bureau of the Commission, which shall keep other members of the Commission informed and present a report on the situation at the next ordinary session of the Commission

Rule 80 Action on Matters of Emergency

1. When the Commission has decided to treat a situation as one of emergency, it shall:
   a. Draw the attention of the Chairperson of the Assembly of Heads of State and Government of the African Union to the matter in accordance with Article 58(3) of the Charter;
   b. Draw the attention of the Peace and Security Council to the matter in accordance with Article 19 of the Protocol on Peace and Security Council;
   c. Inform the Executive Council;
   d. Inform the Chairperson of the African Union Commission of the matter.
2. The Commission as well as its subsidiary mechanisms under the Charter and present Rules, shall also take any appropriate action, including urgent appeals.

Chapter II – Protection Missions

Rule 81 General Provisions

1. If it deems it necessary and advisable, the Commission may carry out a protection mission to a State Party.
2. States Parties shall provide the Commission with an open invitation for protection missions and respond promptly to any request by the Commission for authorisation to undertake a protection mission.

3. Any protection mission agreed upon between the Commission and a State Party shall be conducted in accordance with the Commission's Guidelines for Missions.
4. The expenses incurred by a mission undertaken at the request of any AU organ shall be borne by such organ.

Rule 82 State Party's Obligations

During a protection mission of the Commission the State Party concerned shall:

a. Commit itself not to take any kind of reprisal against any persons or entities who provide the mission with information, testimony or evidence;
b. Guarantee the free movement of the members of the mission throughout the territory of the country, in this regard, provide corresponding facilities, including any necessary internal authorisation;
c. Provide the mission of the Commission with any document that the latter may consider necessary for the preparation of its reports;
d. Take necessary security measures to protect members of the Commission and also to guarantee the smooth running of the mission.

Chapter III – Consideration Of Communications

Section 1 – General Provisions

Rule 83 Records of Communications under Articles 47, 48, 49 and 55 of the Charter

1. The Commission shall receive or note as the case may be, communications or notifications under Articles 47, 48, 49 and 55 of the Charter.
2. The Secretary shall maintain a record of each communication, with a reference number, the names of the parties, the date of registration or notification, and the date of decision or closure of each communication.

Rule 84 Situation of Serious or Massive Violation of Human Rights

1. When the Commission considers that one or more communications relate to a series of serious or massive human rights violations, it shall bring the matter to the attention of the Assembly of Heads of State and Government of the African Union and the Peace and Security Council.
2. The Commission may also, in conformity with Article 5 of the African Court Protocol and Rule 118(3) of the present Rules of Procedure, refer the matter to the African Court.

Rule 85 Other Interventions

The Commission may decide to solicit or accept interventions by parties other than the complainant and the Respondent State that it considers could provide it with information relevant to making a decision on a communication.

Section 2 – Consideration of Communications Received in Conformity with Article 47 of the Charter: Communications Negotiations of States Parties

Rule 86 Submission of a Communication

1. A communication under Article 47 of the Charter shall be submitted to the Chairperson, through the Secretary of the Commission.
2. The communication referred to above shall be in writing and shall contain a comprehensive statement of the facts as well as the provisions of the African Charter alleged to have been violated.
3. Notification of the communication to the State Party concerned, the Chairperson of the African Union Commission and the Chairperson of the Commission shall be done through the most practical and reliable means.
4. The Secretary of the Commission shall, on behalf of the Chairperson, acknowledge receipt, by note verbale, receipt of the communication and request the parties to keep the Commission informed of developments which could arise within the framework of ongoing negotiations.

Section 3 – Consideration Of Communications Received under Articles 48 & 49 of the Charter: Communications – Complaints of States Parties'

Rule 87 Seizure of the Commission

1. Any communication under Articles 48 and 49 of the Charter may be submitted to the Chairperson of the Commission through the Secretary by an interested State Party.
2. The Communication shall contain information on the following or be accompanied particularly by:
   a. Measures taken to resolve the issue pursuant to Article 47 of the African Charter including the text of the initial communication and any subsequent written explanation from the interested States Parties relating to the issue;
   b. Measures taken to exhaust regional or international procedures of settlement or good offices;
   c. Any other procedure of international investigation or international settlement to which the interested States Parties have resorted.

Rule 88 Consideration of the Communication

1. Where, pursuant to Articles 48 and 49 of the African Charter, a communicationis brought before the Commission by a State Party, the Chairperson of the Commission, through the Secretary, shall give notice of such communication to the State Party against which the complaint is made and shall invite it to submit to the Commission its observations in writing on the admissibility of the Communication within ninety (90) days. The observations so obtained in writing shall be immediately communicated to the complaining State Party, which shall respond within ninety (90) days of receipt of the observations.
2. The Commission shall designate one or more of its members as Rapporteur for the communication.
3. Rapporteurs, through the Secretary, may:
   a. Request relevant information on matters connected with the communication from the applicant or the State Party concerned. Such information shall be provided by both parties within ninety (90) days of receipt of such request;
   b. Transmit any information obtained from one party to the other for comments. The parties shall be given ninety (90) days to respond to the observations made by the other party.
4. Prior to the session at which the communication is to be considered, the rapporteurs shall prepare a report on the admissibility of the communication. Such report shall contain:
   a. The relevant facts, including any information or comments obtained under paragraph 3 of this Rule;
   b. The provision(s) of the African Charter alleged to have been violated in the communication;
   c. A recommendation on admissibility and on any other action to be taken, as the case may require.
5. Before deciding upon the admissibility of the communication, the Commission may invite the parties to submit further observations in writing and shall fix a time limit of ninety (90) days for the submission of these observations. The written observations or information shall be transmitted to the opposing party.
6. The Commission may also allow the parties to make additional observations orally.

Rule 89 Decision on Admissibility

1. The Commission shall consider the report of the rapporteurs, decide on the admissibility of the communication, and shall inform the parties accordingly.
2. The Commission shall give reasons for its decision on admissibility.

Rule 90 Amicable Settlement

1. When the Commission declares that a communication is Admissible, it shall place its good offices at the disposal of the interested States Parties with the objective of reaching an amicable settlement under the terms of the African Charter;
2. For the purpose of the Commission's good offices, the bureau of the Commission shall establish contact with the relevant authorities of the States Parties.
3. The bureau shall report its findings and recommendations to the Commission at the Commission's next session.
4. The Commission shall thereafter decide on the appropriate action to take, which may include the following:
   a. appointing a rapporteur;
   b. convening, in consultation with the States Parties concerned, meetings with the aim of achieving an amicable settlement of the dispute;
   c. facilitating the drafting of a Memorandum of Understanding, when the parties accept the principle of an amicable settlement, containing the terms of settlement being proposed.
5. In the case of acceptance of the draft Memorandum of Understanding, the States Parties concerned shall sign the agreement under the auspices of the Commission.
6. The rapporteur shall then prepare a draft report, which shall be submitted to the Commission for adoption at its next session.
7. When adopted, the report shall be sent to the States Parties concerned and communicated to the Assembly.
8. The Commission, through the rapporteur shall then follow up on monitoring the implementation of the terms of the agreement and report on the said implementation to each subsequent ordinary session of the Commission until the settlement is concluded. Such a report shall form part of the activity report of the Commission to the Assembly.

Rule 91 Failure to Settle the Dispute Amicably

1. If the amicable settlement of the dispute fails, the Commission shall request the States Parties concerned to provide, within a period of thirty (30) days, their written submissions.
2. The Commission shall communicate any information obtained from one party to the other for comments. The States Parties concerned shall be given thirty (30) days to respond.
3. The Rapporteur shall prepare a report containing the facts, findings and recommendations for consideration by the Commission.
4. Before adopting the report of the Rapporteur, the Commission may convene a hearing at which it may allow the parties to make additional oral observations.

Rule 92 Decision of the Commission

1. Within twelve months of receipt of a communication, the Commission shall adopt a decision, prepare a report and make recommendations, pursuant to Article 53 of the African Charter following the notification referred to in Article 48 of the African Charter and the present Rules of Procedure.
2. The report of the Commission on the communication shall be communicated to the States Parties concerned through the Secretary.
3. The report of the Commission on the communication shall be submitted as part of the Commission's activity report to the Assembly.

Section 4 – Consideration of Communications Received in Conformity with Article 55 of the African Charter: Other Communications

Sub-Section 1: General Rules

Rule 93 Seizure of the Commission

1. A communication submitted under Article 55 of the African Charter may be addressed to the Chairperson of the Commission through the Secretary by any natural or legal person.
2. The Secretary shall ensure that communications addressed to the Commission contain the following information:
   a. the name, nationality and signature of the person or persons filing it; or in cases where the complainant is a non-governmental entity, the name and signature of its legal representative(s);
   b. whether the complainant wishes that his or her identity be withheld from the State;
   c. the address for receiving correspondence from the Commission and, if available, a telephone number, facsimile number, and email address;
   d. an account of the act or situation complained of, specifying the place, date and nature of the alleged violations;
   e. the name of the victim, in a case where he or she is not the complainant;
   f. any public authority that has taken cognisance of the fact or situation alleged;
   g. the name of the State(s) alleged to be responsible for the violation of the African Charter, even if no specific reference is made to the Article(s) alleged to have been violated;
   h. compliance with the period prescribed in the African Charter for submission of the communication;
   i. any steps taken to exhaust domestic remedies, or if the applicant alleges the impossibility or unavailability of domestic remedies, the grounds in support of such allegation; and

   j. an indication of whether or not the complaint has been submitted to another international settlement proceeding as provided in Article 56(7) of the African Charter.
3. In cases where the victim has not asked for anonymity and is represented by an NGO or other agent, the victim shall be the complainant of record and the fact of representation or agency shall be recognized.
4. In the event that a communication is missing some of the information listed in paragraph 2 of the present Rule, the Secretary shall contact the complainant to furnish it.
5. When the Secretariat is satisfied that all necessary information is in the file of the Communication, it shall transmit the file to the Commission which shall make a decision on seizure.

Rule 94 Representation

1. States Parties shall be represented before the Commission by their representatives.
2. Natural or legal persons may either appear in person or be represented by their appointed representative before the Commission.

Rule 95 Order of Consideration of Communications

Unless otherwise decided, the Commission shall consider communications in the order in which they have been received by the Secretary.

Rule 96 Joinder and Disjoinder of Communications

1. If two or more communications against the same State Party address similar facts, or reveal the same pattern of violation of rights, the Commission may join them and consider them together as a single communication.
2. Notwithstanding paragraph 1 of the present Rule, the Commission may decide not to join the communications if it is of the opinion that the joinder will not serve the interest of justice.
3. Where in accordance with paragraph 1 of the present Rule, the Commission decides to join two or more Communications, it may subsequently, where it deems appropriate, decide to disjoin the Communications.

Rule 97 Working Groups and Rapporteurs on Communications

1. The Commission shall appoint a Rapporteur for each communication from among its members.
2. The Commission may also establish one or more working groups to consider questions of seizure, admissibility and the merits of any communication(s) and to make recommendations to the Commission.

3. The Commission shall consider the recommendations of the Rapporteur(s) and/or the Working Group (s) and make a decision.

Rule 98 Provisional Measures

1. At any time after the receipt of a communication and before a determination on the merits, the Commission may, on its initiative or at the request of a party to the communication, request that the State concerned adopt provisional measures to prevent irreparable harm to the victim or victims of the alleged violation as urgently as the situation demands.
2. If the Commission is not in session at the time that a request for provisional measures is received, the Chairperson, or in his or her absence, the Vice-Chairperson, shall take the decision on the Commission's behalf and shall so inform members of the Commission;
3. After the request for provisional measures has been transmitted to the State Party, the Commission shall send a copy of the letter requesting provisional measures to the victim, the African Union, the Peace and Security Council, and the African Union Commission.
4. The Commission shall request the State Party concerned to report back on the implementation of the provisional measures requested. Such information shall be submitted within fifteen (15) days of the receipt of the request for provisional measures;
5. The granting of such measures and their adoption by the State Party concerned shall not constitute a prejudgment on the merits of a communication.

Rule 99 Procedure for Hearings on Communications

1. At the initiative of the Commission or at the request of one of the parties, a hearing may be held on a communication.
2. During hearings, the Commission shall permit oral presentations by the parties on new or additional facts or arguments or in answer to any questions that it may have concerning all issues relating to the communication.
3. During a hearing on a communication or at any stage prior to the conclusion of the matter, the following may be considered:
   a. The verification of the facts;
   b. Initiation of a friendly settlement;
   c. Consideration on the merits; or
   d. Any other matter pertinent to the communication.
4. A party requesting a hearing, shall do so at least ninety (90) days before the beginning of the session in which the communication is going to be considered.
5. The Rapporteur of the communication, in consultation with the Bureau of the Commission, shall decide upon the request.

6. The Secretary shall inform both parties of the decision on the granting of a hearing within 15 days of the decision referred to under paragraph 5 of the present Rule.
7. If the request for a hearing is accepted, the notification of the hearing shall include the dates and venue of the session, and period of the session during which the hearing is likely to take place.
8. Hearings on communications before the Commission shall be held in camera. Unless the Commission decides otherwise, no person shall be admitted, other than:
   a. The parties to the communication or the representatives duly mandated;
   b. Any person being heard by the Commission as a witness or as an expert;
   c. The persons referred to in Rule 33 (2) or any person whom the Commission may decide to invite under Article 46 of the African Charter.
9. When it considers it in the interest of the proper conduct of a hearing, the Commission may limit the number of parties' representatives or advisers who may appear.
10. The parties shall inform the Commission at least ten days before the date of the opening of the hearing of the names and functions of the persons who will appear on their behalf at the hearing.
11. The Chairperson or his or her representative shall preside over the hearing, and shall verify the identity of any persons before he/she is heard.
12. Any member of the Commission may put questions to the parties or to the persons heard with the permission of the Chairperson;
13. Parties to the communication or their representatives may, with the permission of the Chairperson, put questions to any person heard;
14. The Secretary is responsible for the production of verbatim records of hearings before the Commission. Such records are internal working documents of the Commission. If a party to the communication so requests, the Commission shall provide a copy of such records unless, in the view of the Commission, doing so could create a danger to persons heard;
15. The State Party to the communication shall make an undertaking not to victimise or to take any reprisals against the complainant and/or any person representing them or their family members, or witnesses because of their statements before the Commission.
16. The Commission may receive amicus curiae brief on communication. During the hearing of a communication in which amicus curiae brief has been filed, the Commission, where necessary shall permit the author of the brief or the representative to address the Commission.

Rule 100 Witnesses and Experts

1. The Commission shall determine, at its own initiative, or at the request of one of the parties, when to call witnesses and independent experts of the parties

to the communication whom it considers necessary to hear in a given case. A request to call witness by one of the parties shall not be rejected unless the Commission has good reasons to believe that such request constitutes an abuse of procedure. The notification shall indicate:

a. The parties to the communication;
b. A summary of the facts or issues in relation to which the
c. Commission desires to hear the witness or expert;

2. Any such person may, if they do not have sufficient knowledge of the working languages of the Commission, be authorised by the Chairperson to speak in any other language to be interpreted in one of the Working Languages of the Commission.
3. After establishing the identity of the witnesses or experts the Chairperson of the Commission shall request them to take the following oath:
   a. For witnesses: "I swear/affirm that I will speak the truth, the whole truth and nothing but the truth."
   b. For the experts: "I swear/affirm that my statement will be in accordance with my knowledge, findings and sincere belief."
4. The State Party to the communication shall give an undertaking not to victimise or persecute the witnesses or experts, or carry out reprisals against them or their family members because of their statements or expert opinions given before the Commission.

Rule 101 Inability of a Member of the Commission to Take Part in the Examination of a Communication

1. A member of the Commission shall not be present and take part in the consideration of a communication if he or she:
   a. is a national of the State Party concerned;
   b. has any personal interest in the case;
   c. is engaged in any political or administrative activity or any professional activity that is incompatible with his or her independence or impartiality;
   d. has participated in any capacity in any decision at the national level in relation to the communication; or
   e. has expressed publicly opinions that might be interpreted as reflecting lack of impartiality with respect to the communication.
2. Any question that may arise under paragraph 1 above shall be decided by the Commission without the participation of the member concerned.

Rule 102 Withdrawal of a Member

If, for any reason, a member of the Commission considers that he or she should not take part or continue to take part in the consideration of a communication, he or she shall inform the Chairperson of his or her decision to withdraw.

Rule 103 Preliminary Objection

1. A party desiring to raise a preliminary objection at the stage of admissibility or before the Commission takes a decision on the merits of the communication, shall do so not later than thirty (30) days after receiving notification to submit on admissibility or on the merits. The Commission shall communicate the objection to the other party within fifteen (15) days.
2. A party desiring to respond to a preliminary objection raised by the other party shall submit a written response not later than thirty (30) days after the Secretary of the Commission has transmitted the objection to that party.
3. If no response to a preliminary objection is received within the stipulated period, the Commission shall proceed with the consideration of the preliminary objection on the basis of the available information.
4. When the Commission receives a preliminary objection, it shall first of all determine this objection before any other question relating to the communication.

Rule 104 Legal Aid

1. The Commission may, either at the request of the author of the communication or proprio motu, facilitate free legal aid to the author in connection with the representation of the case;
2. Free legal aid shall only be facilitated where the Commission is convinced:
   a. That it is essential for the proper discharge of the Commission's duties, and to ensure equality of the parties before it; and
   b. The author of the communication has no sufficient means to meet all or part of the costs involved;
3. In case of urgency or when the Commission is not in session, its Chairperson may exercise the powers conferred on the Commission by this Rule. As soon as the Commission is in session, any action that has been taken under this paragraph shall be brought to its attention for confirmation.

Sub-Section 2: Procedures on Admissibility

Rule 105 Submissions of Observations

1. When the Commission has decided to be seized of a communication pursuant to the present Rules, it shall promptly transmit a copy of the complaint to the respondent state. It shall simultaneously inform the complainant of the decision on seizure, and request the complainant to present evidence and arguments on the admissibility within two months.
2. Upon receipt of the complainant's observations on admissibility, the Secretary shall transmit a copy to the respondent state and request the respondent state

to make a written submission, containing its arguments and evidence on the admissibility, within two months of its receipt of the Commission's request. The Secretariat shall, within a week of receipt of the state's submission, provide the complainant with a copy.
3. Upon receiving the observations of the respondent state on admissibility, the complainant may comment on the observations within one month of receipt.
4. In conformity with Rule 88(6), the Commission, while determining Admissibility may ask the parties to present supplementary observations in an oral hearing.

Rule 106 Admissibility of Communications

The Commission shall comply with the requirements of Admissibility under Article 56 of the Charter which are cumulative.

Rule 107 Decision on Admissibility

1. Once it has considered the positions of the parties, the Commission shall make a decision on the admissibility of the communication and the Secretary shall inform the parties accordingly.
2. Once a Communication has been declared admissible, the Commission shall inform the parties and defer the communication to the next session for consideration on the merit.
3. The Commission's decisions on the inadmissibility of communications shall be notified to the parties and attached to its activity report.
4. If the Commission has declared a communication inadmissible this decision may be reviewed at a later date, upon the submission of new evidence, contained in a written request to the Commission by the author.

Sub-Section 3: Procedures for the Consideration of Communications on the Merits

Rule 108 Proceedings

1. Once a Communication has been declared admissible, the Commission shall set a period of sixty (60) days for the complainant to submit observations on the merits. These observations shall be transmitted to the State Party concerned for the submission of its observations within sixty (60) days;
2. Any written statements submitted by the State Party concerned shall be communicated, through the Secretary, to the complainant, who may submit any additional written information or observations within thirty (30) days. This time limit cannot be extended.

Rule 109 Amicable Settlement

1. At any stage of the examination of a communication, the Commission, on its own initiative or at the request of any of the parties concerned, may offer its good offices for an amicable settlement between the parties.
2. The amicable settlement procedure shall be initiated, and may only continue, with the consent of the parties.
3. If it deems it necessary, the Commission may entrust to one or more of its members the task of facilitating negotiations between the parties.
4. The Commission may terminate its intervention in the amicable settlement procedure at the request of one or both parties, within a period of six months, renewable once, when an amicable settlement is not reached.
5. When the Commission receives information from parties that an amicable settlement has been reached, the Commission shall ensure that such amicable settlement:
   a. Complies with or respects the human rights and fundamental freedoms enshrined in the African Charter and other applicable instruments;
   b. Indicates that the victim of the alleged human rights violation or, his/her successors, as the case may be, have consented to the terms of the settlement and are satisfied with the conditions.
   c. Includes an undertaking by the parties to implement the terms of the settlement;
6. When the Commission is satisfied that the requirements of paragraph 5 have been complied with, it shall prepare a report which shall contain:
   a. a brief statement of the facts;
   b. an explanation of the settlement reached;
   c. recommendations by the Commission for steps to be taken by the parties to ensure the maintenance of the settlement;
   d. steps to be taken by the Commission to monitor the parties' compliance with the terms of the settlement.
7. If the terms of the amicable settlement are not implemented within six months, or when the terms do not comply with the requirements under paragraph 5 of the present Rule the Commission shall at the request of the Complainant continue to process the communication in accordance with the relevant provisions of the Charter and the relevant Rules in the present Rules.

Rule 110 Decision on the Merits

1. The Commission, after deliberation on the submissions of both parties, shall adopt a decision on the merits of the communication.
2. The decision shall be in conformity with the Communication Guidelines of the Commission. Upon adoption of a decision on the merits, the Commission shall prepare a report on the communication with the following information:

3. The Commission shall deliberate on communications in private, and all aspects of the discussions shall be confidential.
4. The decision of the Commission shall be signed by the Chairperson and the Secretary and communicated to the parties. In transmitting the decision, the Secretary shall specify to the parties that, pursuant to Article 59(1) of the Charter, the decision is for the parties' information only and is confidential until its publication is authorized by the Assembly.
5. The decision of the Commission shall be annexed to the Commission's Activity Report and posted on the Commission's website as soon as the publication of the activity report is authorized by the Assembly.

Rule 111 Review of the Decision of the Commission on the Merits

1. Once the Commission has taken a decision on the merits, it may, on its own initiative or upon the written request of one of the parties, review the decision.
2. In determining whether to review its decision on the merits, the Commission shall satisfy itself of the following:
   a. that the request is based upon the discovery of some fact of such a nature as to be a decisive factor, which fact was not known to the Commission and the party requesting the review, provided that such ignorance was not due to negligence;
   b. that the application for review is made within six months of the discovery of the new fact;
   c. any other compelling reason or situation that the Commission may deem appropriate or relevant to justify review of a communication, with a view to ensure fairness, justice and respect for human and peoples' rights.
3. No application for review may be made after three years from the date of the decision.

Rule 112 Follow-Up on the Recommendations of the Commission

1. Upon the authorization of the publication of the Commission's activity report by the Assembly, the Secretary shall notify the parties within thirty (30) days that they may disseminate the decision.
2. In the event of a decision against a State Party, the parties shall inform the Commission in writing, within one hundred and eighty (180) days of being informed of the decision in accordance with paragraph one, of all measures, if any, taken or being taken by the State Party to implement the decision of the Commission.

3. Within ninety (90) days of receipt of the State's written response, the Commission may invite the State concerned to submit further information on the measures it has taken in response to its decision.
4. If no response is received from the State, the Commission may send a reminder to the State Party concerned to submit its information within ninety (90) days from the date of the reminder;
5. The Rapporteur for the communication, or any other member of the Commission designated for this purpose, shall monitor the measures taken by the State Party to give effect to the Commission's recommendations on each communication.
6. The Rapporteur may make such contacts and take such action as may be appropriate to fulfill his/her assignment including recommendations for further action by the Commission as may be necessary.
7. At each ordinary session, the Rapporteur shall report during the public session on the implementation of the Commission's recommendations.
8. The Commission shall draw the attention of the Sub-Committee of the Permanent Representatives Committee and the Executive Council on the Implementation of the Decisions of the African Union, to any situations of non-compliance with the Commission's decisions.
9. The Commission shall include information on any follow-up activities in its Activity Report.

Rule 113 Extension of Time

1. Subject to the provisions of Rule 111, when a deadline is fixed for a particular submission, either party may apply to the Commission for extension of the period stipulated.
2. The Commission may grant an extension which shall not exceed one (1) month, and shall not grant more than one extension per party for any given submission.

Part Four: Relationships with the African Court

Chapter I – General Provisions

Rule 114 Complementarity with the African Court

1. Pursuant to Article 2 of the Protocol, the Court shall complement the protective mandate of the Commission as provided for in Articles 30 and 45 (2) of the African Charter.
2. The complementarity relationship between the Commission and the Court is set out and organized by Articles 5, 6(1) & (3), 8 and 33 of the Protocol.

Rule 115 Consultations with the Court

1. In pursuance of Article 2 of the Protocol, the Commission shall meet with the Court at least once a year and whenever necessary to ensure good working relationship between the two institutions.
2. The Bureau of the Commission may meet the Bureau of the Court as often as necessary to undertake any functions assigned to them by the two institutions.
3. The conclusions of the meetings of the Bureau shall be considered and if adopted by the Commission, shall be included in the activity report.
4. The Commission shall consult with the Court before the modification of any of its Rules relating to their relationship.

Rule 116 Interpretation of the Charter by the Commission

1. If the Commission is requested to interpret the Charter under Article 45(3), it shall immediately inform the President of the Court.
2. A copy of the interpretation of the Charter by the Commission shall be sent to the President of the Court as soon as it is adopted.

Rule 117 Advisory Opinion

The Commission may request to be heard by the Court upon being notified by the Court of a request for an advisory opinion pursuant to Article 4(1) of the Protocol.

Rule 118 Seizure of the Court

1. If the Commission has taken a decision with respect to a communication submitted under Articles 48, 49 or 55 of the Charter and the Commission considers that the State has not complied or is unwilling to comply with its recommendations in respect of the communication within the period stated in Rule 112(2), the Commission may submit the Case to the Court pursuant to Article 5 (1) (a) of the Protocol and inform the parties accordingly.
2. If the Commission has made a request for provisional measures against a State Party to the Protocol, in accordance with Rule 98, and considers that the State has not complied with the provisional measures requested, the Commission may pursuant to Article 27 (2) of the Protocol, refer the Case to the Court and inform the complainant and the State concerned.
3. The Commission may, pursuant to Rule 84(2) submit a case before the Court against a State Party that has ratified the Protocol if a situation that, in its view, constitutes one of serious or massive violations of human rights

as provided for under Article 58 of the African Charter, has come to its attention.
4. The Commission may seize the Court with any other case and at any stage of the proceedings.

Rule 119 Admissibility under Article 6 of the Protocol

1. Where, pursuant to Article 6 of the Protocol, the Commission is requested to give its opinion, on the admissibility of a case pending before the Court or where the Court has transferred a case to the Commission, it shall consider the admissibility of this matter in accordance with Article 56 of the Charter and Rules 105, 106 and 107.
2. Upon conclusion of the examination of the admissibility of the case referred to it under Article 6 of the Protocol establishing the Court, the Commission shall immediately transmit its opinion or its decision on the admissibility to the Court.

Rule 120 Representation of the Commission before the Court

When the Commission decides to submit a case to the Court, pursuant to Article 5(1) (a) of the Protocol and Rule 118, it may appoint one or more Commissioners to represent it before the Court. The Commissioner(s) so designated shall be assisted by a Legal Officer of the Commission's Secretariat and/or experts who shall be designated or appointed by the Commission.

Rule 121 Content of the Application and File to the Court

1. When, in pursuance of Article 5 (1) (a) of the Protocol and Rule 120, the Commission decides to bring a case before the Court, it shall submit an application seizing the Court in accordance with the Court Rules, accompanied by a summary of the case and the case file.
2. The Summary shall include the names of the representatives of the commission, the facts of the case and all the relevant provisions of the African Charter which have been violated.
3. Where necessary, the Summary shall include
   a. the date on which the Commission adopted its decision, or adopted and sent the request for provisional measures;
   b. the facts which reveal serious or massive violations;
   c. the date on which the decision of the Commission was transmitted to the State Party concerned;
   d. information relating to the deadline stipulated under Rule 113; and
   e. the parties to the proceedings before the Commission, if applicable.

4. The case file along with the Summary to be transmitted to the Court shall contain all the evidence, documents or information concerning the Communication including documents relating to any attempts to secure a friendly settlement, and the Commission's decision.

Rule 122 Transmission of Cases to the Court and Notification of the Parties

1. The Secretary of the Commission shall transmit to the Court the application signed by the Chairperson, the certified copy of the case file and the summary referred to in Rule 121 in conformity with the Rules of Procedure of the Court. At the request of the Court, the Commission shall transmit the original of the case file.
2. The Secretary shall also immediately notify the Parties who were before the Commission about the referral of the case to the Court and shall transmit copies of the case file and the summary thereof.

Rule 123 Lis Pendens

The Commission shall not consider any communication relating to a case still pending before the Court, unless the case has been formally withdrawn.

Part Five: Relationship with other African Union Organs, Institutions, and Programmes

Rule 124 General Rule

1. The Commission, in fulfilling its mandate, shall establish formal relations of cooperation, including meetings as necessary, with all African Union organs, and institutions and programmes that have a human rights element in their mandate.
2. The Bureau of the Commission may, in addition, meet with the bureaux of these organs, institutions and programmes as often as may be required to ensure their good working relationship.

Rule 125 Relationship with the Policy Organs of the African Union

1. When submitting its Activity Report in accordance with article 54 of the African Charter, the Commission may request the Assembly to take necessary measures to implement its decisions.
2. The Commission shall bring all its recommendations to the attention of the Sub-Committee on the Implementation of the Decisions of the African Union of the Permanent Representatives Committee.

Rule 126 Cooperation with the African Union Commission

1. Prior to the appointment of the Secretary or any staff member of the Commission's Secretariat, the African Union Commission shall consult with the Bureau of the Commission.
2. After transmitting the report on the evaluation of the performance of the Secretary in accordance with Rule 13(3) and 14(2)(c) of the present Rule of Procedure, the Chairperson of the African Union Commission may invite the Bureau of the African Commission for discussion.

Part Six: Final Provisions

Rule 127 Interpretation

In conformity with Article 45(3) of the Charter, the Commission shall interpret the Charter. Rule 128 Amendment of the Rules of Procedure The present Rules of Procedure may be amended by the Commission.

Rule 129 Transitional Provisions

Upon the entry into force of the Protocol on the Statute of the African Court of Justice and Human Rights, all references in the present Rules to provisions of the African Court Protocol or the African Court shall be deemed, where applicable, to refer to the relevant provisions of the Protocol on the Statute of the African Court of Justice and Human Rights or to the African Court of Justice and Human Rights, respectively.

Rule 130 Non-Retroactivity

The present Rules of Procedure shall not have any retrospective effect.

Rule 131 Suspension

The Commission may suspend temporarily, the application of any Rule of the present Rules of Procedure, on condition that such a suspension shall not be incompatible with any applicable decision of the Commission or the Assembly or with any relevant provision of the Charter and that the proposal shall have been submitted 24 hours in advance...

Rule 132 Entry into Force of the Rules of Procedure

The present Rules of Procedure shall enter into force three months after their adoption by a simple majority of members of the Commission present and voting at a session where the rules are scheduled to be adopted.

Appendix III

Protocol to the African Charter on Human and People's Rights on the Establishment of an African Court on Human and People's Rights, June 9, 1998 AU Doc. AU/LEG/EXP/AFCHPR/PROT (III)

Entry into force on 25 January, 2004. The first Judges elected to the Court are: Mr. Fatsah Ouguergouz (Algeria); Mr. Jean Emile Somda (Burkina Faso); Mr. Gerard Niyungeko (Burundi); Ms. Sophia Akuffo (Ghana); Mrs. Kelello Justina Masafo-Guni (Lesotho); Mr. Hamdi Faraj Fanoush (Libya); Mr. Modibo Tounty Guindo (Mali); Mr. Jean Mutsinzi (Rwanda); Mr. El Hadji Guisse (Senegal); Mr. Bernard Ngoepe (South Africa); Mr. George Kanyiehamba (Uganda).

Article 1 ESTABLISHMENT OF THE COURT

There shall be established within the Organization of African Unity an African Court Human and Peoples' Rights hereinafter referred to as "the Court", the organization, jurisdiction and functioning of which shall be governed by the present Protocol.

Article 2 RELATIONSHIP BETWEEN THE COURT AND THE COMMISSION

The Court shall, bearing in mind the provisions of this Protocol, complement the protective mandate of the African Commission on Human and Peoples' Rights hereinafter referred to as "the Commission", conferred upon it by the African Charter on Human and Peoples' Rights, hereinafter referred to as "the Charter".

Article 3 JURISDICTION

The jurisdiction of the Court shall extend to all cases and disputes submitted to it concerning the interpretation and application of the Charter, this Protocol and any other relevant Human Rights instrument ratified by the States concerned.

In the event of a dispute as to whether the Court has jurisdiction, the Court shall decide.

Article 4 ADVISORY OPINIONS

At the request of a Member State of the AU, the AU, any of its organs, or any African organization recognized by the AU, the Court may provide an opinion on any legal matter relating to the Charter or any other relevant human rights instruments, provided that the subject matter of the opinion is not related to a matter being examined by the Commission.

The Court shall give reasons for its advisory opinions provided that every judge shall be entitled to deliver a separate of dissenting decision.

Article 5 ACCESS TO THE COURT

The following are entitled to submit cases to the Court:

The Commission
The State Party, which had lodged a complaint to the Commission
The State Party against which the complaint has been lodged at the Commission
The State Party whose citizen is a victim of human rights violation
African Intergovernmental Organizations

When a State Party has an interest in a case, it may submit a request to the Court to be permitted to join.

The Court may entitle relevant Non Governmental organizations (NGOs) with observer status before the Commission, and individuals to institute cases directly before it, in accordance with article 34 (6) of this Protocol.

Article 6 ADMISSIBILITY OF CASES

The Court, when deciding on the admissibility of a case instituted under article 5 (3) of this Protocol, may request the opinion of the Commission which shall give it as soon as possible.

The Court shall rule on the admissibility of cases taking into account the provisions of article 56 of the Charter.

The Court may consider cases or transfer them to the Commission.

Article 7 SOURCES OF LAW

The Court shall apply the provision of the Charter and any other relevant human rights instruments ratified by the States concerned.

Article 8 CONSIDERATION OF CASES

The Rules of Procedure of the Court shall lay down the detailed conditions under which the Court shall consider cases brought before it, bearing in mind the complementarity's between the Commission and the Court.

Article 9 AMICABLE SETTLEMENT

The Court may try to reach an amicable settlement in a case pending before it in accordance with the provisions of the Charter.

Article 10 HEARINGS AND REPRESENTATION

The Court shall conduct its proceedings in public. The Court may, however, conduct proceedings in camera as may be provided for in the Rules of Procedure.

Any party to a case shall be entitled to be represented by a legal representative of the party's choice. Free legal representation may be provided where the interests of justice so require.

Any person, witness or representative of the parties, who appears before the Court, shall enjoy protection and all facilities, in accordance with international law, necessary for the discharging of their functions, tasks and duties in relation to the Court.

Article 11 COMPOSITION

The Court shall consist of eleven judges, nationals of Member States of the AU, elected in an individual capacity from among jurists of high moral character and of recognized practical, judicial or academic competence and experience in the field of human and peoples' rights.

No two judges shall be nationals of the same State.

Article 12 NOMINATIONS

States Parties to the Protocol may each propose up to three candidates, at least two of whom shall be nationals of that State.

Due consideration shall be given to adequate gender representation in nomination process.

Article 13 LIST OF CANDIDATES

Upon entry into force of this Protocol, the Secretary-general of the AU shall request each State Party to the Protocol to present, within ninety (90) days of such a request, its nominees for the office of judge of the Court.

The Secretary-General of the AU shall prepare a list in alphabetical order of the candidates nominated and transmit it to the Member States of the AU at least thirty days prior to the next session of the Assembly of Heads of State and Government of the AU hereinafter referred to as "the Assembly".

Article 14 ELECTIONS

The judges of the Court shall be elected by secret ballot by the Assembly from the list referred to in Article 13 (2) of the present Protocol.

The Assembly shall ensure that in the Court as a whole there is representation of the main regions of Africa and of their principal legal traditions.

In the election of the judges, the Assembly shall ensure that there is adequate gender representation.

Article 15 TERM OF OFFICE

The judges of the Court shall be elected for a period of six years and may be re-elected only once. The terms of four judges elected at the first election shall expire at the end of two years, and the terms of four more judges shall expire at the end of four years.

The judges whose terms are to expire at the end of the initial periods of two and four years shall be chosen by lot to be drawn by the Secretary-General of the AU immediately after the first election has been completed.

A judge elected to replace a judge whose term of office has not expired shall hold office for the remainder of the predecessor's term.

All judges except the President shall perform their functions on a part-time basis. However, the Assembly may change this arrangement as it deems appropriate.

Article 16 OATH OF OFFICE

After their election, the judges of the Court shall make a solemn declaration to discharge their duties impartially and faithfully.

Article 17 INDEPENDENCE

The independence of the judges shall be fully ensured in accordance with international law.

No judge may hear any case in which the same judge has previously taken part as agent, counsel or advocate for one of the parties or as a member of a national or international court or a commission of enquiry or in any other capacity. Any doubt on this point shall be settled by decision of the Court.

The judges of the Court shall enjoy, from the moment of their election and throughout their term of office, the immunities extended to diplomatic agents in accordance with international law.

At no time shall the judges of the Court be held liable for any decision or opinion issued in the exercise of their functions.

Article 18 INCOMPATIBILITY

The position of judge of the court is incompatible with any activity that might interfere with the independence or impartiality of such a judge or the demands of the office as determined in the Rules of Procedure of the Court.

Article 19 CESSATION OF OFFICE

A judge shall not be suspended or removed from office unless, by the unanimous decision of the other judges of the Court, the judge concerned has been found to be no longer fulfilling the required conditions to be a judge of the Court.

Such a decision of the Court shall become final unless it is set aside by the Assembly at its next session.

Article 20 VACANCIES

In case of death or resignation of a judge of the Court, the President of the Court shall immediately inform the Secretary General of the Organization of African Unity, who shall declare the seat vacant from the date of death or from the date on which the resignation takes effect.

The Assembly shall replace the judge whose office became vacant unless the remaining period of the term is less than one hundred and eighty (180) days.

The same procedure and considerations as set out in Articles 12, 13 and 14 shall be followed for the filling of vacancies.

Article 21 PRESIDENCY OF THE COURT

The Court shall elect its President and one Vice-President for a period of two years. They may be re-elected only once.

The President shall perform judicial functions on a full-time basis and shall reside at the seat of the Court.

The functions of the President and the Vice-President shall be set out in the Rules of Procedure of the Court.

Article 22 EXCLUSION

If the judge is a national of any State, which is a party to a case, submitted to the Court, that judge shall not hear the case.

Article 23 QUORUM

The Court shall examine cases brought before it, if it has a quorum of at least seven judges.

Article 24 REGISTRY OF THE COURT

The Court shall appoint its own Registrar and other staff of the registry from among nationals of Member States of the AU according to the Rules of Procedure.

The office and residence of the Registrar shall be at the place where the Court has its seat.

Article 25 SEAT OF THE COURT

The Court shall have its seat at the place determined by the Assembly from among States parties to this Protocol. However, it may convene in the territory of any Member State of the AU when the majority of the Court considers it desirable, and with the prior consent of the State concerned.

The seat of the Court may be changed by the Assembly after due consultation with the Court.

Article 26 EVIDENCE

The Court shall hear submissions by all parties and if deemed necessary, hold an enquiry. The States concerned shall assist by providing relevant facilities for the efficient handling of the case.

The Court may receive written and oral evidence including expert testimony and shall make its decision on the basis of such evidence.

Article 27 FINDINGS

If the Court finds that there has been violation of a human or peoples' rights, it shall make appropriate orders to remedy the violation, including the payment of fair compensation or reparation.

In cases of extreme gravity and urgency, and when necessary to avoid irreparable harm to persons, the Court shall adopt such provisional measures as it deems necessary.

Article 28 JUDGMENT

The Court shall render its judgment within ninety-(90)-days of having completed its deliberations.

The judgment of the Court decided by majority shall be final and not subject to appeal.

Without prejudice to sub-article 2 above, the Court may review its decision in the light of new evidence under conditions to be set out in the Rules of Procedure.

The Court may interpret its own decision.

The judgment of the Court shall be read in open court, due notice having been given to the parties.

Reasons shall be given for the judgment of the Court.

If the judgment of the court does not represent, in whole or in part, the unanimous decision of the judges, any judge shall be entitled to deliver a separate or dissenting opinion.

Article 29 NOTIFICATION OF JUDGMENT

The parties to the case shall be notified of the judgment of the Court and it shall be transmitted to the Member States of the AU and the Commission.

The Council of Ministers shall also be notified of the judgment and shall monitor its execution on behalf of the Assembly.

Article 30 EXECUTION OF JUDGMENT

The States Parties to the present Protocol undertake to comply with the judgment in any case to which they are parties within the time stipulated by the Court and to guarantee its execution.

Article 31 REPORT

The Court shall submit to each regular session of the Assembly, a report on its work during the previous year. The report shall specify, in particular, the cases in which a State has not complied with the Court's judgment.

Article 32 BUDGET

Expenses of the Court, emoluments and allowances for judges and the budget of its registry, shall be determined and borne by the AU, in accordance with criteria laid down by the AU in consultation with the Court.

Article 33 RULES OF PROCEDURE

The Court shall draw up its Rules and determine its own procedures. The Court shall consult the Commission as appropriate.

Article 34 RATIFICATION

This Protocol shall be open for signature and ratification or accession by any State Party to the Charter.

The instrument of ratification or accession to the present Protocol shall be deposited with the Secretary-General of the AU.

The Protocol shall come into force thirty days after fifteen instruments of ratification or accession have been deposited.

For any State Party ratifying or acceding subsequently, the present Protocol shall come into force in respect of that State on the date of the deposit of its instrument of ratification or accession.

The Secretary-General of the AU shall inform all Member States of the entry into force of the present Protocol.

At the time of the ratification of this Protocol or any time thereafter, the State shall make a declaration accepting the competence of the Court to receive cases under article 5 (3) of this Protocol. The Court shall not receive any petition under article 5 (3) involving a State Party which has not made such a declaration.

Declarations made under sub-article (6) above shall be deposited with the Secretary-General, who shall transmit copies thereof to the State parties.

Article 35 AMENDMENTS

The present Protocol may be amended if a State Party to the Protocol makes a written request to that effect to the Secretary-General of the AU. The Assembly may adopt, by simple majority, the draft amendment after all the State Parties to the present Protocol have been duly informed of it and the Court has given its opinion on the amendment.

The Court shall also be entitled to propose such amendments to the present Protocol, as it may deem necessary, through the Secretary-General of the AU.

The amendment shall come into force for each State Party, which has accepted it thirty days after the Secretary-General of the AU has received notice of the acceptance.

Appendix IV

Protocol on the Statute of the African Court of Justice and Human Rights

TABLE OF CONTENTS PROTOCOL

STATUTE OF THE AFRICAN COURT OF JUSTICE AND HUMAN RIGHTS

PROTOCOL ON THE STATUTE OF THE AFRICAN COURT OF JUSTICE AND HUMAN RIGHTS

The Member States of the African Union, Parties to this Protocol,

RECALLING the objectives and principles enunciated in the Constitutive Act of the African Union, adopted on 11 July 2000 in Lomé, Togo, in particular the commitment to settle their disputes through peaceful means;

BEARING IN MIND their commitment to promote peace, security and stability on the Continent and to protect human and peoples' rights in accordance with the African Charter on Human and Peoples' Rights and other relevant instruments relating to human rights;

CONSIDERING that the Constitutive Act of the African Union provides for the establishment of a Court of Justice charged with hearing, among other things, all cases relating to interpretation or application of the said Act or of all other Treaties adopted within the framework of the Union;

FURTHER CONSIDERING Decisions Assembly/AU/Dec.45 (III) and Assembly/AU/Dec.83 (V) of the Assembly of the Union, adopted respectively at its Third (6–8 July 2004, Addis Ababa, Ethiopia) and Fifth (4–5 July 2005, Sirte, Libya), Ordinary Sessions, to merge the African Court on Human and Peoples' Rights and the Court of Justice of the African Union into a single Court,

FIRMLY CONVINCED that the establishment of an African Court of Justice and Human Rights shall assist in the achievement of the goals pursued by the African Union and that the attainment of the objectives of the African Charter on Human and Peoples' Rights requires the establishment of a judicial organ to supplement and strengthen the mission of the African Commission on Human and Peoples' Rights as well as the African Committee of Experts on the Rights and Welfare of the Child;

TAKING DUE ACCOUNT of the Protocol to the African Charter on Human and Peoples' Rights on the Establishment an African Court on Human and Peoples' Rights, adopted by the Assembly of Heads of States and Governments of the Organization of African Unity on 10 June 1998 at Ouagadougou, Burkina Faso, and which entered into force on 25 January 2004;

TAKING DUE ACCOUNT ALSO of the Protocol of the Court of Justice of the African Union, adopted by the Assembly of the Union on 11 July 2003 in Maputo Mozambique;

RECALLING their commitment to take all necessary measures to strengthen their common institutions and to endow them with the necessary powers and resources to carry out their missions effectively;

COGNIZANT of the Protocol to the African Charter on Human and Peoples' Rights on the Rights of Women in Africa, and the commitments contained in the Solemn Declaration on the gender equality in Africa (Assembly/AU/Decl.12 (III) adopted by the Assembly of the Union respectively at its Second and Third ordinary sessions held in July 2003 and 2004, in Maputo, Mozambique and in Addis Ababa, Ethiopia);

Convinced that that the present Protocol shall supplement the mandate and efforts of other continental treaty bodies as well as national institutions in protecting human rights:

HAVE AGREED AS FOLLOWS:

CHAPTER I
MERGER OF THE AFRICAN COURT ON HUMAN AND PEOPLES' RIGHTS AND THE COURT OF JUSTICE OF THE AFRICAN UNION

Article 1
Replacement of the 1998 and 2003 Protocols

The Protocol to the African Charter on Human and Peoples' Rights on the Establishment of an African Court on Human and Peoples' Rights, adopted on 10 June 1998 in Ouagadougou, Burkina Faso and which entered into force on 25 January 2004, and the Protocol of the Court of Justice of the African Union, adopted on 11 July 2003 in Maputo, Mozambique, are hereby replaced by the present Protocol and Statute annexed as its integral part hereto, subject to the provisions of Article 5, 7 and 9 of this Protocol.

Article 2
Establishment of a single Court

The African Court on Human and Peoples' Rights established by the Protocol to the African Charter on Human and Peoples' Rights on the Establishment of an African Court on Human and Peoples' Rights and the Court of Justice of the African Union established by the Constitutive Act of the African Union, are hereby merged into a single Court and established as "The African Court of Justice and Human Rights".

Article 3
Reference to the single Court in the Constitutive Act

References made to the "Court of Justice" in the Constitutive Act of the African Union shall be read as references to the "African Court of Justice and Human Rights" established under Article 2 of this Protocol.

CHAPTER II
TRANSITIONAL PROVISIONS

Article 4
Term of Office of the Judges of the African Court on Human and Peoples' Rights

The term of office of the Judges of the African Court on Human and Peoples' Rights shall end following the election of the Judges of the African Court of Justice and Human Rights. However, the Judges shall remain in office until the newly elected Judges of the African Court of Justice and Human Rights are sworn in.

Article 5
Cases Pending before the African Court on Human and Peoples' Rights

Cases pending before the African Court on Human and Peoples' Rights, that have not been concluded before the entry into force of the present Protocol, shall be transferred to the Human Rights Section of the African Court of Justice and Human Rights on the understanding that such cases shall be dealt with In accordance with the protocol to the ACHPR on the establishment of the African Court on Human and Peoples' Rights.

Article 6
Registry of the Court

The Registrar of the African Court on Human and Peoples' Rights shall remain in office until the appointment of a new Registrar for the African Court of Justice and Human Rights.

Article 7
Provisional validity of the 1998 Protocol

The Protocol to the African Charter on Human and Peoples' Rights on the Establishment of an African Court on Human and Peoples' Rights shall remain in force for a transitional period not exceeding one (1) year or any other period determined by the Assembly, after entry into force of the present Protocol, to enable the African Court on Human and Peoples' Rights to take the necessary measures for the transfer of its prerogatives, assets, rights and obligations to the African Court of Justice and Human Rights.

CHAPTER III
FINAL PROVISIONS

Article 8
Signature, Ratification and Accession

1. The present Protocol shall be open for signature, ratification or accession by Member States, in accordance with their respective constitutional procedures.
2. The instruments of ratification or accession to the present Protocol shall be deposited with the Chairperson of the Commission of the African Union.
3. Any Member State may, at the time of signature or when depositing its instrument of ratification or accession, or at any time thereafter, make a declaration accepting the competence of the Court to receive cases under Article 30 (f) involving a State which has not made such a declaration.

Article 9
Entry into force

1. The present Protocol and the Statute annexed to it shall, enter into force thirty (30) days after the deposit of the instruments of ratification by fifteen (15) Member States.
2. For each Member State which shall ratify or accede to it subsequently, the present Protocol shall enter into force on the date on which the instruments of ratification or accession are deposited,
3. The Chairperson of the Commission shall inform all Member States of the entry into force of the present Protocol.

Adopted by the 11th Ordinary Session of the Assembly of the Union, In Sharm El-Sheikh, Egypt, 01 July 2008

Annex

STATUTE OF THE AFRICAN COURT OF JUSTICE AND HUMAN RIGHTS

CHAPTER I
GENERAL PROVISIONS

Article 1
Definitions

In this Statute, except otherwise indicated, the following shall mean:

"African Charter" means the African Charter on Human and Peoples' Rights;

"African Commission" means the African Commission on Human and Peoples' Rights;

"African Committee of Experts" means the African Committee of Experts on the Rights and Welfare of the Child;

"African Intergovernmental Organisations" means an organisation that has been established with the aim of ensuring socio-economic integration, and to which some Member States have ceded certain competences to act on their behalf, as well as other sub-regional, regional or inter-African Organisations;

"African Non-Governmental Organizations" means Non-Governmental Organizations at the sub-regional, regional or inter-African levels as well as those in the Diaspora as may be defined by the Executive Council;

"Agent" means a person mandated in writing to represent a party in a case before the Court;

"Assembly" means the Assembly of Heads of State and Government of the Union;

"Chamber(s)" means a Chamber established in accordance with Article 19 of the Statute.

"Constitutive Act" means the Constitutive Act of the African Union;

"Commission": means the Commission of the Union;

"Court" means the African Court of Justice and Human Rights as well as its sections and chambers;

"Executive Council" means the Executive Council of Ministers of the Union;

"Full Court" means joint sitting of the General Affairs and Human Rights Sections of the Court;

"Human Rights Section" means the Human and Peoples' Rights Section of the Court;

"Judge" means a judge of the Court;

"Member State" means a Member State of the Union;

"National Human Rights Institutions" means public institutions established by a state to promote and protect human rights;

"President" means the President of the Court elected in accordance with Article 22(1) of the Statute;

"Protocol" means the Protocol to the Statute of the African Court of Justice and Human Rights;

"Registrar" means the person appointed as such in accordance with Article 22 (4) of the Statute;

"Rules" means the Rules of the Court;

"Section" means the General Affairs or the Human Rights Section of the Court;

"Senior Judge" means the person defined as such in the Rules of Court;

"States Parties" means Member States, which have ratified or acceded to this Protocol;

"Statute" means the present Statute;

"Union" means the African Union established by the Constitutive Act;

"Vice President" means the Vice President of the Court elected in accordance with Article 22 (1) of the Statute.

Article 2
Functions of the Court

1. The African Court of Justice and Human Rights shall be the main judicial organ of the African Union.
2. The Court shall be constituted and function in accordance with the provisions of the present Statute.

CHAPTER II
ORGANIZATION OF THE COURT

Article 3
Composition

1. The Court shall consist of sixteen (16) Judges who are nationals of States Parties. Upon recommendation of the Court, the Assembly, may, review the number of Judges.
2. The Court shall not, at any one time, have more than one judge from a single Member State.

3. Each geographical region of the Continent, as determined by the Decisions of the Assembly shall, where possible, be represented by three (3) Judges except the Western Region which shall have four (4) Judges.

Article 4
Qualifications of Judges

The Court shall be composed of impartial and independent Judges elected from among persons of high moral character, who possess the qualifications required in their respective countries for appointment to the highest judicial offices, or are juristconsults of recognized competence and experience in international law and / or, human rights law.

Article 5
Presentation of Candidates

1. As soon as the Protocol to this Statute enters into force, the Chairperson of the Commission shall invite each State Party to submit, in writing, within a period of ninety (90) days, candidatures to the post of judge of the Court.
2. Each State Party may present up to two (2) candidates and shall take into account equitable gender representation in the nomination process.

Article 6
List of Candidates

1. For the purpose of election, the Chairperson of the Commission shall establish two alphabetical lists of candidates presented as follows:
   i) List A containing the names of candidates having recognized competence and experience in International law; and
   ii) List B containing the names of candidates possessing recognized competence and experience in Human Rights law.
2. States Parties that nominate candidates possessing the competences required on the two lists shall choose the list on which their candidates may be placed.
3, At the first election, eight (8) Judges shall be elected from amongst the candidates of list A and eight (8) from among the candidates of list B. The elections shall be organized in a way as to maintain the same proportion of judges elected on the two lists.
4. The Chairperson of the Commission shall communicate the two lists to Member States, at least thirty (30) days before the Ordinary Session of the Assembly or of the Council, during which the elections shall take place.

Article 7
Election of judges

1. The Judges shall be elected by the Executive Council, and appointed by the Assembly.
2. They shall be elected through secret ballot by a two-thirds majority of Member States with voting rights, from among the candidates provided for in Article 6 of this Statute.
3. Candidates who obtain the two-thirds majority and the highest number of votes shall be elected. However, if several rounds of election are required, the candidates with the least number of votes shall withdraw.
4. The Assembly shall ensure that in the Court as a whole there is equitable representation of the regions and the principal legal traditions of the Continent.
5. In the election of the Judges, the Assembly shall ensure that there is equitable gender representation.

Article 8
Term of Office

1. The Judges shall be elected for a period of six (6) years and may be re-elected only once. However, the term of office of eight (8) judges, four (4) from each section, elected during the first election shall end after four (4) years.
2. The Judges, whose term of office shall end after the initial period of four (4) years, shall be determined for each section, by lot drawn by the Chairperson of the Assembly or the Executive Council, immediately after the first election.
3. A Judge, elected to replace another whose term of office has not expired, shall complete the term of office of his predecessor.
4. All the Judges except the President and the Vice-President, shall perform their functions on a part-time basis.

Article 9
Resignation, Suspension and Removal from Office

1. A Judge may resign his/her position in writing addressed to the President for transmission to the Chairperson of the Assembly through the Chairperson of the Commission.
2. A Judge shall not be suspended or removed from office save, where, on the recommendation of two-thirds majority of the other members, he/she no longer meets the requisite conditions to be a Judge.
3. The President shall communicate the recommendation for the suspension or removal of a Judge to the Chairperson of the Assembly through the Chairperson of the Commission.
4. Such a recommendation of the Court shall become final upon its adoption by the Assembly.

Article 10
Vacancies

1. A vacancy shall arise in the Court under the following circumstances:
   a. Death;
   b. Resignation;
   c. Removal from office.
2. In the case of death or resignation of a Judge, the President shall immediately inform the Chairperson of the Assembly through the Chairperson of the Commission in writing, who shall declare the seat vacant.
3. The same procedure and consideration for the election of a Judge shall also be followed in filling the vacancies.

Article 11
Solemn Declaration

1. After the first election, the Judges shall, at the first session of the Court and in the presence of the Chairperson of the Assembly, make a Solemn Declaration as follows:

" I ,,,,,,,,,,,,,,,,,,,,,,,,,,,, Do solemnly swear (or affirm or declare) that I shall faithfully exercise the duties of my office as Judge of the African Court of Justice and Human Rights of the African Union impartially and conscientiously, without fear or favour, affection or ill will and that I will preserve the integrity of the Court.

2. The Chairperson of the Assembly or his/her duly authorized representative shall administer the Solemn Declaration.
3. Subsequently, the Solemn Declaration shall be made before the President of the Court.

Article 12
Independence

1. The independence of the judges shall be fully ensured in accordance with international law.
2. The Court shall act impartially, fairly and justly.
3. In performance of the judicial functions and duties, the Court and its Judges shall not be subject to the direction or control of any person or body.

Article 13
Conflict of Interest

1. Functions of a Judge are incompatible with all other activities, which might infringe on the need for independence or impartiality of the judicial profession. In case of doubt, the Court shall decide.

2. A Judge shall not exercise the function of agent, or counsel, or lawyer in any case before the Court.

Article 14
Conditions Governing the Participation of Members in the Settlement of a Specific Case

1. Where a particular judge feels he/she has a conflicting interest in a particular case, he/she shall so declare. In any event, he/she shall not participate in the settlement of a case for which he/she was previously involved as agent, counsel or lawyer of one of the parties, or as a member of a national or international Court or Tribunal, or a Commission of enquiry or in any other capacity.
2. If the President considers that a Judge should not participate in a particular case, he/she shall notify the judge concerned. Such notification from the President shall, after agreement by the Court, exclude that Judge from participating in that particular case.
3. A Judge of the nationality of a State Party to a case before the full Court or one of its Sections shall not have the right to sit on the case.
4. Where there is doubt on these points, the Court shall decide.

Article 15
Privileges and Immunities

1. The Judges shall enjoy, from the time of their election and throughout their term of office, the full privileges and immunities extended to diplomatic agents in accordance with international law.
2. The Judges shall be immune from legal proceedings for any act or omission committed in the discharge of their judicial functions.
3. The Judges shall continue, after they have ceased to hold office, to enjoy immunity in respect of acts performed by them when engaged in their official capacity.

Article 16
Sections of the Court

The Court *shall have two* (2) *Sections*; a General Affairs Section composed of eight (8) Judges and a Human Rights Section composed of eight (8) Judges.

Article 17
Assignment of Matters to Sections

1. The General Affairs Section shall be competent to hear all cases submitted under Article 28 of this Statute *save those concerning human and/or peoples' rights issues.*

2. The Human Rights Section shall be competent to hear all cases relating to human and/or peoples rights.

Article 18
Referral of matters to the Full Court

When a Section of the Court is seized with a case, it may, if it deems it necessary refer that case to the Full Court for consideration.

Article 19
Chambers

1. The General Affairs Section and the Human Rights Section may, at any time, constitute one or several chambers. The quorum required to constitute such chambers shall be determined in the Rules of Court.
2. A judgment given by any Section or Chamber shall be considered as rendered by the Court.

Article 20
Sessions

1. The Court shall hold ordinary and extraordinary sessions.
2. The Court shall decide each year on the periods of its ordinary sessions.
3. Extraordinary sessions shall be convened by the President or at the request of the majority of the Judges.

Article 21
Quorum

1. A quorum of nine (9) Judges shall be required for deliberations of the Full Court.
2. A quorum of six (6) Judges shall be required for the deliberations of the General Affairs Section.
3. A quorum of six (6) Judges shall be required for the deliberations of the Human and Peoples' Rights Section.

Article 22
Presidency, Vice-Presidency and Registry

1. At its first ordinary session after the election of the judges, the full Court shall elect its President as well as the Vice-President from the different lists for a period of three (3) years. The President and the Vice-President may be re-elected once.
2. The President shall preside over all sessions of the full Court and those of the Section to which he/she belongs; in the event of being unable to sit, the

President shall be replaced by the Vice president for the full Court and by the most Senior Judge for the sessions of his/her Section.
3. The Vice-President shall preside over all sessions of the section to which he/she belongs. In the event of being unable to sit, the Vice-President shall be replaced by the most Senior Judge of that Section.
4. The Court shall appoint a Registrar and may provide for the appointment of such other officers as may be necessary.
5. The President, the Vice-President and the Registrar shall reside at the seat of the Court.

Article 23
Remuneration of Judges

1. The President and the Vice-President shall receive an annual salary and other benefits.
2. The other Judges shall receive a sitting allowance for each day on which he/she exercises his/her functions.
3. These salaries, allowances and compensation shall be determined by the Assembly, on the proposal of the Executive Council. They may not be decreased during the term of office of the Judges.
4. Regulations adopted by the Assembly on the proposal of the Executive Council shall determine the conditions under which retirement pensions shall be given to the Judges as well as the conditions under which their travel expenses shall be paid.
5. The above-mentioned salaries, allowances and compensation shall be free from all taxation.

Article 24
Conditions of Service of the Registrar and Members of the Registry

The salaries and conditions of service of the Registrar and other Court Officials shall be determined by the Assembly on the proposal of the Court, through the Executive Council.

Article 25
Seat and Seal of the Court

1. The Seat of the Court shall be same as the Seat of the African Court on Human and Peoples' Rights. However, the Court may sit in any other Member State, if circumstances warrant, and with the consent of the Member State concerned. The Assembly may change the seat of the Court after due consultations with the Court.
2. The Court shall have a seal bearing the inscription "The African Court of Justice and Human Rights"

Article 26
Budget

1. The Court shall prepare its draft annual budget and shall submit it to the Assembly through the Executive Council.
2. The budget of the Court shall be borne by the African Union.
3. The Court shall be accountable for the execution of its budget and shall submit report thereon to the Executive Council in conformity with the Financial Rules and Regulations of the African Union.

Article 27
Rules of Court

1. The Court shall adopt rules for carrying out its functions and the implementation of the present Statute. In particular, it shall lay down its own Rules.
2. In elaborating its Rules, the Court shall bear in mind the complementarity it maintains with the African Commission and the African Committee of Experts.

CHAPTER III
COMPETENCE OF THE COURT

Article 28
Jurisdiction of the Court

The Court shall have jurisdiction over all cases and all legal disputes submitted to it in accordance with the present Statute which relate to:

a) the interpretation and application of the Constitutive Act;
b) the interpretation, application or validity of other Union Treaties and all subsidiary legal instruments adopted within the framework of the Union or the Organization of African Unity;
c) the interpretation and the application of the African Charter, the Charter on the Rights and Welfare of the Child, the Protocol to the African Charter on Human and Peoples' Rights on the Rights of Women in Africa, or any other legal instrument relating to human rights, ratified by the States Parties concerned;
d) any question of international law;
e) all acts, decisions, regulations and directives of the organs of the Union;
f) all matters specifically provided for in any other agreements that States Parties may conclude among themselves, or with the Union and which confer jurisdiction on the Court;
g) the existence of any fact which, if established, would constitute a breach of an obligation owed to a State Party or to the Union;
h) the nature or extent of the reparation to be made for the breach of an international obligation.

Article 29
Entities Eligible to Submit Cases to the Court

1. The following entities shall be entitled to submit cases to the Court on any issue or dispute provided for in Article 28:
   a) State Parties to the present Protocol;
   b) The Assembly, the Parliament and other organs of the Union authorized by the Assembly;
   c) A staff member of the African Union on appeal, in a dispute and within the limits and under the terms and conditions laid down in the Staff Rules and Regulations of the Union;
2. The Court shall not be open to States, which are not members of the Union. The Court shall also have no jurisdiction to deal with a dispute involving a Member State that has not ratified the Protocol.

Article 30
Other Entities Eligible to Submit Cases to the Court

The following entities shall also be entitled to submit cases to the Court on any violation of a right guaranteed by the African Charter, by the Charter on the Rights and Welfare of the Child, the Protocol to the African Charter on Human and Peoples' Rights on the Rights of Women in Africa, or any other legal instrument relevant to human rights ratified by the States Parties concerned:
   a) State Parties to the present Protocol;
   b) the African Commission on Human and Peoples' Rights;
   c) the African Committee of Experts on the Rights and Welfare of the Child;
   d) African Intergovernmental Organizations accredited to the Union or its organs;
   e) African National Human Rights Institutions;
   f) Individuals or relevant Non-Governmental Organizations accredited to the African Union or to its organs, subject to the provisions of Article 8 of the Protocol.

Article 31
Applicable Law

1. In carrying out its functions, the Court shall have regard to:
   a) The Constitutive Act;
   b) International treaties, whether general or particular, ratified by the contesting States;
   c) International custom, as evidence of a general practice accepted as law;
   d) The general principles of law recognized universally or by African States;
   e) Subject to the provisions of paragraph 1, of Article 46 of the present Statute, judicial decisions and writings of the most highly qualified publicists of

various nations s well as the regulations, directives and decisions of the Union, as subsidiary means for the determination of the rules of law;

f) Any other law relevant to the determination of the case.

2. This Article shall not prejudice the power of the Court to decide a case *ex aequo et bono,* if the parties agree thereto.

CHAPTER IV
PROCEDURE

Article 32
Official Languages

The official and working languages of the Court shall be those of the Union.

Article 33
Institution of Proceedings before the General Affairs Section

1. Cases brought before the Court by virtue of Article 29 of the present Statute shall be submitted by written application addressed to the Registrar. The subject of the dispute, the applicable law and basis of jurisdiction shall be indicated.
2. The Registrar shall forthwith give notice of the application to the Parties concerned.
3. The Registrar shall also notify, through the Chairperson of the Commission, all Member States and, if necessary, the organs of the Union whose decisions are in dispute.

Article 34
Institution of Proceedings before the Human Rights Section

1. Cases brought before the Court relating to an alleged violation of a human or peoples' right shall be submitted by a written application to the Registrar. The application shall indicate the right (s) alleged to have been violated, and, insofar as it is possible, the provision or provisions of the African Charter on Human and Peoples' Rights, the Charter on the Rights and Welfare of the Child, Protocol to the African Charter on Human and Peoples' Rights on the Rights of Women in Africa or any other relevant human rights instrument, ratified by the State concerned, on which it is based.
2. The Registrar shall forthwith give notice of the application to all parties concerned, as well as the Chairperson of the Commission.

Article 35
Provisional Measures

1. The Court shall have the power, on its own motion or on application by the parties, to indicate, if it considers that circumstances so require any provisional measures which ought to be taken to preserve the respective rights of the parties.
2. Pending the final decision, notice of the provisional measures shall forthwith be given to the parties and the Chairperson of the Commission, who shall inform the Assembly.

Article 36
Representation of Parties

1. The States, parties to a case, shall be represented by agents.
2. They may, if necessary, have the assistance of counsel or advocates before the Court.
3. The organs of the Union entitled to appear before the Court shall be represented by the Chairperson of the Commission or his /her representative.
4. The African Commission, the African Committee of Experts, African Inter-Governmental Organizations accredited to the Union or its organs and African National Human Rights Institutions entitled to appear before the Court shall be represented by any person they choose for that purpose.
5. Individuals and Non-Governmental Organizations accredited to the Union or its organs may be represented or assisted by a person of their choice.
6. The agents and other representatives of parties before the Court, their counsel or advocates, witnesses, and any other persons whose presence is required at the Court shall enjoy the privileges and immunities necessary to the independent exercise of their duties or the smooth functioning of the Court.

Article 37
Communications and Notices

1. Communications and notices addressed to agents or counsel of parties to a case shall be considered as addressed to the parties.
2. For the service of all communications or notices upon persons other than the agents, counsel or advocates of parties concerned, the Court shall direct its request to the government of the State upon whose territory the communication or notice has to be served.
3. The same provision shall apply whenever steps are to be taken to procure evidence on the spot.

Article 38
Procedure before the Court

The procedures before the Court shall be laid out in the Rules of Court, taking into account the complementarity between the Court and other treaty bodies of the Union.

Article 39
Public Hearing

The hearing shall be public, unless the Court, on its own motion or upon application by the parties, decides that the session shall be closed.

Article 40
Record of Proceedings

1. A record of proceedings shall be made at each hearing and shall be signed by the Registrar and the presiding Judge of the session.
2. This record alone shall be authentic.

Article 41
Default Judgment

1. Whenever one of the parties does not appear before the Court, or fails to defend the case against it, the Court shall proceed to consider the case and to give its judgment.
2. The Court shall before doing so, satisfy itself, not only that it has jurisdiction in accordance with Articles 28, 29 and 30 of the present Statute, but also that the claim is well founded in fact and law, and that the other party had due notice.
3. An objection by the party concerned may be lodged against the judgment within ninety (90) days of it being notified of the default judgment. Unless there is a decision to the contrary by the Court, the objection shall not have effect of staying the enforcement of the default judgment.

Article 42
Majority Required for Decision of the Court

1. Without prejudice to the provisions of Article 50(4) of the present Statute, the decisions of the Court shall be decided by a majority of the Judges present.
2. In the event of an equality of votes, the presiding Judge shall have a casting vote.

Article 43
Judgments and Decisions

1. The Court shall render its judgment within ninety (90) days of having completed its deliberations.
2. All judgments shall state the reasons on which they are based.
3. The judgment shall contain the names of the Judges who have taken part in the decision.
4. The judgment shall be signed by all the Judges and certified by the Presiding Judge and the Registrar. It shall be read in open session, due notice having been given to the agents.
5. The Parties to the case shall be notified of the judgment of the Court and it shall be transmitted to the Member States and the Commission.
6. The Executive Council shall also be notified of the judgment and shall monitor its execution on behalf of the Assembly

Article 44
Dissenting Opinion

If the judgment does not represent in whole or in part the unanimous opinion of the Judges, any Judge shall be entitled to deliver a separate or dissenting opinion.

Article 45
Compensation

Without prejudice to its competence to rule on issues of compensation at the request of a party by virtue of paragraph 1(h), of Article 28 of the present Statute, the Court may, if it considers that there was a violation of a human or peoples' right, order any appropriate measures in order to remedy the situation, including granting fair compensation.

Article 46
Binding Force and Execution of Judgments

1. The decision of the Court shall be binding on the parties.
2. Subject to the provisions of paragraph 3, Article 41 of the present Statute, the judgment of the Court is final.
3. The parties shall comply with the judgment made by the Court in any dispute to which they are parties within the time stipulated by the Court and shall guarantee its execution.
4. Where a party has failed to comply with a judgment, the Court shall refer the matter to the Assembly, which shall decide upon measures to be taken to give effect to that judgment.
5. The Assembly may impose sanctions by virtue of paragraph 2 of Article 23 of the Constitutive Act.

Article 47
Interpretation

In the event of any dispute as to the meaning or scope of a judgment, the Court shall construe it upon the request of any party.

Article 48
Revision

1. An application for revision of a judgment may be made to the Court only when it is based upon discovery of a new fact of such nature as to be a decisive factor, which fact was, when the judgment was given, unknown to the Court and also to the party claiming revision, provided that such ignorance was not due to negligence.
2. The proceedings for revision shall be opened by a ruling of the Court expressly recording the existence of the new fact, recognizing that it has such a character as to lay the case open to revision, and declaring the revision admissible on this ground.
3. The Court may require prior compliance with the terms of the judgment before it admits proceedings in revision.
4. The application for revision shall be made within six (6) months of the discovery of the new fact.
5. No application may be made after the lapse of ten (10) years from the date of the judgment.

Article 49
Intervention

1. Should a Member State or organ of the Union consider that it has an interest of a legal nature which may be affected by the decision in the case, it may submit a request to the Court to be permitted to intervene. It shall be for the Court to decide upon this request.
2. If a Member State or organ of the Union should exercise the option offered under paragraph 1 of the present Article, the interpretation contained in the decision shall be equally binding upon it.
3. In the interest of the effective administration of justice, the Court may invite any Member State that is not a party to the case, any organ of the Union or any person concerned other than the claimant, to present written observations or take part in hearings.

Article 50
Intervention in a Case Concerning the Interpretation of the Constitutive Act

1. Whenever the question of interpretation of the Constitutive Act arises, in a case in which Member States other than the parties to the dispute have

expressed an interest, the Registrar shall notify all such States and organs of the Union forthwith.

2. Every State Party and organ of the Union so notified has the right to intervene in the proceedings.
3. The decisions of the Court concerning the interpretation and application of the Constitutive Act shall be binding on Member States and organs of the Union, notwithstanding the provisions of paragraph 1, of Article 46 of this Statute.
4. Any decision made by virtue of this Article shall be made by a qualified majority of at least two (2) votes and in the presence of at least two-thirds of the Judges.

Article 51
Intervention in a Case Concerning the Interpretation of Other Treaties

1. Whenever the question is that of interpretation of other treaties ratified by Member States other than the parties to a dispute, the Registrar shall notify all such States and the organs of the Union forthwith.
2. Every State Party and organ of the Union so notified has the right to intervene in the proceedings, and if it exercises this right, the interpretation given by the judgment shall be equally binding upon it.
3. This Article shall not be applicable to cases relating to alleged violations of a human or peoples' right, submitted by virtue of Articles 29 or 30 of the present Statute.

Article 52
Costs

1. Unless otherwise decided by the Court, each party shall bear its own costs.
2. Should it be required in the interest of justice, free legal aid may be provided for the person presenting an individual communication, under conditions to be set out in the Rules of Court.

CHAPTER V
ADVISORY OPINION

Article 53
Request for Advisory Opinion

1. The Court may give an advisory opinion on any legal question at the request of the Assembly, the Parliament, the Executive Council, the Peace and Security Council, the Economic, Social and Cultural Council (ECOSOCC), the Financial Institutions or any other organ of the Union as may be authorized by the Assembly.

2. A request for an advisory opinion shall be in writing and shall contain an exact statement of the question upon which the opinion is required and shall be accompanied by all relevant documents.
3. A request for an advisory opinion must not be related to a pending application before the African Commission or the African Committee of Experts.

Article 54
Service of Notice

1. The Registrar shall forthwith give notice of the request for an advisory opinion to all States or organs entitled to appear before the Court by virtue of Article 30 of the present Statute.
2. The Registrar shall also, by means of a special and direct communication, notify any State entitled to appear before the Court or any Intergovernmental Organization considered by the Court, or should it not be sitting, by the President, as likely to be able to furnish information on the question, that the Court will be prepared to receive, within a time limit to be fixed by the President, written statements, or to hear, at a public sitting to be held for the purpose, oral statements relating to the question.
3. Should any such State entitled to appear before the Court have failed to receive the special communication referred to in paragraph 2 of this Article, such State may express the desire to submit a written statement or to be heard, and the Court shall decide.
4. States and organizations having presented written or oral statements or both shall be permitted to comment on the statements made by other States or organizations in the form, to the extent, and within the time limits which the Court, or should it not be sitting, the President, shall decide in each particular case. Accordingly, the Registrar shall in due course communicate any such written statements to States and organizations having submitted similar statements.

Article 55
Delivery of Advisory Opinion

The Court shall deliver its advisory opinion in open court, notice having been given to the Chairperson of the Commission and Member States, and other International Organizations directly concerned.

Article 56
Application by Analogy of the Provisions of the Statute Applicable to Contentious Cases

In the exercise of its advisory functions, the Court shall further be guided by the provisions of the present Statute which apply in contentious cases to the extent to which it recognizes them to be applicable.

CHAPTER VI
REPORT TO THE ASSEMBLY

Article 57
Annual Activity Report

The Court shall submit to the Assembly, an annual report on its work during the previous year. The report shall specify, in particular, the cases in which a party has not complied with the judgment of the Court.

CHAPTER VII
PROCEDURE FOR AMENDMENTS

Article 58
Proposed Amendments from a State Party

1. The present Statute may be amended if a State Party makes a written request to that effect to the Chairperson of the Commission, who shall transmit same to Member States within thirty (30) days of receipt thereof.
2. The Assembly may adopt by a simple majority, the proposed amendment after the Court has given its opinion on it.

Article 59
Proposed Amendments from the Court

The Court may propose such amendments to the present Statute as it may deem necessary, to the Assembly through written communication to the Chairperson of the Commission, for consideration in conformity with the provisions of Article 58 of the present Statute.

Article 60
Entry into Force of Amendments

The amendment shall enter into force for every State which has accepted it in conformity with its Constitutional laws thirty (30) days after the Chairperson of the Commission is notified of this acceptance.

Appendix V

Convention Relating to the Status of Refugees, 189 U.N.T.S. 150, Entered into Force April 22, 1954

CHAPTER I
GENERAL PROVISIONS

Article 1. – Definition of the Term "Refugee"

A. For the purposes of the present Convention, the term "refugee" shall apply to any person who:

(1) Has been considered a refugee under the Arrangements of 12 May 1926 and 30 June 1928 or under the Conventions of 28 October 1933 and 10 February 1938, the Protocol of 14 September 1939 or the Constitution of the International Refugee Organization;

Decisions of non-eligibility taken by the International Refugee Organization during the period of its activities shall not prevent the status of refugee being accorded to persons who fulfil the conditions of paragraph 2 of this section;

(2) As a result of events occurring before I January 1951 and owing to well-founded fear of being persecuted for reasons of race, religion, nationality, membership of a particular social group or political opinion, is outside the country of his nationality and is unable, or owing to such fear, is unwilling to avail himself of the protection of that country; or who, not having a nationality and being outside the country of his former habitual residence as a result of such events, is unable or, owing to such fear, is unwilling to return to it.

In the case of a person who has more than one nationality, the term "the country of his nationality" shall mean each of the countries of which he is a national, and a person shall not be deemed to be lacking the protection of the country of his nationality if, without any valid reason based on well-founded fear, he has not availed himself of the protection of one of the countries of which he is a national.

B. (1) For the purposes of this Convention, the words "events occurring before I January 1951" in article 1, section A, shall be understood to mean either (a) "events occurring in Europe before I January 1951"; or (b) "events occurring in Europe or elsewhere before I January 1951"; and each Contracting State shall make a declaration at the time of signature, ratification or accession, specifying which of these meanings it applies for the purpose of its obligations under this Convention.

(2) Any Contracting State which has adopted alternative (a) may at any time extend its obligations by adopting alternative (b) by means of a notification addressed to the Secretary-General of the United Nations.

C. This Convention shall cease to apply to any person falling under the terms of section A if:

(1) He has voluntarily re-availed himself of the protection of the country of his nationality; or

(2) Having lost his nationality, he has voluntarily reacquired it; or

(3) He has acquired a new nationality, and enjoys the protection of the country of his new nationality; or

(4) He has voluntarily re-established himself in the country which he left or outside which he remained owing to fear of persecution; or

(5) He can no longer, because the circumstances in connection with which he has been recognized as a refugee have ceased to exist, continue to refuse to avail himself of the protection of the country of his nationality;

Provided that this paragraph shall not apply to a refugee falling under section A (I) of this article who is able to invoke compelling reasons arising out of previous persecution for refusing to avail himself of the protection of the country of nationality;

(6) Being a person who has no nationality he is, because the circumstances in connection with which he has been recognized as a refugee have ceased to exist, able to return to the country of his former habitual residence;

Provided that this paragraph shall not apply to a refugee falling under section A (I) of this article who is able to invoke compelling reasons arising out of previous persecution for refusing to return to the country of his former habitual residence.

D. This Convention shall not apply to persons who are at present receiving from organs or agencies of the United Nations other than the United Nations High Commissioner for Refugees protection or assistance.

When such protection or assistance has ceased for any reason, without the position of such persons being definitively settled in accordance with the relevant resolutions adopted by the General Assembly of the United Nations, these persons shall ipso facto be entitled to the benefits of this Convention.

E. This Convention shall not apply to a person who is recognized by the competent authorities of the country in which he has taken residence as having the rights and obligations which are attached to the possession of the nationality of that country.

F. The provisions of this Convention shall not apply to any person with respect to whom there are serious reasons for considering that:

   (a) He has committed a crime against peace, a war crime, or a crime against humanity, as defined in the international instruments drawn up to make provision in respect of such crimes;
   (b) He has committed a serious non-political crime outside the country of refuge prior to his admission to that country as a refugee;
   (c) He has been guilty of acts contrary to the purposes and principles of the United Nations.

Article 2. – General Obligations

Every refugee has duties to the country in which he finds himself, which require in particular that he conform to its laws and regulations as well as to measures taken for the maintenance of public order.
eThe Contracting States shall apply the provisions of this Convention to refugees without discrimination as to race, religion or country of origin.

Article 4. – Religion

The Contracting States shall accord to refugees within their territories treatment at least as favourable as that accorded to their nationals with respect to freedom to practise their religion and freedom as regards the religious education of their children.

Article 5. – Rights Granted Apart from this Convention

Nothing in this Convention shall be deemed to impair any rights and benefits granted by a Contracting State to refugees apart from this Convention.

Article 6. – The Term "in the Same Circumstances"

For the purposes of this Convention, the term "in the same circumstances" implies that any requirements (including requirements as to length and conditions of sojourn or residence) which the particular individual would have to fulfil for the enjoyment of the right in question, if he were not a refugee, must be fulfilled by him, with the exception of requirements which by their nature a refugee is incapable of fulfilling.

Article 7. – Exemption from Reciprocity

1. Except where this Convention contains more favourable provisions, a Contracting State shall accord to refugees the same treatment as is accorded to aliens generally.
2. After a period of three years' residence, all refugees shall enjoy exemption from legislative reciprocity in the territory of the Contracting States.
3. Each Contracting State shall continue to accord to refugees the rights and benefits to which they were already entitled, in the absence of reciprocity, at the date of entry into force of this Convention for that State.
4. The Contracting States shall consider favourably the possibility of according to refugees, in the absence of reciprocity, rights and benefits beyond those to which they are entitled according to paragraphs 2 and 3, and to extending exemption from reciprocity to refugees who do not fulfil the conditions provided for in paragraphs 2 and 3.
5. The provisions of paragraphs 2 and 3 apply both to the rights and benefits referred to in articles 13, 18, 19, 21 and 22 of this Convention and to rights and benefits for which this Convention does not provide.

Article 8. – Exemption from Exceptional Measures

With regard to exceptional measures which may be taken against the person, property or interests of nationals of a foreign State, the Contracting States shall not apply such measures to a refugee who is formally a national of the said State solely on account of such nationality. Contracting States which, under their legislation, are prevented from applying the general principle expressed in this article, shall, in appropriate cases, grant exemptions in favour of such refugees.

Article 9. – Provisional Measures

Nothing in this Convention shall prevent a Contracting State, in time of war or other grave and exceptional circumstances, from taking provisionally measures which it considers to be essential to the national security in the case of a particular person, pending a determination by the Contracting State that that person is in fact a refugee and that the continuance of such measures is necessary in his case in the interests of national security.

Article 10. – Continuity of Residence

1. Where a refugee has been forcibly displaced during the Second World War and removed to the territory of a Contracting State, and is resident there, the period

of such enforced sojourn shall be considered to have been lawful residence within that territory.
2. Where a refugee has been forcibly displaced during the Second World War from the territory of a Contracting State and has, prior to the date of entry into force of this Convention, returned there for the purpose of taking up residence, the period of residence before and after such enforced displacement shall be regarded as one uninterrupted period for any purposes for which uninterrupted residence is required.

Article 11. – Refugee Seamen

In the case of refugees regularly serving as crew members on board a ship flying the flag of a Contracting State, that State shall give sympathetic consideration to their establishment on its territory and the issue of travel documents to them or their temporary admission to its territory particularly with a view to facilitating their establishment in another country.

CHAPTER II
JURIDICAL STATUS

Article 12. – Personal Status

1. The personal status of a refugee shall be governed by the law of the country of his domicile or, if he has no domicile, by the law of the country of his residence.
2. Rights previously acquired by a refugee and dependent on personal status, more particularly rights attaching to marriage, shall be respected by a Contracting State, subject to compliance, if this be necessary, with the formalities required by the law of that State, provided that the right in question is one which would have been recognized by the law of that State had he not become a refugee.

Article 13. – Movable and Immovable Property

The Contracting States shall accord to a refugee treatment as favourable as possible and, in any event, not less favourable than that accorded to aliens generally in the same circumstances, as regards the acquisition of movable and immovable property and other rights pertaining thereto, and to leases and other contracts relating to movable and immovable property.

Article 14. – Artistic Rights and Industrial property

In respect of the protection of industrial property, such as inventions, designs or models, trade marks, trade names, and of rights in literary, artistic and scientific works, a refugee shall be accorded in the country in which he has his habitual residence the same protection as is accorded to nationals of that country. In the territory of any other Contracting States, he shall be accorded the same protection as is accorded in that territory to nationals of the country in which he has his habitual residence.

Article 15. – Right of Association

As regards non-political and non-profit-making associations and trade unions the Contracting States shall accord to refugees lawfully staying in their territory the most favourable treatment accorded to nationals of a foreign country, in the same circumstances.

Article 16. – Access to Courts

1. A refugee shall have free access to the courts of law on the territory of all Contracting States.
2. A refugee shall enjoy in the Contracting State in which he has his habitual residence the same treatment as a national in matters pertaining to access to the courts, including legal assistance and exemption from cautio judicatum solvi.
3. A refugee shall be accorded in the matters referred to in paragraph 2 in countries other than that in which he has his habitual residence the treatment granted to a national of the country of his habitual residence.

CHAPTER III
GAINFUL EMPLOYMENT

Article 17. – Wage-Earning Employment

1. The Contracting States shall accord to refugees lawfully staying in their territory the most favourable treatment accorded to nationals of a foreign country in the same circumstances, as regards the right to engage in wage-earning employment.
2. In any case, restrictive measures imposed on aliens or the employment of aliens for the protection of the national labour market shall not be applied to a refugee who was already exempt from them at the date of entry into force of this Convention for the Contracting State concerned, or who fulfils one of the following conditions:
   (a) He has completed three years' residence in the country;
   (b) He has a spouse possessing the nationality of the country of residence. A refugee may not invoke the benefit of this provision if he has abandoned his spouse;

(c) He has one or more children possessing the nationality of the country of residence.

3. The Contracting States shall give sympathetic consideration to assimilating the rights of all refugees with regard to wage-earning employment to those of nationals, and in particular of those refugees who have entered their territory pursuant to programmes of labour recruitment or under immigration schemes.

Article 18. – Self-Employment

The Contracting States shall accord to a refugee lawfully in their territory treatment as favourable as possible and, in any event, not less favourable than that accorded to aliens generally in the same circumstances, as regards the right to engage on his own account in agriculture, industry, handicrafts and commerce and to establish commercial and industrial companies.

Article 19. – Liberal Professions

1. Each Contracting State shall accord to refugees lawfully staying in their territory who hold diplomas recognized by the competent authorities of that State, and who are desirous of practising a liberal profession, treatment as favourable as possible and, in any event, not less favourable than that accorded to aliens generally in the same circumstances.
2. The Contracting States shall use their best endeavours consistently with their laws and constitutions to secure the settlement of such refugees in the territories, other than the metropolitan territory, for whose international relations they are responsible.

CHAPTER IV
WELFARE

Article 20. – Rationing

Where a rationing system exists, which applies to the population at large and regulates the general distribution of products in short supply, refugees shall be accorded the same treatment as nationals.

Article 21. – Housing

As regards housing, the Contracting States, in so far as the matter is regulated by laws or regulations or is subject to the control of public authorities, shall accord to refugees lawfully staying in their territory treatment as favourable as possible and, in any event, not less favourable than that accorded to aliens generally in the same circumstances.

Article 22. – Public Education

1. The Contracting States shall accord to refugees the same treatment as is accorded to nationals with respect to elementary education.
2. The Contracting States shall accord to refugees treatment as favourable as possible, and, in any event, not less favourable than that accorded to aliens generally in the same circumstances, with respect to education other than elementary education and, in particular, as regards access to studies, the recognition of foreign school certificates, diplomas and degrees, the remission of fees and charges and the award of scholarships.

Article 23. – Public Relief

The Contracting States shall accord to refugees lawfully staying in their territory the same treatment with respect to public relief and assistance as is accorded to their nationals.

Article 24. – Labour Legislation and Social Security

1. The Contracting States shall accord to refugees lawfully staying in their territory the same treatment as is accorded to nationals in respect of the following matters;
   (a) In so far as such matters are governed by laws or regulations or are subject to the control of administrative authorities: remuneration, including family allowances where these form part of remuneration, hours of work, overtime arrangements, holidays with pay, restrictions on home work, minimum age of employment, apprenticeship and training, women's work and the work of young persons, and the enjoyment of the benefits of collective bargaining;
   (b) Social security (legal provisions in respect of employment injury, occupational diseases, maternity, sickness, disability, old age, death, unemployment, family responsibilities and any other contingency which, according to national laws or regulations, is covered by a social security scheme), subject to the following limitations:
      (i) There may be appropriate arrangements for the maintenance of acquired rights and rights in course of acquisition;
      (ii) National laws or regulations of the country of residence may prescribe special arrangements concerning benefits or portions of benefits which are payable wholly out of public funds, and concerning allowances paid to persons who do not fulfil the contribution conditions prescribed for the award of a normal pension.
2. The right to compensation for the death of a refugee resulting from employment injury or from occupational disease shall not be affected by the fact that the residence of the beneficiary is outside the territory of the Contracting State.

3. The Contracting States shall extend to refugees the benefits of agreements concluded between them, or which may be concluded between them in the future, concerning the maintenance of acquired rights and rights in the process of acquisition in regard to social security, subject only to the conditions which apply to nationals of the States signatory to the agreements in question.
4. The Contracting States will give sympathetic consideration to extending to refugees so far as possible the benefits of similar agreements which may at any time be in force between such Contracting States and non- contracting States.

CHAPTER V
ADMINISTRATIVE MEASURES

Article 25. – Administrative Assistance

1. When the exercise of a right by a refugee would normally require the assistance of authorities of a foreign country to whom he cannot have recourse, the Contracting States in whose territory he is residing shall arrange that such assistance be afforded to him by their own authorities or by an international authority.
2. The authority or authorities mentioned in paragraph 1 shall deliver or cause to be delivered under their supervision to refugees such documents or certifications as would normally be delivered to aliens by or through their national authorities.
3. Documents or certifications so delivered shall stand in the stead of the official instruments delivered to aliens by or through their national authorities, and shall be given credence in the absence of proof to the contrary.
4. Subject to such exceptional treatment as may be granted to indigent persons, fees may be charged for the services mentioned herein, but such fees shall be moderate and commensurate with those charged to nationals for similar services.
5. The provisions of this article shall be without prejudice to articles 27 and 28.

Article 26. – Freedom of Movement

Each Contracting State shall accord to refugees lawfully in its territory the right to choose their place of residence and to move freely within its territory subject to any regulations applicable to aliens generally in the same circumstances.

Article 27. – Identity Papers

The Contracting States shall issue identity papers to any refugee in their territory who does not possess a valid travel document.

Article 28. – Travel Documents

1. The Contracting States shall issue to refugees lawfully staying in their territory travel documents for the purpose of travel outside their territory, unless compelling reasons of national security or public order otherwise require, and the provisions of the Schedule to this Convention shall apply with respect to such documents. The Contracting States may issue such a travel document to any other refugee in their territory; they shall in particular give sympathetic consideration to the issue of such a travel document to refugees in their territory who are unable to obtain a travel document from the country of their lawful residence.
2. Travel documents issued to refugees under previous international agreements by Parties thereto shall be recognized and treated by the Contracting States in the same way as if they had been issued pursuant to this article.

Article 29. – Fiscal Charges

1. The Contracting States shall not impose upon refugees duties, charges or taxes, of any description whatsoever, other or higher than those which are or may be levied on their nationals in similar situations.
2. Nothing in the above paragraph shall prevent the application to refugees of the laws and regulations concerning charges in respect of the issue to aliens of administrative documents including identity papers.

Article 30. – Transfer of Assets

1. A Contracting State shall, in conformity with its laws and regulations, permit refugees to transfer assets which they have brought into its territory, to another country where they have been admitted for the purposes of resettlement.
2. A Contracting State shall give sympathetic consideration to the application of refugees for permission to transfer assets wherever they may be and which are necessary for their resettlement in another country to which they have been admitted.

Article 31. – Refugees Unlawfully in the Country of Refuge

1. The Contracting States shall not impose penalties, on account of their illegal entry or presence, on refugees who, coming directly from a territory where their life or freedom was threatened in the sense of article 1, enter or are present in their territory without authorization, provided they present themselves without delay to the authorities and show good cause for their illegal entry or presence.

2. The Contracting States shall not apply to the movements of such refugees restrictions other than those which are necessary and such restrictions shall only be applied until their status in the country is regularized or they obtain admission into another country. The Contracting States shall allow such refugees a reasonable period and all the necessary facilities to obtain admission into another country.

Article 32. – Expulsion

1. The Contracting States shall not expel a refugee lawfully in their territory save on grounds of national security or public order.
2. The expulsion of such a refugee shall be only in pursuance of a decision reached in accordance with due process of law. Except where compelling reasons of national security otherwise require, the refugee shall be allowed to submit evidence to clear himself, and to appeal to and be represented for the purpose before competent authority or a person or persons specially designated by the competent authority.
3. The Contracting States shall allow such a refugee a reasonable period within which to seek legal admission into another country. The Contracting States reserve the right to apply during that period such internal measures as they may deem necessary.

Article 33. – Prohibition of Expulsion or Return ("Refoulement")

1. No Contracting State shall expel or return ("refouler") a refugee in any manner whatsoever to the frontiers of territories where his life or freedom would be threatened on account of his race, religion, nationality, membership of a particular social group or political opinion.
2. The benefit of the present provision may not, however, be claimed by a refugee whom there are reasonable grounds for regarding as a danger to the security of the country in which he is, or who, having been convicted by a final judgement of a particularly serious crime, constitutes a danger to the community of that country.

Article 34. – Naturalization

The Contracting States shall as far as possible facilitate the assimilation and naturalization of refugees. They shall in particular make every effort to expedite naturalization proceedings and to reduce as far as possible the charges and costs of such proceedings.

CHAPTER VI
EXECUTORY AND TRANSITORY PROVISIONS

Article 35. – Co-operation of the National Authorities with the United Nations

1. The Contracting States undertake to co-operate with the Office of the United Nations High Commissioner for Refugees, or any other agency of the United Nations which may succeed it, in the exercise of its functions, and shall in particular facilitate its duty of supervising the application of the provisions of this Convention.
2. In order to enable the Office of the High Commissioner or any other agency of the United Nations which may succeed it, to make reports to the competent organs of the United Nations, the Contracting States undertake to provide them in the appropriate form with information and statistical data requested concerning:
   (a) The condition of refugees,
   (b) The implementation of this Convention, and
   (c) Laws, regulations and decrees which are, or may hereafter be, in force relating to refugees.

Article 36. – Information on National Legislation

The Contracting States shall communicate to the Secretary-General of the United Nations the laws and regulations which they may adopt to ensure the application of this Convention.

Article 37. – Relation to Previous Conventions

Without prejudice to article 28, paragraph 2, of this Convention, this Convention replaces, as between Parties to it, the Arrangements of 5 July 1922, 31 May 1924, 12 May 1926, 30 June 1928 and 30 July 1935, the Conventions of 28 October 1933 and 10 February 1938, the Protocol of 14 September 1939 and the Agreement of 15 October 1946.

CHAPTER VII
FINAL CLAUSES

Article 38. – Settlement of Disputes

Any dispute between Parties to this Convention relating to its interpretation or application, which cannot be settled by other means, shall be referred to the International Court of Justice at the request of any one of the parties to the dispute.

Article 39. – Signature, Ratification and Accession

1. This Convention shall be opened for signature at Geneva on 28 July 1951 and shall thereafter be deposited with the Secretary-General of the United Nations. It shall be open for signature at the European Office of the United Nations from 28 July to 31 August 1951 and shall be re-opened for signature at the Headquarters of the United Nations from 17 September 1951 to 31 December 1952.
2. This Convention shall be open for signature on behalf of all States Members of the United Nations, and also on behalf of any other State invited to attend the Conference of Plenipotentiaries on the Status of Refugees and Stateless Persons or to which an invitation to sign will have been addressed by the General Assembly. It shall be ratified and the instruments of ratification shall be deposited with the Secretary-General of the United Nations.
3. This Convention shall be open from 28 July 1951 for accession by the States referred to in paragraph 2 of this article. Accession shall be effected by the deposit of an instrument of accession with the Secretary-General of the United Nations.

Article 40. – Territorial Application Clause

1. Any State may, at the time of signature, ratification or accession, declare that this Convention shall extend to all or any of the territories for the international relations of which it is responsible. Such a declaration shall take effect when the Convention enters into force for the State concerned.
2. At any time thereafter any such extension shall be made by notification addressed to the Secretary-General of the United Nations and shall take effect as from the ninetieth day after the day of receipt by the Secretary- General of the United Nations of this notification, or as from the date of entry into force of the Convention for the State concerned, whichever is the later.
3. With respect to those territories to which this Convention is not extended at the time of signature, ratification or accession, each State concerned shall consider the possibility of taking the necessary steps in order to extend the application of this Convention to such territories, subject, where necessary for constitutional reasons, to the consent of the Governments of such territories.

Article 41. – Federal Clause

In the case of a Federal or non-unitary State, the following provisions shall apply:

(a) With respect to those articles of this Convention that come within the legislative jurisdiction of the federal legislative authority, the obligations of the Federal Government shall to this extent be the same as those of parties which are not Federal States;

(b) With respect to those articles of this Convention that come within the legislative jurisdiction of constituent States, provinces or cantons which are not, under the constitutional system of the Federation, bound to take legislative action, the Federal Government shall bring such articles with a favourable recommendation to the notice of the appropriate authorities of States, provinces or cantons at the earliest possible moment;

(c) A Federal State Party to this Convention shall, at the request of any other Contracting State transmitted through the Secretary-General of the United Nations, supply a statement of the law and practice of the Federation and its constituent units in regard to any particular provision of the Convention showing the extent to which effect has been given to that provision by legislative or other action.

Article 42. – Reservations

1. At the time of signature, ratification or accession, any State may make reservations to articles of the Convention other than to articles 1, 3, 4, 16 (1), 33, 36–46 inclusive.
2. Any State making a reservation in accordance with paragraph I of this article may at any time withdraw the reservation by a communication to that effect addressed to the Secretary-General of the United Nations.

Article 43. – Entry into Force

1. This Convention shall come into force on the ninetieth day following the day of deposit of the sixth instrument of ratification or accession.
2. For each State ratifying or acceding to the Convention after the deposit of the sixth instrument of ratification or accession, the Convention shall enter into force on the ninetieth day following the date of deposit by such State of its instrument of ratification or accession.

Article 44. – Denunciation

1. Any Contracting State may denounce this Convention at any time by a notification addressed to the Secretary-General of the United Nations.
2. Such denunciation shall take effect for the Contracting State concerned one year from the date upon which it is received by the Secretary-General of the United Nations.
3. Any State which has made a declaration or notification under article 40 may, at any time thereafter, by a notification to the Secretary-General of the United Nations, declare that the Convention shall cease to extend to such territory one

year after the date of receipt of the notification by the Secretary-General.
Article 45. - Revision

1. Any Contracting State may request revision of this Convention at any time by a notification addressed to the Secretary-General of the United Nations.
2. The General Assembly of the United Nations shall recommend the steps, if any, to be taken in respect of such request.

Article 46. –Notifications by the Secretary-General of the United Nations

The Secretary-General of the United Nations shall inform all Members of the United Nations and non-member States referred to in article 39:

(a) Of declarations and notifications in accordance with section B of article 1;
(b) Of signatures, ratifications and accessions in accordance with article 39;
(c) Of declarations and notifications in accordance with article 40;
(d) Of reservations and withdrawals in accordance with article 42;
(e) Of the date on which this Convention will come into force in accordance with article 43;
(f) Of denunciations and notifications in accordance with article 44;
(g) Of requests for revision in accordance with article 45.

IN FAITH WHEREOF the undersigned, duly authorized, have signed this Convention on behalf of their respective Governments.

DONE at Geneva, this twenty-eighth day of July, one thousand nine hundred and fifty-one, in a single copy, of which the English and French texts are equally authentic and which shall remain deposited in the archives of the United Nations, and certified true copies of which shall be delivered to all Members of the United Nations and to the non-member States referred to in article 39.

States Parties to the Protocol establishing an African Court on Human and Peoples' Rights.

Algeria, Burkina Faso, Burundi, Côte d'Ivoire, the Comoros, Gabon, the Gambia, Ghana, Kenya, Lesotho, Libya, Mali, Mauritius, Mozambique, Niger, Nigeria, Rwanda, Senegal, South Africa, Togo, and Uganda.

Appendix VI

Protocol Relating to the Status of Refugees

Done at New York, on 31st January 1967

In accordance with article VIII, paragraph 1, the Protocol came into force on 4 October 1967.

Article I

GENERAL PROVISION

1. The States Parties to the present Protocol undertake to apply articles 2 to 34 inclusive of the Convention to refugees as hereinafter defined.
2. For the purpose of the present Protocol, the term "refugee" shall, except as regards the application of paragraph 3 of this article, mean any person within the definition of article 1 of the Convention as if the words "As a result of events occurring before 1 January 1951 and ..." and the words "... as a result of such events", in article 1 A (2) were omitted.
3. The present Protocol shall be applied by the States Parties hereto without any geographic limitation, save that existing declarations made by States already Parties to the Convention in accordance with article 1 B (1) (a) of the Convention, shall, unless extended under article 1 B (2) thereof, apply also under the present Protocol.

Article II

CO-OPERATION OF THE NATIONAL AUTHORITIES WITH THE UNITED NATIONS

1. The States Parties to the present Protocol undertake to co-operate with the Office of the United Nations High Commissioner for Refugees, or any other agency of the United Nations which may succeed it, in the exercise of its functions, and shall in particular facilitate its duty of supervising the application of the provisions of the present Protocol.
2. In order to enable the Office of the High Commissioner, or any other agency of the United Nations which may succeed it, to make reports to the competent organs of the United Nations, the States Parties to the present Protocol undertake to provide them with the information and statistical data requested, in the appropriate form, concerning:

   (a) The condition of refugees;
   (b) The implementation of the present Protocol;
   (c) Laws, regulations and decrees which are, or may hereafter be, in force relating to refugees.

Article III

INFORMATION ON NATIONAL LEGISLATION

The States Parties to the present Protocol shall communicate to the Secretary-General of the United Nations the laws and regulations which they may adopt to ensure the application of the present Protocol.

Article IV

SETTLEMENT OF DISPUTES

Any dispute between States Parties to the present Protocol which relates to its interpretation or application and which cannot be settled by other means shall be referred to the International Court of Justice at the request of any one of the parties to the dispute.

Article V

ACCESSION

The present Protocol shall be open for accession on behalf of all States Parties to the Convention and of any other State Member of the United Nations or member of any of the specialized agencies or to which an invitation to accede may have been addressed by the General Assembly of the United Nations. Accession shall be effected by the deposit of an instrument of accession with the Secretary-General of the United Nations.

Article VI

FEDERAL CLAUSE

In the case of a Federal or non-unitary State, the following provisions shall apply:

(a) With respect to those articles of the Convention to be applied in accordance with article I, paragraph 1, of the present Protocol that come within the legislative jurisdiction of the federal legislative authority, the obligations of the Federal Government shall to this extent be the same as those of States Parties which are not Federal States;
(b) With respect to those articles of the Convention to be applied in accordance with article I, paragraph 1, of the present Protocol that come within the legislative jurisdiction of constituent States, provinces or cantons which are not, under the constitutional system of the federation, bound to take legislative action, the Federal Government shall bring such articles with a favourable recommendation to the notice of the appropriate authorities of States, provinces or cantons at the earliest possible moment;
(c) A Federal State Party to the present Protocol shall, at the request of any other State Party hereto transmitted through the Secretary-General of the United Nations, supply a statement of the law and practice of the Federation and its constituent units in regard to any particular provision of the Convention to be applied in accordance with article I, paragraph 1, of the present Protocol, showing the extent to which effect has been given to that provision by legislative or other action.

Article VII

RESERVATIONS AND DECLARATIONS

1. At the time of accession, any State may make reservations in respect of article IV of the present Protocol and in respect of the application in accordance with article I of the present Protocol of any provisions of the Convention other than those contained in articles 1, 3, 4, 16 (1) and 33 thereof, provided that in the case of a State Party to the Convention reservations made under this article shall not extend to refugees in respect of whom the Convention applies.
2. Reservations made by States Parties to the Convention in accordance with article 42 thereof shall, unless withdrawn, be applicable in relation to their obligations under the present Protocol.
3. Any State making a reservation in accordance with paragraph 1 of this article may at any time withdraw such reservation by a communication to that effect addressed to the Secretary-General of the United Nations.

4. Declaration made under article 40, paragraphs 1 and 2, of the Convention by a State Party thereto which accedes to the present Protocol shall be deemed to apply in respect of the present Protocol, unless upon accession a notification to the contrary is addressed by the State Party concerned to the Secretary-General of the United Nations. The provisions of article 40, paragraphs 2 and 3, and of article 44, paragraph 3, of the Convention shall be deemed to apply mutatis mutandis to the present Protocol.

Article VIII

ENTRY INTO FORCE

1. The present Protocol shall come into force on the day of deposit of the sixth instrument of accession.
2. For each State acceding to the Protocol after the deposit of the sixth instrument of accession, the Protocol shall come into force on the date of deposit by such State of its instrument of accession.

Article IX

DENUNCIATION

1. Any State Party hereto may denounce this Protocol at any time by a notification addressed to the Secretary-General of the United Nations.
2. Such denunciation shall take effect for the State Party concerned one year from the date on which it is received by the Secretary-General of the United Nations.

Article X

NOTIFICATIONS BY THE SECRETARY-GENERAL OF THE UNITED NATIONS

The Secretary-General of the United Nations shall inform the States referred to in article V above of the date of entry into force, accessions, reservations and withdrawals of reservations to and denunciations of the present Protocol, and of declarations and notifications relating hereto.

Article XI

DEPOSIT IN THE ARCHIVES OF THE SECRETARIAT OF THE UNITED NATIONS

A copy of the present Protocol, of which the Chinese, English, French, Russian and Spanish texts are equally authentic, signed by the President of the General Assembly and by the Secretary-General of the United Nations, shall be deposited in the archives of the Secretariat of the United Nations. The Secretary-General will transmit certified copies thereof to all States Members of the United Nations and to the other States referred to in article V above.

Appendix VII

<table>
<tr><td>AFRICAN UNION</td><td rowspan="2"></td><td>UNION AFRICAINE</td></tr>
<tr><td>الاتحاد الأفريقي</td><td>UNIÃO AFRICANA</td></tr>
<tr><td colspan="3">AFRICAN COURT ON HUMAN AND PEOPLES' RIGHTS
COUR AFRICAINE DES DROITS DE L'HOMME ET DES PEUPLES</td></tr>
</table>

FINAL RULES OF COURT FOR PUBLICATION AFTER HARMONIZATION*

PREAMBLE

The Court,

In accordance with the African Charter on Human and Peoples' Rights of 27 June 1981 and the Protocol thereof on the Establishment of an African Court on Human and Peoples' Rights dated 9 June 1998,

And in pursuance of article 33 of the Protocol,

Adopts the following Rules of Court which shall be known as the "Interim Rules of Court".

* These Internal Rules shall replace the Interim Rules of Procedure of 20 June 2008, following the harmonization of the Interim Rules of the Court and the Commission carried out during joint meetings in July 2009 in Arusha, October 2009 in Dakar and April 2010 in Arusha.

Rule 1
Definitions

For the purposes of these Rules, unless the context otherwise indicates:

a. "Assembly" means the Assembly of Heads of State and Government of the African Union;
b. "Charter" means the African Charter on Human and Peoples' Rights;
c. "Commission" means the African Commission on Human and Peoples' Rights;
d. "Constitutive Act" means the Constitutive Act of the African Union;
e. "Court" means the African Court on Human and Peoples' Rights;
f. "Executive Council" means the Executive Council of the African Union;
g. "Judge" means a Member of the Court;
h. "Member State" means a Member State of the African Union;
i. "President" means the President of the Court;
j. "Protocol" means the Protocol to the African Charter on Human and Peoples' Rights on the Establishment of an African Court on Human and Peoples' Rights;
k. "Registrar" means the Registrar of the Court;
l. "Registry" means Registry of the Court;
m. "Rules" mean the present Rules;
n. "State Party" means a State Party to the Protocol to the African Charter on Human and Peoples' Rights on the Establishment of an African Court on Human and Peoples' Rights;
o. "Vice President" means the Vice President of the Court.

PART I – THE COURT

CHAPTER I – MEMBERS OF THE COURT

Rule 2
Term of Office

1. The newly elected Judges will assume duty on the first day of the first ordinary session following their election. Before assuming duty, the elected Judges shall take an oath of office or make a declaration in accordance with Rule 4 of these Rules.
2. Notwithstanding the foregoing sub-rule, outgoing Members of the Court shall remain in office until such time as they are replaced; after they are replaced, they shall continue to sit until the completion of all stages of any case in which the Court has met for an oral hearing prior to the date of replacement.

Rule 3
Precedence

1. The Members of the Court, in the exercise of their functions, are of equal status, irrespective of age, date of election or length of service.
2. Members of the Court shall, except as provided in sub-rule 4 and 5 of this Rule, take precedence according to the date on which their terms of office respectively began pursuant to Rule 2 of these Rules.
3. Members of the Court who assume duty on the same date shall take precedence, in relation to one another, according to seniority of age.
4. A Member of the Court who is re-elected to a new term of office which is continuous with his/her previous term shall retain his/her precedence.
5. The President and the Vice-President of the Court, while holding these offices, shall take precedence before all other Members of the Court.
6. The Member of the Court who is, in accordance with the foregoing sub-rules, next in precedence after the President and the Vice-President, is in these Rules designated as "the Senior Member of the Court". Whenever that Member is unable to act, the Member of the Court who is next after him in precedence and able to act shall be considered the Senior Member of the Court.

Rule 4
Oath of Office or Solemn Declaration

1. Pursuant to article 16 of the Protocol, each Member of the Court shall make the following oath or solemn declaration: "I .... (full names of Judge) do swear or solemnly declare that I will perform my duties and exercise my powers as a Member of the Court honourably, faithfully, impartially and conscientiously, and that I will preserve the confidentiality of its deliberations even after my term of office has expired".
2. This oath/declaration shall be taken/made in a public sitting as soon as possible after his/her election, and if necessary, a special public sitting shall be held for this purpose.
3. A Member of the Court who is re-elected shall take/make a new oath/declaration only if his/her new term is not continuous with his/her previous one.

Rule 5
Incompatibility

1. In accordance with the terms of article 18 of the Protocol, during their term in office, no Members of the Court shall participate in any other activity of a nature that will compromise the independence and impartiality of such a Judge or the demands of the office.

2. In particular, the Members of the Court may not hold political, diplomatic or administrative positions or function as government legal advisers at the national level.
3. Each Member of the Court shall declare any other activities to the Court.

Rule 6
Resignation

1. In the event of the resignation of a Member of the Court, the notice of resignation shall be tendered to the President of the Court, who shall notify the Chairperson of the African Union Commission of the same. Upon the latter notification, the seat shall be considered vacant.
2. Where the Member of the Court who decides to resign is the President, he/she shall announce his/her decision to the Vice President who shall notify the Chairperson of the African Union Commission and the resignation shall take effect in accordance with the terms of sub-rule 1 of the present Rule.

Rule 7
Suspension or Removal

1. Where the application of article 19(1) of the Protocol is under consideration, the President or, if the circumstances so require, the Vice-President, shall inform the Member of the Court concerned accordingly, in a written statement which shall include the grounds thereof and any relevant evidence. He/she shall, subsequently, at a private session of the Court specially convened for the purpose, be afforded an opportunity of making a statement, of furnishing any information or explanations he/she wishes to give, and of supplying answers, orally or in writing, to any questions put to him/her. At a further private session, at which the Member of the Court concerned shall not be present, the matter shall be considered; each Member of the Court shall state his/her opinion and, if requested, a vote shall be taken.
2. Any decision to suspend or remove a Member of the Court shall be communicated to the Chairperson of the African Union Commission.

Rule 8
Inability to Sit, Exemption and Withdrawal

1. Any Member of the Court who is unable to attend a sitting of the Court shall notify the President as early as possible.
2. In accordance with article 22 of the Protocol, any Member of the Court who is a national of a State that is party to a case shall abstain from hearing that case.

3. A Member of the Court shall also abstain from hearing cases in which the State by virtue of which he/she was elected is a party.
4. No Member of the Court shall take part in the consideration of any case if:
   a) he/she has previously acted, in relation to the case, as agent, counsel or advocate for one of the parties, or as a member of a national or international court or a commission of inquiry or in any other capacity;
   b) he/she has a personal interest in the case, including a spousal, parental or other close family, personal or professional relationship, or a subordinate relationship with any of the parties;
   c) he/she has expressed opinions publicly, through the communications media, in writing, through his or her public actions or otherwise, that may, objectively adversely affect his or her impartiality;
   d) for any other reason, his/her independence or impartiality may, legitimately, be called into doubt;
5. If a Member intends to withdraw for any of the aforesaid reasons he/she shall, accordingly, notify the President of the Court, who shall exempt such Judge from participation in the hearing of the matter.
6. In the event of any doubt as to the existence of any of the grounds for withdrawal listed in this Rule, the Member concerned shall make his/her disclosures to the Court, and deliberations and voting on the matter shall be carried out in his/her absence.

CHAPTER II – THE OFFICE OF THE PRESIDENT AND VICE-PRESIDENT

Rule 9
Term of Office

1. The President and Vice President shall be elected for a period of two (2) years and may be re-elected only once. However, none of them may continue to hold office should they cease to be a Member of the Court.
2. The term of office of the President and Vice President shall begin to run on the commencement date of the terms of office of the Members of the Court elected in a biennial election, pursuant to Rule 2 of these Rules.
3. The elections of the President and Vice-President shall be held on the above mentioned date or shortly thereafter. The outgoing President or Vice-President, if still a Member of the Court, shall continue to exercise the functions of his/her office until the election has taken place.
4. If for any reason, the President or the Vice President ceases to be a Member of the Court before the expiry of his/her term of office, the Court shall elect a successor for the remainder of the term.

Rule 10
Elections

1. If on the date of the election to the Presidency, the outgoing President is still a Member of the Court, he/she shall conduct the election. If he/she has ceased to be a Member of the Court, is unable to act, or is himself/herself a candidate, the election shall be conducted by the Member of the Court exercising the functions of the Presidency pursuant to Rule 12, sub-rule 1 of these Rules.
2. The vote shall be taken by secret ballot after the Member of the Court acting as President indicates the number of votes required to be elected.
3. The Member of the Court obtaining the votes of the absolute majority of all the Judges of the Court shall be declared elected.
4. If no Member of the Court obtains the absolute majority required during the first ballot, the Judge having obtained the least number of votes shall withdraw. If during the second ballot no candidate receives the majority required, a third round shall take place between the two candidates having obtained the greatest number of votes. An additional round or additional rounds shall take place until one candidate has achieved the required majority. In the event of a tied vote, preference shall be given to the Judge having precedence under the terms of Rule 3 of these Rules.
5. The Member of the Court who is elected President shall take office immediately.
6. The incoming President shall conduct the election of the Vice President, either at the same or at the following sitting. The provisions of sub-rule 2 to 5 above shall also apply to this election.

Rule 11
Functions

1. The functions of the President are to:
   a) represent the Court;
   b) preside at the sittings of the Court;
   c) direct the work and supervise the administration of the Court;
   d) promote the activities of the Court;
   e) present a detailed Annual Report to the Court on the Court's activities and on his/her own activities as President over the year;
   f) pursuant to article 31 of the Protocol, prepare and present an Annual Report to the Assembly;
   g) carry out any other duties assigned to him/her by the Protocol or the present Rules, or entrusted to him/her by the Court.

2. The Vice-President shall assist the President in performing his/her functions. He/she shall replace him/her in the event of inability to act or of a vacancy in the presidency, or at the request of the President.

Rule 12
Exercise of Functions

1. In the event of the office of the President becoming vacant or the President being unable to act, his/her functions shall be performed by the Vice-President and, in default, by the Senior Member of the Court.
2. When the President is precluded from hearing a case under the terms of article 22 of the Protocol and Rule 8 hereof, he/she shall continue to act as President for all purposes save in respect of the said case; the same shall apply to the Vice President.
3. The President shall take the necessary measures to ensure the continuous exercise of the functions of the presidency at the Seat of the Court. In the event of his/her absence, he/she may, so far as is compatible with the Protocol and the present Rules, arrange for these functions to be exercised by the Vice President or in default, by the Senior Member of the Court.
4. If the President decides to resign the Presidency, he/she shall communicate his decision in writing to the Court through the Vice President, or, failing that, through the Senior Member of the Court. If the Vice President decides to resign from his office, he/she shall communicate his/her decision to the President.

Rule 13
Adequate Gender Representation, Main Legal Traditions and Main Regions of Africa

In electing to office or making appointments governed by this Chapter and Part II of these Rules, the Members of the Court shall pursue, to the greatest extent possible, a policy aimed at securing a balanced representation of gender, the principal legal traditions and the main regions of Africa.

CHAPTER III – INTERNAL FUNCTIONING OF THE COURT

Rule 14
Ordinary Sessions

1. The Court shall hold four ordinary sessions per annum, each of which shall last about fifteen days.

2. The sessions of the Court shall be convened on the dates set by the Court during its previous session. Under exceptional circumstances, the President may, in consultation with the other Members of the Court, change the dates of a session.
3. The invitation letter shall indicate the dates, agenda, duration and venue of the session as well as any other relevant information. The letter shall be sent to the Members of the Court at least thirty (30) calendar days before the session is held.

Rule 15
Extraordinary Sessions

1. Extraordinary sessions may also be convened by the President on his own initiative or at the request of a majority of the Members of the Court.
2. The invitation letter shall indicate the dates, agenda, duration and venue of the sessions as well as any other relevant information. The letter shall be sent to the Members of the Court at least fifteen (15) calendar days before the session is held.

Rule 16
Venue of Meeting

The sessions shall normally take place at the Seat of the Court. However, the Court may, pursuant to article 25 (1) of the Protocol, decide to sit in the territory of any other Member State of the African Union.

Rule 17
Quorum

1. The quorum of seven (7) Judges stipulated under article 23 of the Protocol shall apply to all sittings of the Court.
2. If at the commencement of a sitting, the quorum is not met, the President shall adjourn it.
3. If during a sitting, the quorum ceases to exist, the President shall adjourn the sitting.

Rule 18
Official and Working Languages

1. The official languages of the Court shall be the official languages of the African Union.
2. The working languages of the Court shall be the working languages of the African Union. However, the Court may, whenever the need arises, select one or more of these languages as its working languages.

3. Notwithstanding the provisions of sub-rules1 and 2 of this Rule, the Court may permit any person appearing before it to use a language of his or her choice, if it is shown that he or she does not have sufficient knowledge of any of the official languages of the Court.
4. The terms and conditions for obtaining interpreters for implementation of sub-rule 3 of this Rule shall be determined by the Court.

Rule 19
Internal Judicial Practice and Practice Directions

Subject to the provisions of the Protocol and these Rules, the judicial practice and procedure followed by the Court shall be governed by relevant resolutions or practice directions of the Court.

PART II: THE REGISTRY

Rule 20
Composition and Organisation of the Registry

1. The Registry shall comprise the Registrar, the Deputy Registrar, and such other staff as the Court may require for the effective exercise of its functions.
2. The Court shall prescribe the organisation of the Registry.
3. Instructions for the Registry shall be drawn up by the Court.
4. The staff of the Registry shall be subject to Staff Rules and Regulations drawn up by the Court.

Rule 21
Appointment and Term of Office of the Registrar

1. The Court shall appoint its Registrar.
2. Candidates for the position of Registrar shall be of the highest moral standing and shall possess the necessary legal, administrative and linguistic knowledge and experience for the discharge of the function s linked to the post.
3. The Registrar shall be appointed for a term of five years. He/she may be re-appointed.
4. The process of recruiting the Registrar shall be conducted in accordance with the procedure established by the Court and consistent with the norms of the African Union.
5. The applications shall include all relevant information concerning the applicant, and in particular, information as to age, nationality, sex, current occupation, academic qualifications as well as the knowledge and experience required in sub-rule 2 above.

Rule 22
Appointment and Term of Office of the Deputy Registrar

1. The Court shall appoint a Deputy Registrar.
2. The provisions of Rule 21 of these Rules shall apply to the appointment and term of office of the Deputy Registrar.

Rule 23
Oath/Solemn Declaration

1. Upon assumption of office, the Registrar shall take the following oath/make the following declaration before the Court: "I ... (full names of Registrar) swear/solemnly declare that I will discharge the duties incumbent upon me as Registrar of the African Court on Human and Peoples' Rights with all loyalty, discretion and good conscience; that I will preserve the confidentiality of the information to which I have access in the exercise, or due to the exercise of my functions, and that I will faithfully observe all the provisions of the Protocol and of the Rules of the Court."
2. Upon assumption of office, the Deputy Registrar shall take a similar oath or make a similar declaration before the Court.
3. These oaths/declarations shall be recorded in the minutes of the Court.

Rule 24
Appointment of the Other Staff of the Registry

1. Other staff members of the Registry shall be appointed by the Court under such terms and conditions as it shall determine in accordance with the norms of the African Union. Appointments to such other positions as the Court shall determine may, however, be made by the Registrar with the approval of the President.
2. Upon assumption of duty, every staff member shall take the following oath/make the following declaration before the President, in the presence of the Registrar: "I .... (full names of official) swear/solemnly declare that I will discharge the duties incumbent upon me as an official of the Registry of the African Court on Human and Peoples' Rights with all loyalty, discretion and good conscience; that I will preserve the confidentiality of the information to which I have access in the exercise or due to the exercise of my functions, and that I will faithfully observe all the provisions of the Protocol and of the Rules of the Court."

Rule 25
Functions of the Registrar

1. The Registrar shall assist the Court in the exercise of its judicial function and shall be in charge of the general administration of the Court's Registry. He or

she shall be responsible for the supervision and coordination of all the operations and activities of the Registry.

2. In the discharge of his/her duties, the Registrar shall:
   a) keep, in such form as may be prescribed by the Court, a General List of all cases, entered and numbered in the order in which the documents instituting proceedings or requesting an advisory opinion are received in the Registry;
   b) be the regular channel of communication to and from the Court, and in particular effect all communications, notifications and transmission of documents required by the Protocol or by these Rules and ensure that the date of dispatch and receipt thereof are readily verifiable;
   c) transmit to the parties copies of all pleadings and documents annexed thereto upon receipt thereof in the Registry;
   d) be present, in person or by his/her duly qualified representative, at the sittings of the Court, and be responsible for the preparation of minutes of such sittings;
   e) sign the minutes referred to in subparagraph (d) above;
   f) inspect documentation submitted to the Court to establish authenticity thereof;
   g) have custody of the seal, the official stamp and all the records and archives of the Court;
   h) make arrangements for such provision or verification of translations and interpretations into the Court's official languages as the Court may require;
   i) be responsible for the printing and publication of the Court's judgments, advisory opinions and orders, the pleadings and statements, and minutes of public sittings in each case, and of such other documents as the Court may direct to be published;
   j) communicate to the government of the country in which the Court is sitting, and any other governments which may be concerned, the necessary information as to the persons from time to time entitled, under the Protocol and any relevant agreements, to privileges, immunities, or facilities;
   k) transmit documents to the Members of the Court, States party to the Protocol and to the Chairperson of the African Union Commission as well as other organs of the African Union where required;
   l) deal with enquiries concerning the Court and its work;
   m) prepare the draft budget of the Court;
   n) be responsible for the sound management of all accounts and financial administration in accordance with the applicable financial rules of the African Union and the financial regulations of the Court;
   o) assist in maintaining relations between the Court and the departments of the African Union Commission as well as those of the other organs of the African Union;

p) ensure that information concerning the Court and its activities is made accessible to governments, the highest national courts of justice, professional associations, learned societies, faculties and schools of law, and public information media;

3. The Court may entrust additional duties to the Registrar.
4. In the exercise of his/her functions, the Registrar shall work under the direction and supervision of the President and be answerable to the Court.

PART III: JURISDICTION

Rule 26
Jurisdiction

1. Pursuant to the Protocol, the Court shall have jurisdiction:
   a) to deal with all cases and all disputes submitted to it concerning interpretation and application of the Charter, the Protocol and any other relevant human rights instrument ratified by the States concerned;
   b) to render an advisory opinion on any legal matter relating to the Charter or any other relevant human rights instruments, provided that the subject of the opinion is not related to a matter being examined by the Commission;
   c) to promote amicable settlement in cases pending before it in accordance with the provisions of the Charter;
   d) to interpret a judgment rendered by itself; and
   e) to review its own judgment in light of new evidence in conformity with Rule 67 of these Rules.
2. In the event of a dispute as to whether the Court has jurisdiction, the Court shall decide.

PART IV: CONTENTIOUS PROCEDURE

CHAPTER I: GENERAL PROVISIONS

Rule 27
Phases of Proceedings

1. The procedure before the Court shall consist of written, and if necessary, oral proceedings.
2. The written procedure shall consist of the communication to the Court, the parties, as well as the Commission, as appropriate, of applications, statements of the case, defences and observations and of replies if any, as well as all papers and documents in support, or of certified copies thereof.

3. The oral proceedings shall consist of a hearing by the Court of representatives of parties, witnesses, experts, or such other persons as the Court may decide to hear.

Rule 28
Representation

Every party to a case shall be entitled to be represented or to be assisted by legal counsel and/or by any other person of the party's choice.

Rule 29
Relations between the Court and the Commission

1.
   a. In pursuance of Article 2 of the Protocol, the Court shall meet with the Commission at least once a year and whenever necessary to ensure a good working relationship between the two institutions.
   b. The Bureau of the Court may meet the Bureau of the Commission as often as necessary.
2. In accordance with Article 33 of the Protocol, the Court shall consult the Commission, as appropriate, on any amendment of its rules, and any issues of procedure, governing the relationship between the two institutions.
3.
   a. In a case brought before the Court by the Commission under Article 5(1)(a) of the Protocol, its application shall be accompanied by its Report as well as all documents pertaining to the proceedings.
   b. The Court may, if necessary, hear one or more Commissioners assisted by such Legal Officers of the Commission's Secretariat and/or experts as the Commission shall designate or appoint.
   c. The Court may also, if it deems it necessary, hear, under Rule 45 of the Rules, the individual or NGO that initiated a communication to the Commission pursuant to Article 55 of the Charter.
4. Where, pursuant to Article 6(1) of the Protocol, the Court decides to solicit the opinion of the Commission on the admissibility of a case, it shall transmit to the Commission a copy of the pertinent sections of the case file, indicating the time limit within which it wishes to receive the opinion.
5.
   a. Where the Court decides to transfer a case to the Commission pursuant to Article 6(3) of the Protocol, it shall transmit to the Commission a copy of the entire pleadings so far filed in the matter accompanied by a summary report. At the request of the Commission, the Court may also transmit the original case file.
   b. The Registrar shall immediately notify the parties who were before the Court about the transfer of the case to the Commission.

6. For the purpose of examining an application brought before it, relating to issues in a communication before the Commission, the Court shall ascertain that the said communication has been formally withdrawn.

Rule 30
Legal Costs

Unless otherwise decided by the Court, each party shall bear its own costs.

Rule 31
Legal Assistance

Pursuant to article 10 (2) of the Protocol, the Court may, in the interest of justice and within the limits of the financial resources available, decide to provide free legal representation and/or legal assistance to any party.

Rule 32
Cooperation of the States

1. The States Parties to a case have the obligation to cooperate so as to ensure that all notices, communications or summonses addressed to persons residing in their territory or falling under their jurisdiction are duly executed.
2. The same rule shall apply to any proceeding that the Court decides to conduct or order in the territory of a State Party to a case.
3. When the performance of any of the measures referred to in the preceding paragraphs requires the cooperation of any other State, the President shall request the government concerned to provide the requisite assistance.

CHAPTER II: WRITTEN PROCEEDINGS

Rule 33
Access to the Court

1. Pursuant to the provisions of articles 5 and 34 (6) of the Protocol, the following are entitled to submit cases to the Court:
   a. The Commission;
   b. The State Party which has lodged an application to the Commission;
   c. The State Party against which an application has been lodged at the Commission;
   d. The State Party whose citizen is a victim of a human rights violation;
   e. An African Intergovernmental Organization;
   f. An individual or a Non-Governmental Organization which has observer status before the Commission provided the requirements of article 34(6) of the Protocol are met.

2. In accordance with article 5(2) of the Protocol, a State Party which has an interest in a case may submit a request to the Court to be permitted to join in accordance with the procedure established in Rule 53 of these Rules.

Rule 34
Commencement of Proceedings

1. The Applicant shall file in the Court Registry, one (1) copy of the application containing a summary of the facts of the case and of the evidence intended to be adduced.

The said application shall be signed by the Applicant or by his/her representative.

The Registrar shall acknowledge receipt of the application.

2. Any application addressed to the Court shall give clear particulars of the Applicant and of the party or parties against whom such application has been brought. The application shall also contain the names and addresses of the persons designated as the Applicant's representatives.
3. The application shall be written in one of the official languages of the Court, and the original forwarded to the Court Registry.
4. The application shall specify the alleged violation, evidence of exhaustion of local remedies or of the inordinate delay of such local remedies as well as the orders or the injunctions sought. All applications filed by individuals and Non-Governmental Organizations shall meet the other admissibility conditions as set out in article 56 of the Charter and Rule 40 of these Rules.
5. Any Applicant who on his/her own behalf or on behalf of the victim wishes to be granted reparation pursuant to article 27(1) of the Protocol shall include the request for the reparation in the application in accordance with sub-rule 4 above. The amount of the reparation and the evidence relating thereto may be submitted subsequently within the time limit set by the Court.
6. The Registrar shall effect service of the application on the other party by registered post together with a request to acknowledge receipt.

Rule 35
Transmission of Applications

1. Upon the receipt of an application filed in accordance with article 5(1) and (3) of the Protocol, the Registrar shall transmit a copy thereof together with any annexes, to the President and other Members of the Court.
2. Unless otherwise decided by the Court, the Registrar shall forward copies of the application where applicable to the:
   a) State Party against which the application has been filed, in accordance with Rule 34 (6) of these Rules;
   b) State Party whose citizen is a victim of the alleged violation;

   c) State Party against which an application has been filed at the Commission;
   d) Commission;
   e) Individual or legal entity or the Non-Governmental Organization that has filed an application at the Commission by virtue of article 55 of the Charter.
3. The Registrar shall also inform the Chairperson of the African Union Commission and through him/her, the Executive Council of the African Union, and all the other States Parties to the Protocol, of the filing of the application;
4. In forwarding applications as stipulated in sub-rules 2 and 3 of this Rule, the Registrar shall invite:
   a) the Respondent State Party to indicate, within thirty (30) days of receipt of the application, the names and addresses of its representatives;
   b) any other State Party that may wish to intervene in the proceedings under article 5(2) of the Protocol, to inform the Registrar accordingly, within the time stipulated in Rule 53;
   c) if applicable, the Commission to forward to the Registrar, within thirty (30) days the names and addresses of its representatives;

Rule 36
Registration and Transmission of Pleadings

1. All pleadings received by the Registrar shall be registered and a copy thereof transmitted to the other party.
2. The Registrar shall acknowledge receipt of all such pleadings.

Rule 37
Time Limit for Reply

The State Party against which an application has been filed shall respond thereto within sixty (60) days provided that the Court may, if the need arises, grant an extension of time.

Rule 38
Dismissal of Application without Merit

Whenever the Court finds that there is no merit in an application, it shall dismiss such application giving reasons for its decision, and may not have to summon the parties to the hearing, provided its decision and the reasons thereof are communicated to all the parties.

Rule 39
Preliminary Examination of the Competence of the Court and of Admissibility of Applications

1. The Court shall conduct preliminary examination of its jurisdiction and the admissibility of the application in accordance with articles 50 and 56 of the Charter, and Rule 40 of these Rules.
2. Pursuant to sub-rule 1 of this Rule, the Court may request the parties to submit any factual information, documents or other material considered by the Court to be relevant.

Rule 40
Conditions for Admissibility of Applications

Pursuant to the provisions of article 56 of the Charter to which article 6(2) of the Protocol refers, applications to the Court shall comply with the following conditions:

1. disclose the identity of the Applicant notwithstanding the latter's request for anonymity;
2. comply with the Constitutive Act of the Union and the Charter;
3. not contain any disparaging or insulting language;
4. not be based exclusively on news disseminated through the mass media;
5. be filed after exhausting local remedies, if any, unless it is obvious that this procedure is unduly prolonged;
6. be filed within a reasonable time from the date local remedies were exhausted or from the date set by the Court as being the commencement of the time limit within which it shall be seized with the matter; and
7. not raise any mater or issues previously settled by the parties in accordance with the principles of the Charter of the United Nations, the Constitutive Act of the African Union, the provisions of the Charter or of any legal instrument of the African Union.

Rule 41
Filing of Documents

The Court may, before the commencement of or during the course of the proceedings, call upon the parties to file any pertinent document or to provide any relevant explanation. The Court shall formally note any refusal to comply.

CHAPTER III: ORAL PROCEEDINGS

Rule 42
Fixing of the Date of Hearing

When the case is ready for hearing, the President shall, after consulting the parties or the representatives of the Commission, if applicable, fix the date of the hearing. The Registrar shall notify them accordingly.

Rule 43
Public Hearings

1. Cases shall be heard in open court.
2. However, the Court may, of its own accord or at the request of a party, hold its hearings *in camera* if, in its opinion, it is in the interest of public morality, safety or public order to do so.
3. Whenever the Court orders that any proceedings shall not be conducted in public, the Court shall give one or more of the reasons specified in sub-rule 2 of this Rule as the basis of its decision. The parties or their legal representatives shall be permitted to be present and heard *in camera*.

Rule 44
Conduct of Hearings

The Presiding Judge shall conduct the hearing. He/she shall prescribe the order in which the representatives of the parties and where applicable, the representatives of the Commission, are to be heard.

Rule 45
Measures for Taking Evidence

1. The Court may, of its own accord, or at the request of a party, or the representatives of the Commission, where applicable, obtain any evidence which in its opinion may provide clarification of the facts of a case. The Court may, *inter alia*, decide to hear as a witness or expert or in any other capacity any person whose evidence, assertions or statements it deems likely to assist it in carrying out its task.
2. The Court may ask any person or institution of its choice to obtain information, express an opinion or submit a report to it on any specific point.
3. The Court may, at any time during the proceedings, assign one or more of its Members to conduct an enquiry, carry out a visit to the scene or take evidence in any other manner.

Rule 46
Witnesses, Experts and Other Persons

1. The Registrar shall issue summons to any witness, expert or other person the Court decides to hear.
2. After verification of his/her identity and before giving evidence, every witness shall take the following oath or make the following solemn declaration:

"I swear/solemnly declare upon my honour and conscience that I will tell the truth, the whole truth and nothing but the truth."

The oath or solemn declaration shall be recorded.

3. After verification of his/her identity and before carrying out his/her task, every expert shall take the following oath or make the following solemn declaration:

"I swear/solemnly declare that I will discharge my functions as expert on my honour and conscience."

The oath or solemn declaration shall be recorded.

4. The oath or declaration referred to in sub-rules 2 and 3 of this Rule shall be taken or made before the Court.
5. The Court shall rule on any challenge arising from an objection to a witness or expert.

Rule 47
Questions Put During Hearings

1. The Presiding Judge, or any Judge, may put questions to the representatives of the parties, and if applicable, the representative of the Commission, the witnesses, experts, and other persons appearing before the Court.
2. The witnesses, experts and other persons who appear before the Court may be examined by the representatives of the parties, and if applicable by the representatives of the Commission. The persons referred to in this paragraph may be subjected to cross-examination, followed by a re-examination.

Rule 48
Verbatim Record of Hearings

1. The Registrar shall be responsible for making a verbatim record of each hearing. The verbatim record shall include the:
    a) composition of the Court at the hearing;
    b) list of the persons appearing before the Court;
    c) text of statements made, questions put and answers given;
    d) text of any decision delivered by the Court during the hearing.
2. The representatives of the parties, and the representatives of the Commission, if applicable, shall receive the verbatim record of their arguments, statements or evidence, in order that they may, under the responsibility of the

Registrar, make corrections, provided that such corrections do not affect the substance of what was said. The Registrar shall fix the time-limits granted for this purpose.
3. Once corrected, the verbatim record shall be signed by the President and the Registrar; and shall then constitute a true reflection of the proceedings.

Rule 49
Recording of Hearings

The proceedings of the hearing shall be recorded and such recordings shall be conserved in the archives of the Court.

Rule 50
New Evidence

No party may file additional evidence after the closure of pleadings except by leave of Court.

CHAPTER IV: SPECIFIC PROCEDURES

Rule 51
Interim Measures

1. Pursuant to article 27(2) of the Protocol, the Court may, at the request of a party, the Commission or on its own accord, prescribe to the parties any interim measure which it deems necessary to adopt in the interest of the parties or of justice.
2. In case of extreme urgency, the President may convene an extraordinary session of the Court to decide on measures to be taken. He/she may, in this regard, and by all reliable means, enlist the views of the Members not present.
3. The Court shall duly notify the parties to the case, the Commission, the Assembly, the Executive Council and the African Union Commission of the aforesaid interim measures.
4. In the Annual Report submitted by the Court to the Assembly pursuant to article 31 of the Protocol, the Court shall disclose the interim measures it ordered during the period under review. In the event of non-compliance with these measures by the State concerned, the Court shall make all such recommendations as it deems appropriate.
5. The Court may invite the parties to provide it with information on any issue relating to implementation of the interim measures adopted by it.

Rule 52
Preliminary Objections

1. Any party served with the application may raise preliminary objections to any part or parts thereof.
2. Preliminary objections shall be raised at the latest before the date fixed by the Court for the filing of the first set of pleadings to be submitted by the party who intends to raise the objections.
3. The submission of preliminary objections shall not cause the proceedings on the substantive case to be suspended unless the Court so decides. In any case, the Court shall rule on the objections or incorporate its ruling in its decision on the substantive case.
4. Every preliminary objection shall set out the facts and the law on which the objection is based as well as the submissions and a list of the documents in support, if any; it shall also specify any evidence which the party intends to produce. Certified copies of all supporting documents shall be attached.
5. Where a party raises a preliminary objection, the Court shall invite the other party to submit, its written observations in reply before ruling on the preliminary objection, the Court may decide to invite the parties to submit further observations in writing.
6. Before deciding on the preliminary objection, the Court may, on the request of a party, or of its own accord, decide to hold a hearing if it deems it necessary.
7. The Court shall give reasons for its ruling on the preliminary objection.

Rule 53
Intervention

1. An application for leave to intervene, in accordance with article 5 (2) of the Protocol shall be filed as soon as possible, and, in any case, before the closure of the written proceedings.
2. The application shall state the names of the Applicant's representatives. It shall specify the case to which it relates, and shall set out:
   a) the legal interest which, in the view of the State applying to intervene, has been affected;
   b) the precise object of the intervention; and
   c) the basis of the jurisdiction which, in the view of the State applying to intervene, exists between it and the parties to the case.
3. The application shall be accompanied by a list of the supporting documents attached thereto and shall be duly reasoned.
4. Certified copies of the application for leave to intervene shall be communicated forthwith to the parties to the case, who shall be entitled to submit their

written observations within a time-limit to be fixed by the Court, or by the President if the Court is not in session. The Registrar shall also transmit copies of the application to any other concerned entity mentioned in Rule 35 of these Rules.
5. If the Court rules that the application is admissible, it shall fix a time limit within which the intervening State shall submit its written observations. Such observations shall be forwarded by the Registrar to the parties to the case, who shall be entitled to file written observations in reply within the timeframe fixed by the Court.
6. The intervening State shall be entitled, in the course of the oral proceedings, if any, to present its submissions in respect of the subject of the intervention.

Rule 54
Joinder of Cases and Pleadings

The Court may at any stage of the pleadings either on its own volition or in response to an application by any of the parties, order the joinder of interrelated cases and pleadings where it deems it appropriate, both in fact and in law.

Rule 55
Judgments in Default

1. Whenever a party does not appear before the Court, or fails to defend its case, the Court may, on the application of the other party, pass judgment in default after it has satisfied itself that the defaulting party has been duly served with the application and all other documents pertinent to the proceedings.
2. Before acceding to the application of the party before it, the Court shall satisfy itself that it has jurisdiction in the case, and that the application is admissible and well founded in fact and in law.

Rule 56
Out-of-Court Settlement

1. Parties to a case may settle their dispute amicably at any time before the Court gives its judgment.
2. Any settlement between the parties shall be reported to the Court, which shall render judgment limited to a brief statement on the facts and the solution adopted.
3. However, the Court may, having regard to its discretion under the Protocol, decide to proceed with a case notwithstanding the notice of such amicable settlement.

Rule 57
Amicable Settlement Under the Auspices of the Court

1. Pursuant to article 9 of the Protocol, the Court may promote amicable settlement of cases pending before it. To that end, it may contact the parties and take appropriate measures to facilitate amicable settlement of the dispute, based on respect for human and peoples' rights as recognized by the Charter.
2. Any negotiations entered into with a view to reaching an amicable settlement shall be confidential and without prejudice to the parties' observations in the proceedings before the Court. No written or oral communication and no offer of concession made as part of such negotiations shall be mentioned or referred to in the proceedings before the Court.
3. In the event of an amicable settlement of a case, the Court shall render a judgment, which shall be limited to a brief statement of the facts and of the solution adopted.
4. However, pursuant to its discretion under the Protocol, the Court may decide to proceed with the hearing of the application notwithstanding the notice of amicable settlement.

Rule 58
Discontinuance

Where an Applicant notifies the Registrar of its intention not to proceed with the case, the Court shall take due note thereof, and shall strike the application off the Court's cause list. If at the date of receipt by the Registry of the notice of the intention not to proceed with the case, the Respondent State has already taken measures to proceed with the case, its consent shall be required.

CHAPTER V: JUDGMENTS OF THE COURT

Rule 59
Decision of the Court

1. Upon the conclusion of the hearing of a case, the Court shall close the proceedings for its deliberations and judgment.
2. The decision of the Court shall be rendered by the Court within ninety (90) days from the date of completion of the deliberations.

Rule 60
Court's Deliberations

1. The deliberations of the Court shall be held *in camera* and shall remain confidential.

2. Only Judges who were Members of the Panel that heard the case shall participate in the deliberations of the Court.
3. The decision of the Court shall be made by a majority of the Members of the Panel present.
4. In the event of a tied vote, the Presiding Judge shall have a casting vote.
5. Any Member of the Court who heard the case may deliver a separate or dissenting opinion.

Rule 61
Judgment

1. In accordance with article 28(6) of the Protocol, every judgment of the Court shall state the reasons on which it is based.
2. The judgment shall indicate the names of Judges who have taken part in the deliberations.
3. The judgment shall be signed by all the Judges and certified by the Presiding Judge and the Registrar. It shall be read in open Court, due notice having been given to the parties.
4. Subject to article 28(3) of the Protocol, the judgment of the Court shall be final.
5. The judgment of the Court shall be binding on the parties.

Rule 62
Contents of Judgments

A judgment shall contain:

a) the date on which it was delivered;
b) the names of the parties;
c) the names of the representatives of the parties;
d) a summary of the proceedings;
e) the submissions of the parties, and as may be required, those of the Commission's representatives;
f) a statement of the facts of the case;
g) the legal grounds;
h) the operative provisions of the judgment;
i) the decision, if any, on costs;
j) the number of Judges constituting the majority;
k) a statement as to the authentic text of the judgment.

Rule 63
Judgment on Reparation

The Court shall rule on the request for the reparation, submitted in accordance with Rule 34 (5) of these Rules, by the same decision establishing the violation of a human and peoples' right or, if the circumstances so require, by a separate decision.

Rule 64
Notification of Judgment

1. In accordance with article 29 of the Protocol, the Court shall duly notify the parties to the case, the Commission, the Assembly, the African Union Commission and any person or institution concerned of the judgment by certified true copies thereof.
2. The Executive Council shall also be notified of the judgment and shall monitor its execution on behalf of the Assembly.
3. The original copy of the judgment, duly signed and sealed, shall be conserved in the archives of the Court.

Rule 65
Publication of Judgments

Final judgments of the Court shall be published in accordance with Rule 25(2)(i), under the authority of the Registrar.

Rule 66
Application for Interpretation of a Judgment

1. Pursuant to article 28(4) of the Protocol, any party may, for the purpose of executing a judgment, apply to the Court for interpretation of the judgment within twelve months from the date the judgment was delivered unless the Court, in the interest of justice, decides otherwise.
2. The application shall be filed in the Registry. It shall state clearly the point or points in the operative provisions of the judgment on which interpretation is required.
3. Upon the instruction of the Court, the Registrar shall transmit the application for interpretation to any other parties concerned and shall invite them to submit their written comments, if any, within the time limit established by the President. The President shall also fix the date for the hearing of the application, in the event the Court decides to hold one. The Court's decision shall take the form of a judgment.
4. When considering an application for interpretation, the Court shall be composed of the same Judges who delivered judgment on the substantive case. However, where it is not possible for any Judge to participate in the proceedings, such Judge shall, if necessary, be replaced.
5. An application for interpretation shall not stay the execution of the judgment unless the Court decides otherwise.

Rule 67
Request for Review of a Judgment

1. Pursuant to article 28(3) of the Protocol, a party may apply to the Court to review its judgment in the event of the discovery of evidence, which was not within the knowledge of the party at the time the judgment was delivered. Such application shall be filed within six (6) months after that party acquired knowledge of the evidence so discovered.
2. The application shall specify the judgment in respect of which revision is requested, contain the information necessary to show that the conditions laid down in sub-rule 1 of this Rule have been met, and shall be accompanied by a copy of all relevant supporting documents. The application as well as the supporting documents shall be filed in the Registry.
3. Upon the instructions of the Court, the Registrar shall transmit a copy of the application to any other party/parties concerned and shall invite them to submit written observations, if any, within the time limit set by the President. The President shall also fix the date of the hearing should the Court decide to hold one. The Court shall rule on the admissibility of such application and its decision shall take the form of a judgment.
4. If the application is declared admissible, the Court shall, after consultation with the parties, determine the time limit for all future proceedings on the substance of the application it may deem necessary.
5. An application for review shall not stay the execution of a judgment unless the Court decides otherwise.

PART V: ADVISORY PROCEDURE

Rule 68
Request for Advisory Opinion

1. Requests for advisory opinions pursuant to article 4 of the Protocol may be filed with the Court by a Member State, by the African Union, by any organ of the African Union or by an African Organization recognized by the African Union. The request shall be on legal matters and shall state with precision the specific questions on which the opinion of the Court is being sought.
2. Any request for advisory opinion shall specify the provisions of the Charter or of any other international human rights instrument in respect of which the advisory opinion is being sought, the circumstances giving rise to the request as well as the names and addresses of the representatives of the entities making the request.

3. The subject matter of the request for advisory opinion shall not relate to an application pending before the Commission.

Rule 69
Transmission of Request for Advisory Opinion

Subsequent to the receipt of a request for advisory opinion, the Registrar shall transmit copies thereof to Member States, the Commission and to any other interested entity.

Rule 70
Written Submissions

1. The Court shall establish the time limit for the filing of written submissions by States Parties and by any other interested entity.
2. Any other States Parties may submit written submissions on any of the issues raised in the request. Any other interested entity may be authorized by the Court to do the same.

Rule 71
Oral Proceedings

After consideration of the written submissions, the Court shall decide whether or not there should be oral proceedings, and if so, shall fix a date for such hearing.

Rule 72
Application of Provisions Relating to Contentious Procedure

The Court shall apply, *mutatis mutandis* the provisions of Part IV of these Rules to the extent that it deems them to be appropriate and acceptable.

Rule 73
Advisory Opinion

1. The delivery of an advisory opinion shall take place in open Court. However, where the circumstances so require, the Court may decide otherwise.
2. Pursuant to article 4(2) of the Protocol, the Court's advisory opinion shall be accompanied by reasons, and any Judge who has participated in the hearing of an advisory request shall be entitled to deliver a separate or dissenting opinion.
3. A copy of the advisory opinion will be transmitted to Member States, the Commission and any other interested party.

PART VI: MISCELLANEOUS

Rule 74
Amendments

1. These Rules may be amended only by the Court.
2. A proposal to amend any Rule of the Court shall be submitted in writing to the President who shall, accordingly, direct the Registrar to notify all Judges.
3. The proposed amendment shall contain the Rule to be a mended and its proposed replacement, if any.
4. Members of the Court shall be notified of the date and venue of the meeting at which the proposed amendment shall be discussed, ninety (90) days prior to the date of the said meeting.
5. No amendment of a Rule shall be passed unless it is supported by not less than seven Judges of the Court

Rules 75
Adoption

These Rules shall be adopted by not less than seven Judges of the Court and signed by the President.

Rule 76
Entry into Force and Authentic Text

These Rules, the texts of which in the working languages of the Court are equally authentic, shall enter into force on 2 June 2010.

Done at Arusha, United Republic of Tanzania, this second Day of June in the Year Two Thousand and Ten.

(Signed) Jean Mutsinzi
President

Signed (Aboubakar Diakité)
Registrar

Convention Governing the Specific Aspects of Refugee Problems in Africa, 1001 U.N.T.S. 45, *entered into force* June 20, 1974.

Article 1

Definition of the term "Refugee"

1. For the purposes of this Convention, the term "refugee" shall mean every person who, owing to well-founded fear of being persecuted for reasons of race, religion, nationality, membership of a particular social group or political opinion, is outside the country of his nationality and is unable or, owing to such fear, is unwilling to avail himself of the protection of that country, or who, not having a nationality and being outside the country of his former habitual residence as a result of such events is unable or, owing to such fear, is unwilling to return to it.
2. The term "refugee" shall also apply to every person who, owing to external aggression, occupation, foreign domination or events seriously disturbing public order in either part or the whole of his country of origin or nationality, is compelled to leave his place of habitual residence in order to seek refuge in another place outside his country of origin or nationality.
3. In the case of a person who has several nationalities, the term "a country of which he is a national" shall mean each of the countries of which he is a national, and a person shall not be deemed to be lacking the protection of the country of which he is a national if, without any valid reason based on well-founded fear, he has not availed himself of the protection of one of the countries of which he is a national.
4. This Convention shall cease to apply to any refugee if: (a) he has voluntarily re-availed himself of the protection of the country of his nationality, or, (b) having lost his nationality, he has voluntarily reacquired it, or, (c) he has acquired a new nationality, and enjoys the protection of the country of his new nationality, or, (d) he has voluntarily re-established himself in the country which he left or outside which he remained owing to fear of persecution, or, (e) he can no longer, because the circumstances in connection with which he was recognized as a refugee have ceased to exist, continue to refuse to avail himself of the protection of the country of his nationality, or, (f) he has committed a serious non-political crime outside his country of refuge after his admission to that country as a refugee, or, (g) he has seriously infringed the purposes and objectives of this Convention.
5. The provisions of this Convention shall not apply to any person with respect to whom the country of asylum has serious reasons for considering that: (a) he has committed a crime against peace, a war crime, or a crime against humanity, as defined in the international instruments drawn up to make provision in respect of such crimes; (b) he committed a serious non-political crime outside

the country of refuge prior to his admission to that country as a refugee; (c) he has been guilty of acts contrary to the purposes and principles of the Organization of African Unity; (d) he has been guilty of acts contrary to the purposes and principles of the United Nations.

6. For the purposes of this Convention, the Contracting State of Asylum shall determine whether an applicant is a refugee.

Article 2

Asylum

1. Member States of the AU shall use their best endeavours consistent with their respective legislations to receive refugees and to secure the settlement of those refugees who, for well-founded reasons, are unable or unwilling to return to their country of origin or nationality.
2. The grant of asylum to refugees is a peaceful and humanitarian act and shall not be regarded as an unfriendly act by any Member State.
3. No person shall be subjected by a Member State to measures such as rejection at the frontier, return or expulsion, which would compel him to return to or remain in a territory where his life, physical integrity or liberty would be threatened for the reasons set out in Article I, paragraphs 1 and 2.
4. Where a Member State finds difficulty in continuing to grant asylum to refugees, such Member State may appeal directly to other Member States and through the AU, and such other Member States shall in the spirit of African solidarity and international co-operation take appropriate measures to lighten the burden of the Member State granting asylum.
5. Where a refugee has not received the right to reside in any country of asylum, he may be granted temporary residence in any country of asylum in which he first presented himself as a refugee pending arrangement for his resettlement in accordance with the preceding paragraph.
6. For reasons of security, countries of asylum shall, as far as possible, settle refugees at a reasonable distance from the frontier of their country of origin.

Article 3

Prohibition of Subversive Activities

1. Every refugee has duties to the country in which he finds himself, which require in particular that he conforms with its laws and regulations as well as with measures taken for the maintenance of public order. He shall also abstain from any subersive activities against any Member State of the AU.
2. Signatory States undertake to prohibit refugees residing in their respective territories from attacking any State Member of the AU, by any activity likely to cause tension between Member States, and in particular by use of arms, through the press, or by radio.

Article 4

Non-Discrimination
Member States undertake to apply the provisions of this Convention to all refugees without discrimination as to race, religion, nationality, membership of a particular social group or political opinions.

Article 5

Voluntary Repatriation
1. The essentially voluntary character of repatriation shall be respected in all cases and no refugee shall be repatriated against his will.
2. The country of asylum, in collaboration with the country of origin, shall make adequate arrangements for the safe return of refugees who request repatriation.
3. The country of origin, on receiving back refugees, shall facilitate their resettlement and grant them the full rights and privileges of nationals of the country, and subject them to the same obligations.
4. Refugees who voluntarily return to their country shall in no way be penalized for having left it for any of the reasons giving rise to refugee situations. Whenever necessary, an appeal shall be made through national information media and through the Administrative Secretary-General of the AU, inviting refugees to return home and giving assurance that the new circumstances prevailing in their country of origin will enable them to return without risk and to take up a normal and peaceful life without fear of being disturbed or punished, and that the text of such appeal should be given to refugees and clearly explained to them by their country of asylum.
5. Refugees who freely decide to return to their homeland, as a result of such assurances or on their own initiative, shall be given every possible assistance by the country of asylum, the country of origin, voluntary agencies and international and intergovernmental organizations, to facilitate their return.

Article 6

Travel Documents
1. Subject to Article III, Member States shall issue to refugees lawfully staying in their territories travel documents in accordance with the United Nations Convention relating to the Status of Refugees and the Schedule and Annex thereto, for the purpose of travel outside their territory, unless compelling reasons of national security or public order otherwise require. Member States may issue such a travel document to any other refugee in their territory.
2. Where an African country of second asylum accepts a refugee from a country of first asylum, the country of first asylum may be dispensed from issuing a document with a return clause.

3. Travel documents issued to refugees under previous international agreements by States Parties thereto shall be recognized and treated by Member States in the same way as if they had been issued to refugees pursuant to this Article.

Article 7

Co-operation of the National Authorities with the Organization of African Unity
In order to enable the Administrative Secretary-General of the Organization of African Unity to make reports to the competent organs of the Organization of African Unity, Member States undertake to provide the Secretariat in the appropriate form with information and statistical data requested concerning:

(a) the condition of refugees; (b) the implementation of this Convention, and (c) laws, regulations and decrees which are, or may hereafter be, in force relating to refugees.

Article 8

Cooperation with the Office of the United Nations High Commissioner for Refugees

1. Member States shall co-operate with the Office of the United Nations High Commissioner for Refugees.
2. The present Convention shall be the effective regional complement in Africa of the 1951 United Nations Convention on the Status of Refugees.

Article 9

Settlement of Disputes
Any dispute between States signatories to this Convention relating to its interpretation or application, which cannot be settled by other means, shall be referred to the Commission for Mediation, Conciliation and Arbitration of the Organization of African Unity, at the request of any one of the Parties to the dispute.

Article 10

Signature and Ratification

1. This Convention is open for signature and accession by all Member States of the Organization of African Unity and shall be ratified by signatory States in accordance with their respective constitutional processes. The instruments of ratification shall be deposited with the Administrative Secretary-General of the Organization of African Unity.
2. The original instrument, done if possible in African languages, and in English and French, all texts being equally authentic, shall be deposited with the Administrative Secretary-General of the Organization of African Unity.

3. Any independent African State, Member of the Organization of African Unity, may at any time notify the Administrative Secretary-General of the Organization of African Unity of its accession to this Convention.

Article 11

Entry into force
This Convention shall come into force upon deposit of instruments of ratification by one-third of the Member States of the Organization of African Unity.

Article 12

Amendment
This Convention may be amended or revised if any member State makes a written request to the Administrative Secretary-General to that effect, provided however that the proposed amendment shall not be submitted to the Assembly of Heads of State and Government for consideration until all Member States have been duly notified of it and a period of one year has elapsed. Such an amendment shall not be effective unless approved by at least two-thirds of the Member States Parties to the present Convention.

Article 13

Denunciation
1. Any Member State Party to this Convention may denounce its provisions by a written notification to the Administrative Secretary-General.
2. At the end of one year from the date of such notification, if not withdrawn, the Convention shall cease to apply with respect to the denouncing State.

Article 14

Upon entry into force of this Convention, the Administrative Secretary-General of the AU shall register it with the Secretary-General of the United Nations, in accordance with Article 102 of the Charter of the United Nations.

Article 15

Notifications by the Administrative Secretary-General of the Organization of African Unity

The Administrative Secretary-General of the Organization of African Unity shall inform all Members of the Organization: (a) of signatures, ratifications and accessions in accordance with Article X; (b) of entry into force, in accordance with Article XI; (c) of requests for amendments submitted under the terms of Article XII; (d) of denunciations, in acccordance with Article XIII.

State Parties

Countries	Ratification/accession
Algeria	24 May 1974
Angola	30 Apr 1981
Benin	26 Feb 1973
Burkina Faso	19 Mar 1974
Burundi	31 Oct 1975
Cameroon	07 Sep 1975
Cape Verde	16 Feb 1989
Central African Republic	23 Jul 1970
Chad	12 Aug 1981
Congo	16 Jan 1971
Egypt	12 Jun 1980
Equatorial Guinea	08 Sep 1980
Ethiopia	15 Oct 1973
Gabon	21 Mar 1986
Gambia	12 Nov 1980
Ghana	19 Jun 1975
Guinea	18 Oct 1972
Guinea Bissau	27 Jun 1989
Kenya	23 Jun 1992
Lesotho	18 Nov 1983
Liberia	01 Oct 1971
Libyan Arab Jamahiriya	25 Apr 1981
Malawi	04 Nov 1987
Mali	10 Oct 1981
Mauritania	22 Jul 1972
Mozambique	22 Feb 1989
Niger	16 Sep 1971
Nigeria	23 May 1986
Rwanda	19 Nov 1979
Senegal	01 Apr 1971
Seychelles	11 Sep 1980
Sierra Leone	28 Dec 1987
Sudan	24 Dec 1972
Swaziland	16 Jan 1989
Tanzania	10 Jan 1975
Togo	10 Apr 1970
Tunisia	17 Nov 1989
Uganda	24 Jul 1987
Zaire	14 Feb 1973
Zambia	30 Jul 1973
Zimbabwe	28 Sep 1985

Appendix VIII

Protocol to the African Charter on Human and Peoples' Rights on the Rights of Women in Africa, Adopted by the 2nd Ordinary Session of the Assembly of the Union, Maputo, July 11–August 13, 2003. Entry into Force 25th November 2005

Article 1

Definitions

For the purpose of the present Protocol:

a) "African Charter" means the African Charter on Human and Peoples' Rights;
b) "African Commission" means the African Commission on Human and Peoples' Rights;
c) "Assembly" means the Assembly of Heads of State and Government of the African Union;
d) "AU" means the African Union;
e) "Constitutive Act" means the Constitutive Act of the African Union;
f) "Discrimination against women" means any distinction, exclusion or restriction or any differential treatment based on sex and whose objectives or effects compromise or destroy the recognition, enjoyment or the exercise by women,

regardless of their marital status, of human rights and fundamental freedoms in all spheres of life;

g) "Harmful Practices" means all behaviour, attitudes and/or practices which negatively affect the fundamental rights of women and girls, such as their right to life, health, dignity, education and physical integrity;
h) "NEPAD" means the New Partnership for Africa's Development established by the Assembly;
i) "States Parties" means the States Parties to this Protocol;
j) "Violence against women" means all acts perpetrated against women which cause or could cause them physical, sexual, psychological, and economic harm, including the threat to take such acts; or to undertake the imposition of arbitrary restrictions on or deprivation of fundamental freedoms in private or public life in peace time and during situations of armed conflicts or of war;
k) "Women" means persons of female gender, including girls;

Article 2

Elimination of Discrimination against Women

1. States Parties shall combat all forms of discrimination against women through appropriate legislative, institutional and other measures. In this regard they shall:
   a) include in their national constitutions and other legislative instruments, if not already done, the principle of equality between women and men and ensure its effective application;
   b) enact and effectively implement appropriate legislative or regulatory measures, including those prohibiting and curbing all forms of discrimination particularly those harmful practices which endanger the health and general well-being of women;
   c) integrate a gender perspective in their policy decisions, legislation, development plans, programmes and activities and in all other spheres of life;
   d) take corrective and positive action in those areas where discrimination against women in law and in fact continues to exist;
   e) support the local, national, regional and continental initiatives directed at eradicating all forms of discrimination against women.
2. States Parties shall commit themselves to modify the social and cultural patterns of conduct of women and men through public education, information, education and communication strategies, with a view to achieving the elimination of harmful cultural and traditional practices and all other practices which are based on the idea of the inferiority or the superiority of either of the sexes, or on stereotyped roles for women and men.

Article 3

Right to Dignity

1. Every woman shall have the right to dignity inherent in a human being and to the recognition and protection of her human and legal rights;
2. Every woman shall have the right to respect as a person and to the free development of her personality;
3. States Parties shall adopt and implement appropriate measures to prohibit any exploitation or degradation of women;
4. States Parties shall adopt and implement appropriate measures to ensure the protection of every woman's right to respect for her dignity and protection of women from all forms of violence, particularly sexual and verbal violence.

Article 4

The Rights to Life, Integrity and Security of the Person

1. Every woman shall be entitled to respect for her life and the integrity and security of her person. All forms of exploitation, cruel, inhuman or degrading punishment and treatment shall be prohibited.
2. States Parties shall take appropriate and effective measures to:
   a) enact and enforce laws to prohibit all forms of violence against women including unwanted or forced sex whether the violence takes place in private or public;
   b) adopt such other legislative, administrative, social and economic measures as may be necessary to ensure the prevention, punishment and eradication of all forms of violence against women;
   c) identify the causes and consequences of violence against women and take appropriate measures to prevent and eliminate such violence;
   d) actively promote peace education through curricula and social communication in order to eradicate elements in traditional and cultural beliefs, practices and stereotypes which legitimise and exacerbate the persistence and tolerance of violence against women;
   e) punish the perpetrators of violence against women and implement programmes for the rehabilitation of women victims;
   f) establish mechanisms and accessible services for effective information, rehabilitation and reparation for victims of violence against women;
   g) prevent and condemn trafficking in women, prosecute the perpetrators of such trafficking and protect those women most at risk;
   h) prohibit all medical or scientific experiments on women without their informed consent;
   i) provide adequate budgetary and other resources for the implementation and monitoring of actions aimed at preventing and eradicating violence against women;

j) ensure that, in those countries where the death penalty still exists, not to carry out death sentences on pregnant or nursing women.
k) ensure that women and men enjoy equal rights in terms of access to refugee status, determination procedures and that women refugees are accorded the full protection and benefits guaranteed under international refugee law, including their own identity and other documents;

Article 5

Elimination of Harmful Practices

States Parties shall prohibit and condemn all forms of harmful practices which negatively affect the human rights of women and which are contrary to recognised international standards. States Parties shall take all necessary legislative and other measures to eliminate such practices, including:
a) creation of public awareness in all sectors of society regarding harmful practices through information, formal and informal education and outreach programmes;
b) prohibition, through legislative measures backed by sanctions, of all forms of female genital mutilation, scarification, medicalisation and para-medicalisation of female genital mutilation and all other practices in order to eradicate them;
c) provision of necessary support to victims of harmful practices through basic services such as health services, legal and judicial support, emotional and psychological counselling as well as vocational training to make them self-supporting;
d) protection of women who are at risk of being subjected to harmful practices or all other forms of violence, abuse and intolerance.

Article 6

Marriage

States Parties shall ensure that women and men enjoy equal rights and are regarded as equal partners in marriage. They shall enact appropriate national legislative measures to guarantee that:
a) no marriage shall take place without the free and full consent of both parties;
b) the minimum age of marriage for women shall be 18 years;
c) monogamy is encouraged as the preferred form of marriage and that the rights of women in marriage and family, including in polygamous marital relationships are promoted and protected;
d) every marriage shall be recorded in writing and registered in accordance with national laws, in order to be legally recognised;
e) the husband and wife shall, by mutual agreement, choose their matrimonial regime and place of residence;

f) a married woman shall have the right to retain her maiden name, to use it as she pleases, jointly or separately with her husband's surname;
g) a woman shall have the right to retain her nationality or to acquire the nationality of her husband;
h) a woman and a man shall have equal rights, with respect to the nationality of their children except where this is contrary to a provision in national legislation or is contrary to national security interests;
i) a woman and a man shall jointly contribute to safeguarding the interests of the family, protecting and educating their children;
j) during her marriage, a woman shall have the right to acquire her own property and to administer and manage it freely.

Article 7

Separation, Divorce and Annulment of Marriage

States Parties shall enact appropriate legislation to ensure that women and men enjoy the same rights in case of separation, divorce or annulment of marriage. In this regard, they shall ensure that:
a) separation, divorce or annulment of a marriage shall be effected by judicial order;
b) women and men shall have the same rights to seek separation, divorce or annulment of a marriage;
c) in case of separation, divorce or annulment of marriage, women and men shall have reciprocal rights and responsibilities towards their children. In any case, the interests of the children shall be given paramount importance;
d) in case of separation, divorce or annulment of marriage, women and men shall have the right to an equitable sharing of the joint property deriving from the marriage.

Article 8

Access to Justice and Equal Protection before the Law

Women and men are equal before the law and shall have the right to equal protection and benefit of the law. States Parties shall take all appropriate measures to ensure:
a) effective access by women to judicial and legal services, including legal aid;
b) support to local, national, regional and continental initiatives directed at providing women access to legal services, including legal aid;
c) the establishment of adequate educational and other appropriate structures with particular attention to women and to sensitise everyone to the rights of women;
d) that law enforcement organs at all levels are equipped to effectively interpret and enforce gender equality rights;

e) that women are represented equally in the judiciary and law enforcement organs;
f) reform of existing discriminatory laws and practices in order to promote and protect the rights of women.

Article 9

Right to Participation in the Political and Decision-Making Process

1. States Parties shall take specific positive action to promote participative governance and the equal participation of women in the political life of their countries through affirmative action, enabling national legislation and other measures to ensure that:
   a) women participate without any discrimination in all elections;
   b) women are represented equally at all levels with men in all electoral processes;
   c) women are equal partners with men at all levels of development and implementation of State policies and development programmes.
2. States Parties shall ensure increased and effective representation and participation of women at all levels of decision-making.

Article 10

Right to Peace

1. Women have the right to a peaceful existence and the right to participate in the promotion and maintenance of peace.
2. States Parties shall take all appropriate measures to ensure the increased participation of women:
   a) in programmes of education for peace and a culture of peace;
   b) in the structures and processes for conflict prevention, management and resolution at local, national, regional, continental and international levels;
   c) in the local, national, regional, continental and international decision making structures to ensure physical, psychological, social and legal protection of asylum seekers, refugees, returnees and displaced persons, in particular women;
   d) in all levels of the structures established for the management of camps and settlements for asylum seekers, refugees, returnees and displaced persons, in particular, women;
   e) in all aspects of planning, formulation and implementation of post conflict reconstruction and rehabilitation.
3. States Parties shall take the necessary measures to reduce military expenditure significantly in favour of spending on social development in general, and the promotion of women in particular.

Article 11

Protection of Women in Armed Conflicts

1. States Parties undertake to respect and ensure respect for the rules of international humanitarian law applicable in armed conflict situations which affect the population, particularly women.
2. States Parties shall, in accordance with the obligations incumbent upon them under the international humanitarian law, protect civilians including women, irrespective of the population to which they belong, in the event of armed conflict.
3. States Parties undertake to protect asylum seeking women, refugees, returnees and internally displaced persons, against all forms of violence, rape and other forms of sexual exploitation, and to ensure that such acts are considered war crimes, genocide and/or crimes against humanity and that their perpetrators are brought to justice before a competent criminal jurisdiction.
4. States Parties shall take all necessary measures to ensure that no child, especially girls under 18 years of age, take a direct part in hostilities and that no child is recruited as a soldier.

Article 12

Right to Education and Training

1. States Parties shall take all appropriate measures to:
   a) eliminate all forms of discrimination against women and guarantee equal opportunity and access in the sphere of education and training;
   b) eliminate all stereotypes in textbooks, syllabuses and the media, that perpetuate such discrimination;
   c) protect women, especially the girl-child from all forms of abuse, including sexual harassment in schools and other educational institutions and provide for sanctions against the perpetrators of such practices;
   d) provide access to counselling and rehabilitation services to women who suffer abuses and sexual harassment;
   e) integrate gender sensitisation and human rights education at all levels of education curricula including teacher training.
2. States Parties shall take specific positive action to:
   a) promote literacy among women;
   b) promote education and training for women at all levels and in all disciplines, particularly in the fields of science and technology;
   c) promote the enrolment and retention of girls in schools and other training institutions and the organisation of programmes for women who leave school prematurely.

Article 13

Economic and Social Welfare Rights

States Parties shall adopt and enforce legislative and other measures to guarantee women equal opportunities in work and career advancement and other economic opportunities. In this respect, they shall:

a) promote equality of access to employment;
b) promote the right to equal remuneration for jobs of equal value for women and men;
c) ensure transparency in recruitment, promotion and dismissal of women and combat and punish sexual harassment in the workplace;
d) guarantee women the freedom to choose their occupation, and protect them from exploitation by their employers violating and exploiting their fundamental rights as recognised and guaranteed by conventions, laws and regulations in force;
e) create conditions to promote and support the occupations and economic activities of women, in particular, within the informal sector;
f) establish a system of protection and social insurance for women working in the informal sector and sensitise them to adhere to it;
g) introduce a minimum age for work and prohibit the employment of children below that age, and prohibit, combat and punish all forms of exploitation of children, especially the girl-child;
h) take the necessary measures to recognise the economic value of the work of women in the home;
i) guarantee adequate and paid pre and post-natal maternity leave in both the private and public sectors;
j) ensure the equal application of taxation laws to women and men;
k) recognise and enforce the right of salaried women to the same allowances and entitlements as those granted to salaried men for their spouses and children;
l) recognise that both parents bear the primary responsibility for the upbringing and development of children and that this is a social function for which the State and the private sector have secondary responsibility;
m) take effective legislative and administrative measures to prevent the exploitation and abuse of women in advertising and pornography.

Article 14

Health and Reproductive Rights

1. States Parties shall ensure that the right to health of women, including sexual and reproductive health is respected and promoted. This includes:

a) the right to control their fertility;
b) the right to decide whether to have children, the number of children and the spacing of children;
c) the right to choose any method of contraception;
d) the right to self protection and to be protected against sexually transmitted infections, including HIV/AIDS;
e) the right to be informed on one's health status and on the health status of one's partner, particularly if affected with sexually transmitted infections, including HIV/AIDS, in accordance with internationally recognised standards and best practices;
f) the right to have family planning education.

2. States Parties shall take all appropriate measures to:
a) provide adequate, affordable and accessible health services, including information, education and communication programmes to women especially those in rural areas;
b) establish and strengthen existing pre-natal, delivery and post-natal health and nutritional services for women during pregnancy and while they are breast-feeding;
c) protect the reproductive rights of women by authorising medical abortion in cases of sexual assault, rape, incest, and where the continued pregnancy endangers the mental and physical health of the mother or the life of the mother or the foetus.

Article 15

Right to Food Security

States Parties shall ensure that women have the right to nutritious and adequate food. In this regard, they shall take appropriate measures to:
a) provide women with access to clean drinking water, sources of domestic fuel, land, and the means of producing nutritious food;
b) establish adequate systems of supply and storage to ensure food security.

Article 16

Right to Adequate Housing

Women shall have the right to equal access to housing and to acceptable living conditions in a healthy environment. To ensure this right, States Parties shall grant to women, whatever their marital status, access to adequate housing.

Article 17

Right to Positive Cultural Context

1. Women shall have the right to live in a positive cultural context and to participate at all levels in the determination of cultural policies.
2. States Parties shall take all appropriate measures to enhance the participation of women in the formulation of cultural policies at all levels.

Article 18

Right to a Healthy and Sustainable Environment

1. Women shall have the right to live in a healthy and sustainable environment.
2. States Parties shall take all appropriate measures to:
   a) ensure greater participation of women in the planning, management and preservation of the environment and the sustainable use of natural resources at all levels;
   b) promote research and investment in new and renewable energy sources and appropriate technologies, including information technologies and facilitate women's access to, and participation in their control;
   c) protect and enable the development of women's indigenous knowledge systems;
   d) regulate the management, processing, storage and disposal of domestic waste;
   e) ensure that proper standards are followed for the storage, transportation and disposal of toxic waste.

Article 19

Right to Sustainable Development

Women shall have the right to fully enjoy their right to sustainable development. In this connection, the States Parties shall take all appropriate measures to:

a) introduce the gender perspective in the national development planning procedures;
b) ensure participation of women at all levels in the conceptualisation, decision-making, implementation and evaluation of development policies and programmes;
c) promote women's access to and control over productive resources such as land and guarantee their right to property;

d) promote women's access to credit, training, skills development and extension services at rural and urban levels in order to provide women with a higher quality of life and reduce the level of poverty among women;
e) take into account indicators of human development specifically relating to women in the elaboration of development policies and programmes; and
f) ensure that the negative effects of globalisation and any adverse effects of the implementation of trade and economic policies and programmes are reduced to the minimum for women.

Article 20

Widows' Rights

States Parties shall take appropriate legal measures to ensure that widows enjoy all human rights through the implementation of the following provisions:
a) that widows are not subjected to inhuman, humiliating or degrading treatment;
b) a widow shall automatically become the guardian and custodian of her children, after the death of her husband, unless this is contrary to the interests and the welfare of the children;
c) a widow shall have the right to remarry, and in that event, to marry the person of her choice.

Article 21

Right to Inheritance

1. A widow shall have the right to an equitable share in the inheritance of the property of her husband. A widow shall have the right to continue to live in the matrimonial house. In case of remarriage, she shall retain this right if the house belongs to her or she has inherited it.
2. Women and men shall have the right to inherit, in equitable shares, their parents' properties.

Article 22

Special Protection of Elderly Women

The States Parties undertake to:
a) provide protection to elderly women and take specific measures commensurate with their physical, economic and social needs as well as their access to employment and professional training;
b) ensure the right of elderly women to freedom from violence, including sexual abuse, discrimination based on age and the right to be treated with dignity.

Article 23

Special Protection of Women with Disabilities

The States Parties undertake to:

a) ensure the protection of women with disabilities and take specific measures commensurate with their physical, economic and social needs to facilitate their access to employment, professional and vocational training as well as their participation in decision-making;
b) ensure the right of women with disabilities to freedom from violence, including sexual abuse, discrimination based on disability and the right to be treated with dignity.

Article 24

Special Protection of Women in Distress

The States Parties undertake to:

a) ensure the protection of poor women and women heads of families including women from marginalized population groups and provide the an environment suitable to their condition and their special physical, economic and social needs;
b) ensure the right of pregnant or nursing women or women in detention by providing them with an environment which is suitable to their condition and the right to be treated with dignity.

Article 25

Remedies

States Parties shall undertake to:

a) provide for appropriate remedies to any woman whose rights or freedoms, as herein recognised, have been violated;
b) ensure that such remedies are determined by competent judicial, administrative or legislative authorities, or by any other competent authority provided for by law.

Article 26

Implementation and Monitoring

1. States Parties shall ensure the implementation of this Protocol at national level, and in their periodic reports submitted in accordance with Article 62 of the African Charter, indicate the legislative and other measures undertaken for the full realisation of the rights herein recognised.

2. States Parties undertake to adopt all necessary measures and in particular shall provide budgetary and other resources for the full and effective implementation of the rights herein recognised.

Article 27

Interpretation

The African Court on Human and Peoples' Rights shall be seized with matters of interpretation arising from the application or implementation of this Protocol.

Article 28

Signature, Ratification and Accession

1. This Protocol shall be open for signature, ratification and accession by the States Parties, in accordance with their respective constitutional procedures.
2. The instruments of ratification or accession shall be deposited with the Chairperson of the Commission of the AU.

Article 29

Entry into Force

1. This Protocol shall enter into force thirty (30) days after the deposit of the fifteenth (15) instrument of ratification.
2. For each State Party that accedes to this Protocol after its coming into force, the Protocol shall come into force on the date of deposit of the instrument of accession.
3. The Chairperson of the Commission of the AU shall notify all Member States of the coming into force of this Protocol.

Article 30

Amendment and Revision

1. Any State Party may submit proposals for the amendment or revision of this Protocol.
2. Proposals for amendment or revision shall be submitted, in writing, to the Chairperson of the Commission of the AU who shall transmit the same to the States Parties within thirty (30) days of receipt thereof.
3. The Assembly, upon advice of the African Commission, shall examine these proposals within a period of one (1) year following notification of States Parties, in accordance with the provisions of paragraph 2 of this article.

4. Amendments or revision shall be adopted by the Assembly by a simple majority.
5. The amendment shall come into force for each State Party, which has accepted it thirty (30) days after the Chairperson of the Commission of the AU has received notice of the acceptance.

Article 31

Status of the Present Protocol

None of the provisions of the present Protocol shall affect more favourable provisions for the realisation of the rights of women contained in the national legislation of States Parties or in any other regional, continental or international conventions, treaties or agreements applicable in these States Parties.

Article 32

Transitional Provisions

Pending the establishment of the African Court on Human and Peoples' Rights, the African Commission on Human and Peoples' Rights shall be the seized with matters of interpretation arising from the application and implementation of this Protocol.

Adopted by the 2nd Ordinary Sessionof the Assembly of the Union
Maputo, 11 July 2003.
States Parties

Comoros, Cape-Verde, Djibouti, The Gambia, Libya, Lesotho, Mali, Malawi, Mauritania, Namibia, Nigeria, Rwanda, South Africa, Senegal, and Togo.

Appendix IX

International Conference on the Great Lakes Region/Protocol on the Property Rights of Returning Persons[1]

Preamble

We, heads of State and government of the Member States of the International Conference on the Great Lakes Region;

Considering our Declaration on Peace, Security, Democracy and Development in the Great Lakes Region adopted on 20th November 2004 in Dar-es-Salaam;

Reaffirming our commitment to its implementation on behalf of our peoples, particularly its Article 69 under which the Member States committed themselves to ensure that refugees and displaced persons, upon return to their areas of origin, recover their property with the assistance of the local traditional and administrative authorities;

Expressing our commitment to comply with the right of everyone to own property under the Universal Declaration of Human Rights 1948, and the guarantee of the right to property in the African Charter on Human and Peoples' Rights 1981;

---

[1] This Protocol was prepared by the author on behalf of the Member States of the International Conference on the Great Lakes Region. It was adopted by the Member States in December 2006.

Conscious that property disputes arising from claims by internally displaced persons and refugees when returning to their places of origin can be a hindrance to the attainment of the durable solutions of voluntary repatriation and reintegration;
Deeply concerned that the failure to resolve such disputes can be a source of recurrent conflict in the Great Lakes Region;

*A*gree as follows:

Article 1

Definitions

In this Protocol, unless the context otherwise requires, the following mean:

1. **Children:** human beings below the age of eighteen years, unless under the law applicable to the children, majority is attained earlier, as defined by the Convention on the Rights of the Child;
2. **Communities:** communities, pastoralists and other groups, whose livelihood has a special dependency on and attachment to their lands, in accordance with the provisions of the International Covenant on Civil and Political Rights 1966, the African Charter on Human and Peoples' Rights;
3. **Internally Displaced Persons:** persons or groups of persons who have been forced or obliged to flee or to leave their homes or places of habitual residence, in particular as a result of or in order to avoid the effects of armed conflict, situations of generalized violence, violations of human rights or natural or human-made disasters, and who have not crossed an internationally recognized State border;
4. **Internally Displaced Persons:** also means persons or groups of persons forced or obliged to flee or to leave their homes or places of habitual residence, in particular as a result of or in order to avoid the effects of development induced displacement and who have not crossed an internationally recognized State border;
5. **Property:** the autonomous possessions of economic value such as, moveable and immoveable property including land, corporeal and incorporeal possessions like intellectual property or copy right, money, pecuniary gains, debts, and contractual rights;
6. **Refugees:** Every person who has a well-founded fear of being persecuted for reasons of race, religion, nationality, membership of a particular social group or political opinion, is outside the country of his nationality and is unable, or owing to such fear, is unwilling to avail himself of the protection of that country; or who, not having a nationality and being outside the country of his former habitual residence as a result of such events, is unable or, owing to such fear, is unwilling to return to it, as defined by the United

Nations Convention relating to the Status of Refugees 1951 and as amended by the United Nations Protocol relating to the Status of Refugees 1967;
7. **Refugee:** also applies to every person who, owing to external aggression, occupation, foreign domination or events seriously disturbing public order in either part or the whole of his country of origin or nationality, is compelled to leave his place of habitual residence in order to seek refuge in another place outside his country of origin or nationality, as defined by the African Union Convention governing the specific aspects of refugee problems in Africa 1969;
8. **Returnees:** internally displaced persons and refugees who return to their original places of residence in their country of origin;
9. Sub-Committee of Experts: the Sub-Committee of Experts established under the Coordinating Committee of the Programme of Action on Humanitarian, Social and Environmental Issues.

Article 2

Objectives

The objectives of this Protocol are to:

1. Encourage Member States to provide legal protection for the property of internally displaced persons and refugees in countries of their origin in the Great Lakes Region;
2. Establish legal principles according to which Member States shall ensure that refugees and internally displaced persons, upon return to their areas of origin, recover their property with the assistance of the local traditional and administrative authorities;
3. Provide a legal basis for resolving disputes arising from the recovery of property previously occupied or owned by Internally displaced persons and refugees in the Great Lakes Region;
4. Provide special protection for the property of returning women, children, and communities with special attachment to land in the Great Lakes Region;
5. Ensure legal remedies for the loss or destruction of the property of internally displaced persons and refugees, and persons resettled or relocated elsewhere due to the construction of large scale development projects in the territories of the Member States.

Article 3

General Principles of Protection

1. Member States accept that the following general principles shall form the basis of the legal protection of the property of internally displaced persons and

refugees, and those resettled or relocated elsewhere due to development induced displacement:

a. The right of everyone, including internally displaced persons and refugees, to own property in accordance with the Universal Declaration of Human Rights and the relevance of the International Covenant on Civil and Political Rights as well as that of the International Covenant on Economic, Social and Cultural Rights 1966, and the guarantee of the right to property under the African Charter on Human and Peoples' Rights;
b. The guarantee of equal protection of the law for all persons, inclusive of Internally displaced persons and refugees, in keeping with the provisions of the International Covenant on Civil and Political Rights, and the African Charter on Human and Peoples' Rights;
c. Non-discrimination under the International Convention on the Elimination of All Forms of Racial Discrimination 1965;
d. Non-discrimination against women under the International Convention on the Elimination of All Forms of Discrimination Against Women 1979, and the Protocol to the African Charter on Human and Peoples' Rights on the Rights of Women in Africa 2003, with respect to the protection of the property of women Internally displaced persons and refugees;
e. The ratification of, and compliance with, the Convention on the Elimination of All Forms of Discrimination Against Women 1979, the Protocol to the African Charter on Human and Peoples' Rights on the Rights of Women in Africa 2003 and the African Charter on the Rights and Welfare of the Child 1990;
f. Implementation of the Convention on the Rights of the Child 1989.

2. Member States undertake, subject to the applicable laws of armed conflict, to protect property belonging to internally displaced persons and refugees in all possible circumstances, and in particular, against the following acts:
   a. Pillage;
   b. Direct or indiscriminate attacks or other acts of violence;
   c. Being used to shield military operations or objectives;
   d. Being made the object of reprisal;
   e. Being destroyed or appropriated as a form of collective punishment.
3. Member States shall ensure that the property of internally displaced persons and refugees shall be protected in all possible circumstances against arbitrary and illegal appropriation, occupation or use, taking into account the United Nations Principles on Housing and Property restitution.
4. Nothing in this Protocol shall affect the right of Internally displaced persons and refugees to take legal action aimed at recovering their properties through national courts and/or the African Commission or African Court on Human and Peoples' Rights.
5. Statutes of limitations of the Member States shall, where applicable, be without prejudice to the provisions of this Protocol.

Article 4

Recovery and Restoration of the Property of Internally Displaced Persons and Refugees and Resettled Persons

1. Member States shall assist internally displaced persons and refugees and/or resettled internally displaced persons to recover, to the extent possible, their property and possessions which they left behind or were dispossessed of upon their displacement.
2. When recovery of such property and possessions is not possible, Member States shall provide or assist such persons in obtaining appropriate compensation as provided for in Article 8.
3. In particular, Member States shall:
   a. Elaborate legislative procedures under which the local traditional and administrative authorities referred to in Article 69 of the Dar-es-Salaam Declaration, can assist to recover the property of returning refugees and displaced persons;
   b. Establish simplified formal judicial procedures to enable Internally displaced persons and refugees to lodge formal claims relating to the loss or recovery of their property;
   c. Establish alternative and informal community based mechanisms and processes for resolving property disputes, with simple requirements of proof of ownership based upon reliable and verifiable testimony;
   d. Establish an affordable property registration scheme under which title to property, including land, held under both customary and statutory land tenure systems is recognized.
4. The obligation of Member States to accord legal protection to the properties of internally displaced persons and refugees shall be binding on all successive Governments in each of the Member States.
5. Member States may exercise the authority of the State to acquire or expropriate property abandoned by internally displaced persons or refugees in compelling and overwhelming circumstances which are justified in the general interest of the public or community, provided that such acquisition or expropriation shall be carried out under procedures prescribed by law.
6. A Member State that acquires or expropriates property belonging to internally displaced persons or refugees shall maintain a fair balance between their right to own such property and the acquisition or expropriation of that property by ensuring that:
   a. Internally displaced persons or refugees shall not disproportionately or unreasonably bear the burden of the loss of their property without being compensated or restituted for such loss;
   b. The loss of the property of internally displaced persons or refugees does not violate other related rights, such as their right to family life, home and adequate housing.

Article 5

Protection of the Property of Returning Spouses

1. Member States undertake to deal with special claims of protection by returning spouses, single parents, and single women with respect to disputes on the ownership of family or other property when a displaced spouse is deceased.
2. Member States undertake to eliminate gender based discrimination against women according to the International Convention on the Elimination of All Forms of Discrimination Against Women, the African Charter on Human and Peoples' Rights and the Protocol to the African Charter on Human and Peoples' Rights on the Rights of Women in Africa.
3. Member States shall give effect to the legal capacity of returning women and all women, including single women, to own land and other property in their own right, without discrimination of any kind.
4. Any land or property registration scheme established under Article 4(1)(d) shall accord women the legal capacity to register title to land or property owned by them under both customary and statutory land tenure systems so as to enable them to own such land or property in their own right, and to avoid conflicting claims relating to their ownership of such land or property.
5. Member States undertake to ensure that legislative, administrative, legal and other mechanisms shall be established to guarantee that returning spouses succeed to the property of their deceased spouses.

Article 6

Protection of the Property of Returning Children and Orphans

1. Member States shall address the plight of all returning children, without discriminating between girls and boys, orphans, children born out of wedlock, and adopted children, where such children are likely to be disinherited, or dispossessed, of family property. In particular, Member States shall guarantee:
   a. The protection of these children's right to inherit family property when both parents died during displacement or refuge;
   b. Legal arrangements for holding these children's inheritance of property in trust until they attain legal capacity;
   c. Protection of the property interests of children in national laws on inheritance and succession, based upon the principle of the best interest of the child;
   d. To harmonize national laws on the attainment of the legal capacity of children at the age of 18 in accordance with the Convention on the Rights of the Child;

e. To harmonize national laws on inheritance and succession, taking into account the principle of the best interest of the child;
f. Adherence to the best interest of the child as the overriding principle applicable to all returning children who are orphaned or have lost both parents while in displacement or refuge;
g. Rapid and unimpeded access by children to the enjoyment or use of the property of their deceased parents.

Article 7

Protection of the Property of Returning Communities

1. Member States recognize special protection of the property of returning communities, pastoralists and other groups whose mode of livelihood depends on special attachment to their lands in situations where such communities or groups exist.
2. Member States shall ensure that such communities, pastoralists or other groups, shall be reintegrated in areas previously occupied them.
3. When such reintegration or return is not possible, these communities shall be provided in all possible cases with lands at least equal in value to those previously occupied by them.
4. Where alternative lands of equal value cannot be allocated, an appropriate compensation package shall be made available as provided for in the national legislation of the Member States.

Article 8

Compensation

1. Member States undertake responsibility for compensating the loss of the property of internally displaced persons and refugees in situations where they are directly responsible for such loss.
2. Member States undertake to establish a framework for enabling the compensation of internally displaced persons and refugees by those responsible for the loss of the property of internally displaced persons and refugees in situations where Member States bear no direct responsibility for such loss.
3. Member States shall determine an appropriate compensation package for the loss of the property of internally displaced persons and refugees on the basis of national legislation which shall set out the terms of such a compensation package.

Article 9

Monitoring

1. A Sub-Committee of Experts established under the Coordinating Committee of the Programme of Action on Humanitarian, Social and Environmental Issues and which has specific responsibility for land and property issues shall ensure that this Protocol is implemented in the Member States.

Article 10

Final Provisions

1. This Protocol shall be an integral part of the Pact and shall not be subject to separate signature and ratification by the Member States.
2. For any Member State which has ratified the Pact in terms set out in Article 30 of the Pact, this Protocol shall automatically enter into force at the same time as the Pact in accordance with Article 33 of the Pact.
3. Nothing contained in this Protocol shall be construed to be contrary to the provisions of the Pact, the Constitutive Act of the African Union, and the Charter of the United Nations.

Appendix X

Conclusions and Recommendations of the Consultative Meeting between the African Commission on Human and Peoples' Rights and the United Nations High Commissioner for Refugees

Addis Ababa, 20 and 21 March 2003

A Consultative Meeting between the African Commission on Human and Peoples' Rights (ACHPR) and the United Nations High Commissioner for Refugees (UNHCR), was convened in Addis Ababa, Ethiopia, on Thursday 20th and Friday 21st March 2003. The main objective of the meeting was to examine ways to strengthen co-operation between the two institutions in order to more effectively promote and protect the rights of refugees, asylum seekers, returnees and other persons of concern under their respective mandates. The following are the conclusions and recommendations adopted by the Consultative Meeting.

Conclusions

1. Historically, Africa has been at the forefront of the struggle to uphold refugee protection. The only existing regional refugee instrument is the 1969 AU Convention Governing the Specific Aspects of Refugee Problems in Africa, which has become a model of progressive refugee protection throughout the world.

2. The Agenda for Protection, adopted in October 2002 by the Executive Committee of UNHCR at the end of the Global Consultations process, reflects the main concerns of African States and provides a framework for addressing refugee problems in Africa. The Comprehensive Implementation Plan (CIP) may be seen as the effective regional complement to the Agenda for Protection. It was adopted by the AU/UNHCR Meeting of Government and Non-Government Technical Experts held in Conakry, Guinea, in March 2000, in commemoration of the 30th Anniversary of the 1969 AU Refugee Convention. The CIP has since been endorsed both by the 72nd Session of the AU Council of Ministers meeting in Lome, Togo, and by the Assembly of Heads of State and Government of Member States of the AU at their 37th Session in Lusaka, Zambia, in July 2001. The Agenda for Protection and the CIP will continue to guide action in the priority areas identified by UNHCR and the African Union.
3. The situation of refugees, asylum seekers, returnees and other persons of concern in Africa should not be viewed as insurmountable or hopeless; there are many situations which have been resolved through the cessation of hostilities and the signing of peace agreements, which have enabled thousands of refugee to return home, for example to Mozambique and Namibia. Other situations, such as in Angola and Sierra Leone, are in the process of being addressed.
4. On the other hand, the continent is faced with a constant problem of inadequate resources which has sometimes resulted in limited commitment to refugee protection and in very low standards of assistance to refugees, particularly to women and children, for instance in the critically important areas of food and education.
5. Furthermore, in certain instances the presence of armed elements within refugee camps and settlements may endanger the national security of the host state and leads to other negative consequences for refugees, including forced military recruitment, the diversion of humanitarian assistance and an insecure environment.
6. The habitual hospitality of African States has been severely tested over recent years because of the environmental impact of the presence of large populations in host countries, combined with the strain on infrastructural resources and the insecurity which States perceive as accompanying the presence of large refugee populations. Notwithstanding such constraints, many African countries continue to grant asylum to refugees and therefore deserve recognition and support.
7. Refugees are endowed with the same rights and responsibilities as all other human beings. The specific rights of refugees are an integral part of human rights and are universal, indivisible, inter-dependent and inter-related. Where national laws on refugees are inadequate or non-existent, general human rights law should therefore be invoked to protect refugees.
8. However, international human rights protection mechanisms generally lack adequate enforceability because of the limited or non-existent sanctions

applicable to states which fail to comply with their obligations. This is particularly the case of international refugee law.

9. While laws and regulations exist in many African countries which could be used to protect the rights of refugees, returnees, asylum seekers and other persons of concern, these are not always widely known and may therefore not be adequately utilized.
10. Under its mandate, the African Commission on Human and Peoples' Rights is charged with overseeing implementation of the 1981 African Charter on Human and Peoples' Rights, which includes the right to seek and obtain asylum from persecution. This offers an opportunity to better monitor implementation of the 1969 AU Convention by States Parties through the various mechanisms at the disposal of the Commission.
11. However, the Commission is seriously under-resourced. Its members are expected to deal with the full range of human rights problems throughout the continent, but there are only eleven members who work part-time. Therefore, the capacity of the Commission through its support structure must be strengthened, to enable it to more effectively address human rights abuses on the continent.
12. Internally displaced persons are present across the continent, but no formal structures exist to address their plight, which has resulted in gaps in the response of the international community to this widespread humanitarian problem.

Recommendations

1. UNHCR and the ACHPR should formulate procedures and methodologies for operationalising the Memorandum of Understanding (MoU) which will be signed to strengthen cooperation between the two institutions. This will enhance refugee protection in Africa through the use of the ACHPR's mandate to monitor implementation of the 1969 AU Convention by States Parties.
2. UNHCR and the ACHPR should undertake joint public information and awareness campaigns to sensitize refugees, asylum seekers, returnees and other persons of concern about their rights and duties, as well as civil society about the important contribution that refugees can make towards the development of their host communities, if they are enabled to exercise their rights and become economically productive.
3. The ACHPR and UNHCR should encourage African States to put in place national laws and policies for the protection of refugee rights, and to establish concrete implementation mechanisms accordingly.
4. The ACHPR and UNHCR should encourage the protection of refugee women and children, in particular, through the establishment of judicial or quasi-judicial mechanisms to enforce their rights in cases of sexual and gender-based violence and exploitation.

5. The ACHPR, in collaboration with UNHCR, should promote the observance by States of the guidelines on the protection of IDPs, which have been developed by the Secretary General's Special Representative on Internally Displaced Persons.
6. The Co-ordinating Committee on Assistance to Refugees, operating within the framework of the African Union, should be entrusted with the task of studying how the 1969 AU Convention may be complemented in order to effectively respond to the challenges posed by refugee movements on the continent. In particular, the Committee should examine the possibility of promoting the adoption of an annul Decision by the Summit of Heads of State and Government, dealing with one specific refugee-related issue of concern to Member States of the African Union. Such Decision would guide action by states in dealing with specific problems which are not adequately addressed by the 1969 AU Convention, for example the maintenance of the civilian and humanitarian character of refugee camps, sexual and gender-based violence and exploitation, protection in mass influx situations, mechanisms for international solidarity and burden sharing. Furthermore, the Committee should also examine the feasibility of promoting the adoption of a Protocol to the 1969 AU Convention which would expand its scope to cover issues not adequately addressed therein.
7. In furtherance of the above, the ACHPR should be invited to become a Member of the Coordinating Committee on Assistance to Refugees.
8. UNCHR and the ACHPR should endeavour to build partnerships for the protection of refugee rights with the UN High Commissioner for Human Rights, with relevant organs of the African Union as well as with civil society groups and organisations.
9. The linkages between mandates and activities of the African Union's Conflict Prevention, Management and Resolution Mechanism, the ACHPR and UNHCR should be explored, with a view to contributing to ongoing efforts to address the root causes of refugee movements within the context of human rights remedies and humanitarian action.
10. The link between impunity and the growing refugee problem in Africa should be made, and avenues explored for holding the perpetrators of gross violations of human rights accountable for their acts. In this regard, the role which may be played by the future African Court on Human and Peoples' Rights should be carefully explored.

Appendix XI

The Addis Ababa Document on Refugees and Forced Population Displacements in Africa

Adopted by the AU/UNHCR Symposium on Refugees and Forced Population Displacements in Africa – 10 SEPTEMBER 1994 ADDIS ABABA, ETHIOP1A.

Held in Commemoration of the twenty-fifth anniversary of the adoption of the 1969 AU Convention Governing the Specific Aspects of Refugee Problems in Africa and the twentieth year of its entry into force.

CONTENTS

(a) Refugee Repatriation
(b) Inter-African Resettlement

VII. Other Populations in Need of Protection and Humanitarian Assistance
VIII. Emergency Preparedness and Response
IX. From Relief and Humanitaian Assistance to Socio-Economic Sustainability
X. Institutional Aspects

PART THREE

FOLLOW-UP

PART ONE

INTRODUCTION

1. The AU/UNHCR Commemorative Symposium on Refugees and Forced Population Displacements in Africa took place in Addis Ababa, Ethiopia, from 8 to 10 September 1994. The symposium was held to commemorate the twenty-fifth anniversary of the adoption of the 1969 AU Convention Governing the Specific Aspects of Refugee Problems in Africa (the "1969 AU Convention") and the twentieth year of its entry into force on 20 June 1974.
2. The Symposium brought together representatives of almost all the Member States of the Organization of African Unity (AU) and a number of the Member States of the Executive Committee of the Programme of the United Nations High Commissioner for Refugees. Also represented were relevant organizations of the United Nations system, other inter-governmental organizations, non-governmental organizations, and academics from various parts of the world.
3. The participants in the Symposium have noted with satisfaction the important contribution that the 1969 AU Convention has made to refugee protection and solutions in Africa. It has also inspired other regions of the world. While acknowledging the challenges facing the Convention, the Symposium reaffirmed its belief in the continued validity of the Convention as the regional foundation for providing protection and finding solutions for refugees in Africa. The Symposium also believed that the Convention provided a good basis for developing the legal tools and mechanisms for solving the problems of refugees and forced population displacements as a whole.
4. There have been positive developments in finding solutions for refugees in Africa, such as the successfully completed repatriation of South African refugees in 1993 and the continuing return home of over one million Mozambique refugees. However, new refugee emergencies have also occurred in many parts of the Continent. In fact, the refugee population in Africa has grown more than 10 times, from 700,000 to over 7,000,000,in the twenty-five years since the Convention came into existence in 1969. Moreover, in addition to the 7,000,000 refugees, one third of the world total, there are an estimated 20 million

internally displaced persons on the African continent. But while the displacement crisis is growing, the political, financial and material support towards protecting and assisting refugees can no longer be taken for granted, as a result of various global developments.

5. The refugee flows impose intolerable security, social and economic burdens on the countries that have generously provided and continue to provide asylum. More seriously, the are symptomatic of the tragedy of the ethnic conflicts, social disintegration and political anarchy prevailing in some countries in Africa.
6. Thus, the anniversaries of the 1969 AU Convention provide an opportunity not only to review the achievements of and challenges facing the Convention, but also to draw attention to the continuing urgency of the refugee and displacement crisis in Africa.
7. The recommendations contained in this document do not lose sight of many important initiatives, recommendations, decisions, declarations and plans of action which have preceded this Symposium, in Africa and elsewhere, and which have an important bearing on the refugee issue. Thus, in formulating its recommendations, the Symposium has drawn inspiration from, among others, the Recommendations of the Pan-African Conference on_the Situation of Refugees in africa, (Arusha, Tanzania, 7 – 17 May 1979, "The Arusha Recommendations"); the African Charter on Human and People's Rights of 1981; The Second International Conference on Assistance to Refugees in Africa (1984, "ICARA II Recommendations"); the Oslo Declaration and Plan of Action on the Plight of Refugees. Returnees and Displaced Persons in Southern Africa ("SARRED", August 1988); the Khartoum Declaration on Africa's Refugee Crisis Adopted by the Seventeenth Extra-Ordinary Session of the AU Commission of Fifteen on Refugees (Khartoum, Sudan, 20 – 24 September 1990); the Declaration Framework of Cooperation and Action Programme of the Horn of Africa Summit on Humanitarian Issues (Addis Ababa, Ethiopia, April 1992); the African Humanitarian Initiative for Sustainable Development (l993); the Cairo Declaration on the Establishment Within the AU of a Mechanism for Conflict Prevention Management and Resolution (Cairo, June 1993); the Addis Ababa PARINAC Conclusions and Recommendations, (March 1994); the Oslo PARINAC Declaration and Plan of Action (Oslo, June 1994); and the Tunis Declaration on the 1969 AU Convention Governing the Specific Aspects of Refugee – Problems in Africa (Tunis, June 1994).

PART TWO

RECOMMENDATIONS

I. ROOT CAUSES OF REFUGEE FLOWS AND OTHER FORCED POPULATION DISPLACEMENTS

8. Refugee flow are a symbol of the crises which afflict many societies in Africa. In particular, most of the refugee flows are the result of armed conflicts and

civil strife. Ethnic intolerance; the abuse of human rights on a massive scale; the monopolization of political and economic power; refusal to respect democracy or the results of free and fair elections; resistance to popular participation in governance; and poor management of public affairs all play a part in forcing people to flee their normal places of residence.

9. External factors have also played a part in at least contributing to forced population displacements. Historically, the main cause of coerced population displacements has been colonialism. Today, there is no question that international economic forces have contributed to the widespread poverty in Africa and to the widening gap between the poor and the rich. In many African countries, there is competition over scarce resources, and the human and physical environment has suffered degradation. Some States can no longer carry out the critical functions of government, including the control of national territory; oversight over the nation's resources; extraction of revenue; maintenance of an adequate national infrastructure; rendering of basic services such as sanitation, education, and housing; and governance and maintenance of law and order. All these factors contribute in one or- another way to the root causes of displacement.
10. The Symposium has focused much of its discussions on the root causes of displacement and the imperative need to carry out preventive measures. Recognizing that conflicts are the major cause of displacement in Africa today, the participants echoed many times over the urgency of talking energetic measures to prevent conflicts or resolve them expeditiously after they have started. They cal]ed for decisive national and international measures to create stable, viable and progressive societies. Otherwise, refugee displacements would continue unabated, and prospects for the return of refugees to their countries origin would also remain elusive.

Recommendation One

The Member Stares of the Organization of African Unity (AU) and the AU Secretariat, in collaboration with the relevant inter-governmental and non-governmental organizations, should examine all factors which cause or contribute to civil conflicts, with a view to elaborate a Comprehensive Plan of Action for tackling the root causes of refugee flows and other displacements. Among others, the following issues should be examined: ethnic strife and conflict; the role of the arms trade tn causing or exacerbating conflicts in Africa; the establishment of a firm foundation for democratic institutions and governance; the respect of human rights; the promotion of economic development and social progress, the obstacles to providing protection and humanitarian assistance to displaced persons; and the inter-relationship between humanitarian, political and military actions at an international level.

Recommendation Two

The political leadership of Africa should rise up to the challenges of practicing politics of inclusion and popular participation in national affairs, creating a firm foundation for responsible and accountable governance, and promoting social progress, economic development and a just and fair society.

Recommendation Three

In this context, the Symposium notes with satisfaction the activities of the AU in conflict prevention and resolution. Bearing in mind the beneficial effects of such activities in preventing or reducing displacement, the Symposium:

(i) recommends that the linkage between the activities of the AU in conflict prevention, management and resolution and those on behalf of refugees and internally displaced persons should be strengthened.
(ii) urges organizajtions involved in refugee and other displacement issues, and the international community at large, to support the activities of the AU in conflict prevention, management and resolution.
(iii) in particular, encourages those organizaiions, and the international community at large, to contribute generously to the AU Peace Fund and to provide human resources, technical support advisory services and equipment to support the above-mentioned activities, in conformity with the relevant AU guidelines.
(iv) further encourages them to support the AU in elaborating and expanding its activities in the fields of human rights monitoring, the promotion of human rights and humanitarian law, election monitoring, the management of political transitions, and the development of early warning systems at national, sub-regional and continental levels.

Recommendation Four

The Symposium urges all parties involved in armed conflicts to respect the principles and norms of humanitarian law, particularly those aimed at protecting civilians from the effects of war, preventing their being subjected to attack, reprisals or starvation, or being displaced in conditions contrary to the provisions of Additional Protocol 11 to the 1949 Geneva Conventions on the laws of war.

II. THE 1969 AU CONVENTION GOVERNING THE SPECIFIC ASPECTS OF REFUGEE PROBLEMS IN AFRICA

11. As a regional complement of the 1951 United Nations Convention Relating to the Status of Refugees and its 1967 Protocol, the 1969 AU Convention has been a strong pillar for refugee protection and solutions in Africa. It has enabled the

provision of asylum to refugees and the implementation of voluntary repatriation in a way that has consolidated brotherhood and comity among African States. It has also inspired the development of favourable refugee laws, policies and practices in Africa and indeed in other regions of the world, most notably in the Latin American region. The Convention remains the only international legal instrument which contains elaborate principles on the voluntary repriatation of refugees.

Recommendation Five

The Symposium reaffirms irs belief in the continuing validity of the 1969 AU Convention as the cornerstone of refugee protection and solutions in Africa. In this regard, and in order to implement the Convention more effectively, it is recommended that States:

(i) which have not already done so should ratify the Convention.
(ii) should uphold the principles of the Convention on the humanitarian nature of asylum, prohibit activities inconsistent with refugee status, safeguard refugees against refoulement or expulsion, actively promote voluntary repatriation, respect the principle of voluntariness in repatriation, and practice burden-sharing and solidarity among States.
(iii) should enact the necessary legislation and regulations so as to give effect nationally to the Convention and its principles.
(iv) with the support of the AU, UNHCR, and other relevant organizations, provide training to government officials on the provisions of the 1969 AU Convention and the principles of refugee protection in general, as well as promote those standards among the refugee and national populations as a whole.
(v) should courageously resist temptations to whittle down, through national policies, laws or practices, obligations and standards contained in the Convention.

Recommendation Six

Those regions of the world in which international or regional legal systems for refugee protection do not exist, or where the applicable regimes are under review, should consider the relevance of the 1969 AU Convention. ln this regard, the Symposium highlights the Convention's broad definition of a refugee, at provisions on the non-projection of refugees at borders and the prohibition of refoulement of refugees, and the respect of the voluntariness of refugee repatriation.

III. REFUGEE PROTECTION IN AFRICA

12. Most of the African States have acceded to the three major international instruments on refugees. 45 States have acceded to the 1951 Convention; 46 to

the 1967 Protocol and 42 to the 1969 AU Convention. Only 4 States in Africa have not yet acceded to at least one of these instruments. Throughout the continent, countries are generous towards refugees and many practice liberal asylum policies.

13. Nevertheless, the institution of asylum and the system of refugee protection are under tremendous stress in Africa. The large number of refugees seeking asylum in countries already themselves experiencing tremendous social and economic hardships, has brought into question the very capacity of nations to co?e with refugees. In a number of countries, the basic principles of refugee protection are not being upheld. Refugees have been arrested and detained without charge. Others have been resumed against their will to places where their lives may be in danger. Yet others have been restricted to refugee camps or to remote, inaccessible locations where they are sometimes exposed to banditry, rape and other forms of criminality. Many have not been able to enjoy social, economic and civil rights.
14. This is partly the result of a combination of political, security, social and economic constraints whereby States are able to abide by their international legal obligations only under the most difficult and burden-some circumstances. Unfortunately, because of a global recession and the increased number of persons seeking asylum and humanitarian assistance world-wide, the international community's financial and material support to lighten the burden on African host countries has diminished.

Recommendation Seven

African States should abide by the letter and spirit of the I969 AU Convention and continue to uphold their traditional hospitality rewards refugees and their liberal asylum policies. In particular:

(i) Refugees seeking admission into the territory of another Stare should not be rejected at the border or returned to territories where their lives may be endangered. Accordingly, Governments should nor close their borders in order to refuse refugees admission.

(ii) Governments should use their best endeavors to treat refugees recording to the standards established under refugee law. In particular, they should ensure the personal safety of refugees, local them in areas which are accessible, safe and where basic services and amenities can be provided, and enable them to regain a normal way of life.

Recommendation Eight

The international community, the United Nations, the United Nations High Commissioner for Refugees, and other relevant organizations, should support and assist host Governments in fulfilling their responsibilities towards refugees in a manner consistent with the principles of refugee law on the one hand, and legitimate national security, social and economic interests on the other hand. In particular, financial, material and technical assistance should be mode available to:

(i) ensure that the social and economic structures, community services, and the environment of host countries or communities are not unduly stretched as a result of having to host massive numbers of refugees.
(ii) provide food, water, shelter, sanitation and medical services on a timely basis so that refugees and local populations alike are not put in a life-endangering situation.
(iii) determine the refugee status of persons seeking asylum, and to ensure that those who do not need or deserve international protection do not abuse the humanitarian institution of asylum.
(iv) enable Governments to respond effectively to situations which may contribute to a deterioration in security, law and order in the refugee-hosting areas. In this regard, priority should be placed on isolating and disarming individuals or groups among the refugee populations who may be armed and threatening the lives of innocent refugees, local citizens, and humanitarian personnel, or engaging in other criminal acts.
(v) further to the preceding recommendation, to trace and impound for safe custody or destruction, dangerous weapons illegally circulating or hidden in refugee-hosting arras.
(vi) create or strengthen national institutions to manage and deal with refugee matters at central, provincial and distinct levels; build adequate and well-trained human resources capacity; and to have such technical and logistic resources as will enable Governments to respond to and administer all aspects of refugee problems.

IV. MATERIAL ASSISTANCE TO REFUGEES

15. The principles of international solidarity and burden-sharing have traditionally provided the foundation for the response by the international community to refugee problems. It is now evident that African countries cannot sustain the burdens of hosting refugees on their own. Yet, because of "compassion fatigue" or "donor fatigue", financial and material resources for refugee programmes in Africa from the developed countries are declining. In recent emergency situations, the response of the international community has been hesitant and characterized by poor preparedness and limited resources.
16. Moreover, in all parts of the world, measures taken to meet diverse national interests have not always conformed to the objectives of refugee protection in all cases. To avoid illegal migration and reduce the abuse of asylum procedures, measures such as interdiction on the high seas, visa restrictions and carrier sanctions have been instituted. Likewise, new refugee categorations

have been devised along with a more restrictive interpretation of the refugee definition in the 1951 Convention. In addition, concepts such as "safe countries of origin", "temporary protection", safety zones", "in-country processing and "safe return" have been developed.

17. These measures, while taken to safeguard various national interests, have had the effect of imposing restrictive migratory controls and raised concerns that genuine refugees are being deterred from being able to seek and enjoy asylum. On the other hand, in some countries, such measures have the effect of denying entry to refugees.

Recommendation Nine

Donor countries, and relevant intergovernmental and non-governmental organizations, should provide financial, material and technical assistance to the African asylum countries hosting refugee populations. In cases of large-scale influxes, such assistance should necessarily be provided on a timely basis in order that lives are nol lost.

Recommendation Ten

The refugee crisis cannot be addressed effectively through rigid and regionalized approaches. The Symposium recommends that this problem be addressed in a global and comprehensive manner, as it will ultimately affect every region of the world. Likewise, countries should strive for effective cooperation and mal assistance on refugee, displacement and migratory issues, the same way they collaborate on security, economic and environmental matters.

Recommendation Eleven

The Symposium appeals for genuine international solidarity and burden-sharing to be brought back to the centre.

Index